Practice and Learn

Ages 7-9

Editors
Karen Froloff
Dona Herweck Rice
Gisela Lee

Editorial Manager
Karen J. Goldfluss, M.S. Ed.

Editor-in-Chief
Sharon Coan, M.S. Ed.

Illustrators
Sue Fullam
Agi Palinay
Wendi Wright-Davis

Cover Artist
Denise Bauer

Art Coordinator
Denice Adorno

Imaging
James Edward Grace
Alfred Lau
Ralph Olmedo, Jr.

Product Manager
Phil Garcia

Publishers
Rachelle Cracchiolo, M.S. Ed.
Mary Dupuy Smith, M.S. Ed.

Part 1 Compiled and Written by
Karen Froloff

Part 2 Compiled and Written by
Dona Herweck Rice

Copyright © 2003 Teacher Created Materials, Inc.
ISBN-0-7439-6455-1
Made in U.S.A.

Table of Contents
Part 1

Introduction

To Teachers and Parents

The wealth of knowledge a person gains throughout his or her lifetime is impossible to measure, and it will certainly vary from person to person. However, regardless of the scope of knowledge, the foundation for all learning remains a constant. All that we know and think throughout our lifetimes is based upon fundamentals, and these fundamentals are the basic skills upon which all learning develops.

Practice and Learn—Ages 7–9 is a book that reinforces a variety of second and thrird grade basic skills.

Part 1 emphasizes those skills generally covered in second grade while Part 2 covers skills usually taught in third grade. Skills are reinforced in these areas:

- Grammar
- Spelling and Phonics
- Writing
- Reading
- Handwriting
- Math

This book was written with the wide range of student skills and ability levels of seven to nine-year olds students in mind. Both teachers and parents can benefit from the variety of pages provided in this book. A parent can use the book to work with his or her child to provide an introduction to new material or to reinforce material already familiar to the child. Similarly, a teacher can select pages that provide additional practice for concepts taught in the classroom. When tied to what is being covered in class, pages from this book make great homework reinforcement. The work sheets provided in this book are ideal for use at home as well as in the classroom. Research shows us that skill mastery comes with exposure and drill. To be internalized, concepts must be reviewed until they become second nature. Parents may certainly foster the classroom experience by exposing their children to the necessary skills whenever possible, and teachers will find that these pages perfectly complement their classroom needs.

Keep in mind that skills can be reinforced in nearly every situation, and such reinforcement need not be invasive or forced. As parents, consider your use of basic skills throughout your daily business, and include your children in the process. For example, while grocery shopping, let your child manage the coupons, finding the correct products and totaling the savings. Also, allow your child to measure detergent for the washing machine or help to prepare a meal by measuring the necessary ingredients. You might even consider as a family the time allocated to commercials during a television show you are watching, and calculate how much of the allotted time goes to advertisements. There are, likewise, countless ways that teachers can reinforce skills throughout a school day. For example, assign each child a number and when taking roll, call out math problems with those numbers as the answers. The children will answer "present" when they calculate the problems and realize that their numbers are the answers.

Basic skills are utilized every day in untold ways. Make the practice of them part of your children's or students' routines. Such work done now will benefit them in countless ways throughout their lives.

Practice
and
Learn

Part 1

What Is This?

Use a red crayon to color all uppercase letter sections.

Use a yellow crayon to color all lowercase letter sections.

Use a blue crayon to color all sections with uppercase and lowercase letter partners that match.

Use the color green to color all sections with uppercase and lowercase letter partners that do not match.

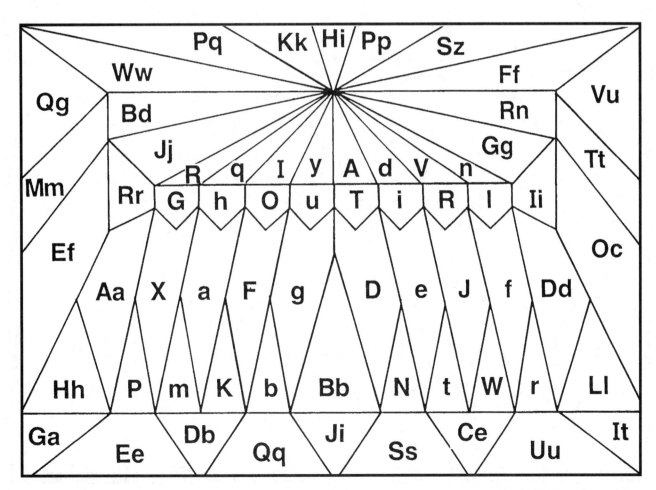

Alphabet Balloons

Color the balloons that have uppercase and lowercase letter partners. (They must be the same letter.)

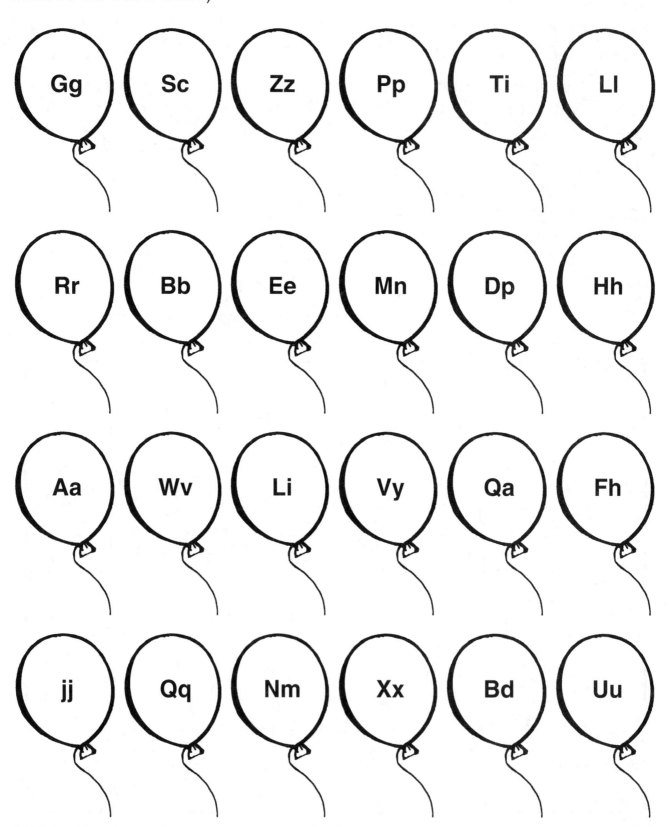

Capital Practice

Practice printing each of these capital letters. Print each letter five times.

Queen
Alice

A _____

B _____

C _____

D _____

E _____

F _____

G _____

H _____

I _____

J _____

K _____

L _____

M _____

Capital Practice *(cont.)*

Practice printing each of these capital letters. Print each letter five times.

N _____

O _____   K ing

P _____   Z achary

Q _____

R _____

S _____

T _____

U _____

V _____

W _____

X _____

Y _____

Z _____

Hidden Reptiles

Color spaces with dots brown. Color spaces with uppercase letters blue. Color spaces with lowercase letters green. What reptiles did you find?

Slithering Snake Trail

The snake needs to get to his hole. There is only one safe way for him to get there. Draw a line on the trail of lowercase letters to help him get there safely.

Animal Antics

Circle the words that contain letters that make the short A sound, as in the title, *Animal Antics.*

1. A hungry alligator opened wide,
2. An albatross accidentally flew inside.
3. "Ahh!" screamed the albatross. "What shall I do?"
4. Then he tickled that 'gator with a feather or two.
5. The alligator sneezed, "A-a-a-choo!"
6. Out that albatross safely flew.

Circle the hidden letters in the picture that make the short A sound.

Color the animals that have the short A sound in their names.

Animal Crossword

Write the animal names in the crossword puzzle.

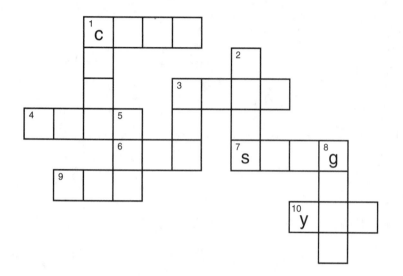

Across

1.

3.

4.

6.

7.

9.

10.

Down

1.

2.

3.

5.

8.

Eskimo Exit

Circle the letters that make the short E sound, as in the title, *Eskimo Exit.*

1. "Make an exit!" yelled the elk. "Trouble is near."
2. "Ehhh?" asked the Eskimo. "I can't hear."
3. "Make an exit!" yelled the elk. "A polar bear is near."
4. "Ehhh?" asked the Eskimo. "I can't hear."
5. "Make an exit!" yelled the elk, but he could not hear.
6. 'Twas the end of the Eskimo. Oh dear, oh dear.

Circle the letters in the picture that make the short E sound.

Color the animals that have the short E sound in their names.

Entrance and Exit

Find the spaces that have a short E picture. Color the spaces red. The path you color will lead you from the entrance to the exit.

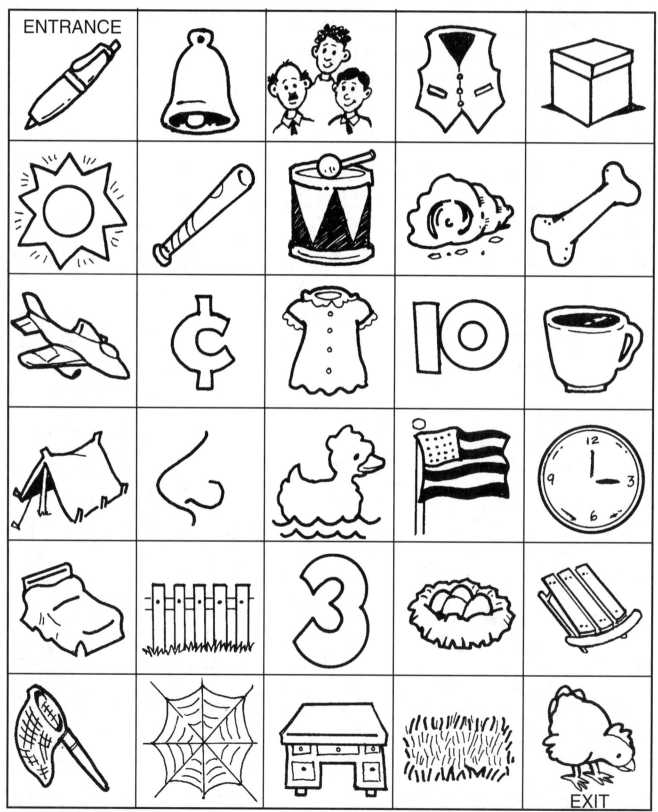

Iguana's Mealtime

Circle the letters that make the short I soun, as in the word *iguana*.

1. The iguana saw an insect passing by.

2. "Ick!" said the iguana. "I won't eat a fly."

3. The iguana saw a fish swimming near.

4. "That would make me sick, I fear."

5. Then the iguana saw some fruit that looked quite sweet.

6. "Now that looks inviting," said the iguana, beginning to eat.

Circle each uppercase or lowercase I in the picture.

Color the animals that have the short I sound in their names.

Short I Igloo

Color the parts of the igloo that have a short I picture on them.

Frog on a Log

Circle the letters that make the short O sound, as in the words *frog* and *log*.

1. Once there was a lazy frog who wouldn't get off his log.
2. "Get off that log and take a job," said another frog.
3. "Exercise!" warned another, "or else you're going to rot."
4. The lazy frog just wouldn't move from his favorite spot.
5. A fox spied that lazy frog who wouldn't hop, trot, or jog.
6. Now you can be sure, there is one less bump on a log.

Circle the letters in the picture that make the short O sound.

Color the animals that have the short O sound in their names.

Rhymes with Spot

Color the circles that have words that rhyme with *spot* yellow. Find and circle the 12 rhyming words in the puzzle.

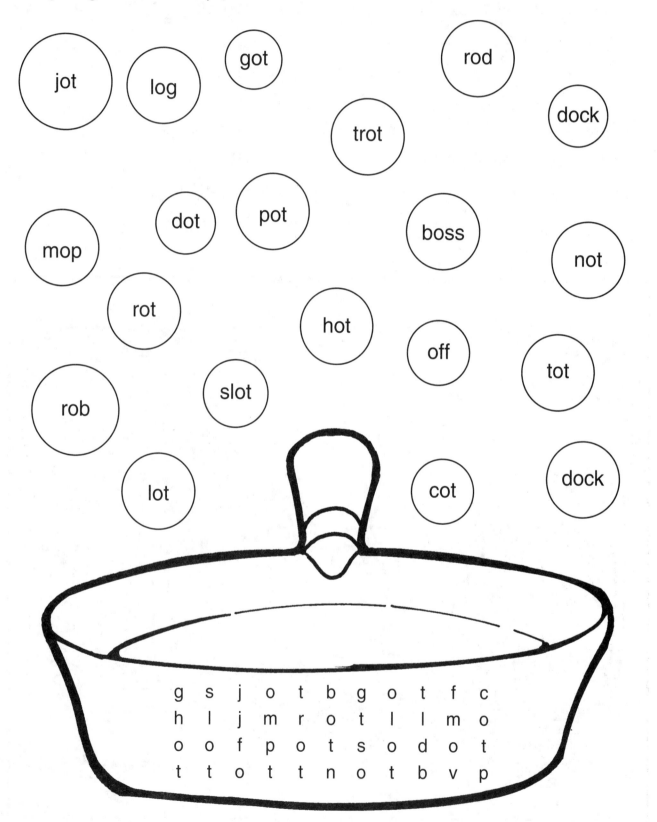

Uh ... I Don't Know

Circle the letters that make the short U sound, as in *Uh*.

1. "Where can I live?" asked the little bug to the bug in the mug.
2. "Uh...I don't know," said the bug, giving him a shrug.
3. "Where can I live?" asked the little bug to the bug in the jug.
4. "Uh...I don't know," said the bug, giving him a shrug.
5. "Where can I live?" asked little bug to the bug in the rug.
6. "I'll share my rug," said the bug, giving him a hug.

Circle the letters in the picture that make the short U sound.

Color the animals that have the short U sound in their names.

Cub in a Tub

Unscramble the letters on each bubble to spell short U words. Find and circle the words in the puzzle.

1. dbu _____

2. dum _____

3. gud _____

4. gru _____

5. gub _____

6. buc _____

7. tuc _____

8. ugn _____

9. bru _____

10. utg _____

11. sbu _____

12. ubt _____

```
c  d  u  g  q  m  u  d  p
t  b  u  d  t  z  b  r  s
u  l  n  u  u  c  g  u  n
g  r  u  g  b  u  g  b  h
m  c  u  t  l  b  b  u  s
```

Crayons

Color the crayons with **short A** pictures red.

Color the crayons with **short E** pictures yellow.

Color the crayons with **short I** pictures green.

Color the crayons with **short O** pictures orange.

Color the crayons with **short U** pictures blue.

Extraordinary Eggs

Write the vowel that you hear in each picture.

1.
_____

2.
_____

3.
_____

4.
_____

5.
_____

6.
_____

7.
_____

8.
_____

9.
_____

10.
_____

11.
_____

12.
_____

13.
_____

14.
_____

15.
_____

16.
_____

Scaly Snake

Use **yellow** crayon to color each section with a picture of a long A word. Color the other sections **red**.

Colorful Toucan

The letters *ai* make the long A sound. Unscramble these "ai" words. Then use the color code to color a section of the toucan.

Black: tail, maid, praise, gain **Red:** stain, main

Yellow: nail, mail **Orange:** fail, pail, bail

Green: chain, pain, paid, sail, jail

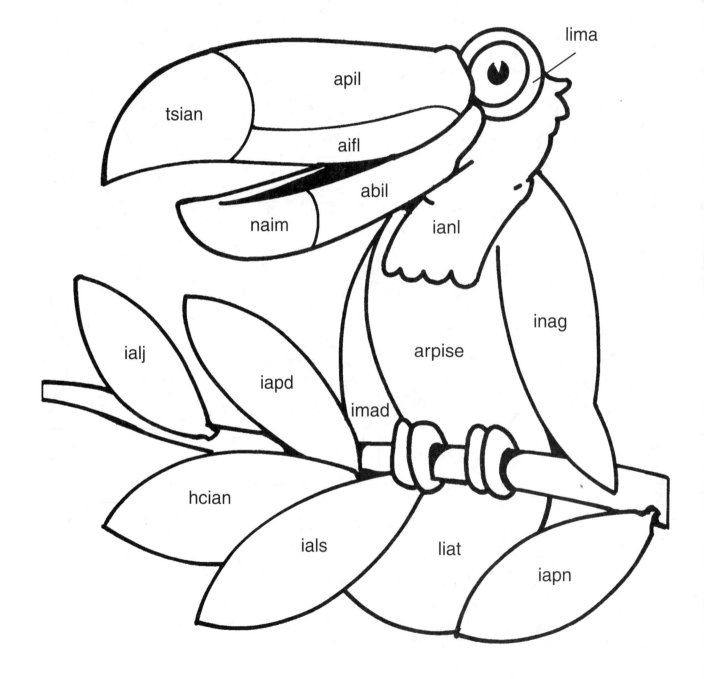

Tray of Treats

Add *ay* to the letters on the treats to make the long A sound. Write the words on the lines. Learn to spell all 12 words.

Magic E Genie

An *e* can change a short vowel word into a long vowel word just like magic. Add a silent *e* to the end of each short A word. Write the new long A words on the lines.

_____   _____   _____

_____   _____   _____

_____   _____   _____

_____   _____   _____

_____   _____   _____

Teepee Patches

Color in the patches on the teepee that have pictures of long E words as in the word *teepee*.

Long E Puzzle

The letters *ee* make the long E sound. To complete the crossword puzzle, use these double *e* words.

breeze	street	tweet
feet	teeth	week
freezer	three	tweeze
see	tree	

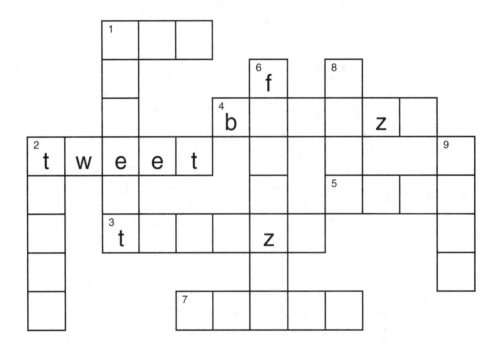

Across

1. When you look, you ___.

2. A sound that a bird makes is a _____.

3. To _____ means to pull something out with a tweezer.

4. A gentle wind is called a _____.

5. Apples grow on a ____.

7. The number that comes after two is _____.

Down

1. Another name for a road is a _____.

2. You should brush your _____ after eating.

6. A place to keep ice is called the _____.

8. You wear shoes on your ____.

9. There are seven days in one ____.

Twelve Long E Words

The letters *ea* can make the long E sound. Fill in the missing letters to spell 12 long E words.

1. ____ ea ____ ____

2. ____ ea

3. ____ ea ____

4. ____ ea ____ ____

5. ____ ea

6. ____ ea ____

7. ____ ea ____

8. ____ eas

9. ____ ea ____

10. ____ ea ____

11. ____ ea ____

12. ____ ea ____ ____

Spider Web

Use a blue crayon to color all sections of the spider's web with pictures of long I words such as *spider*.

Strike Three

Cross out in each row across the three balls that do not have words with the long I sound.

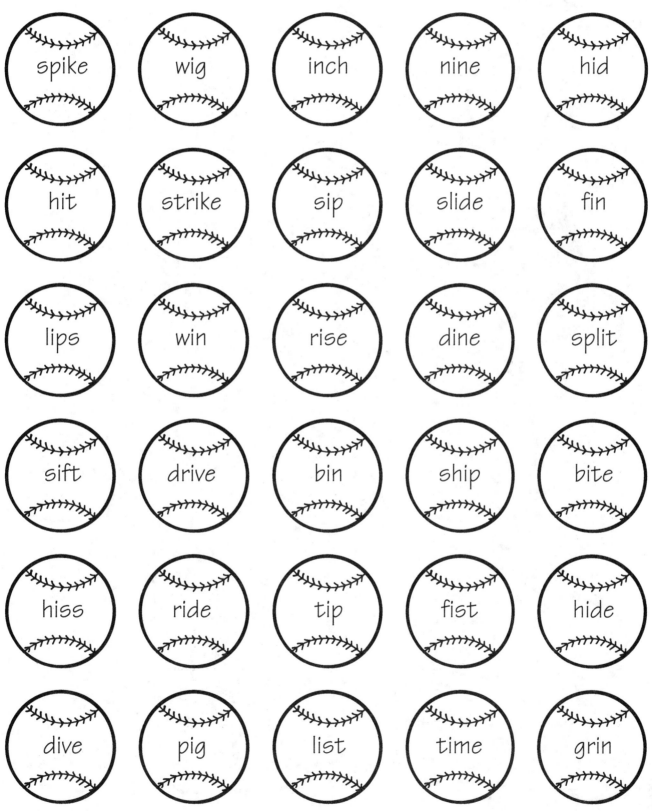

Nice Slice of Pie

Write a rhyming long I word on each cherry. You may pick a word on the pie or choose your own.

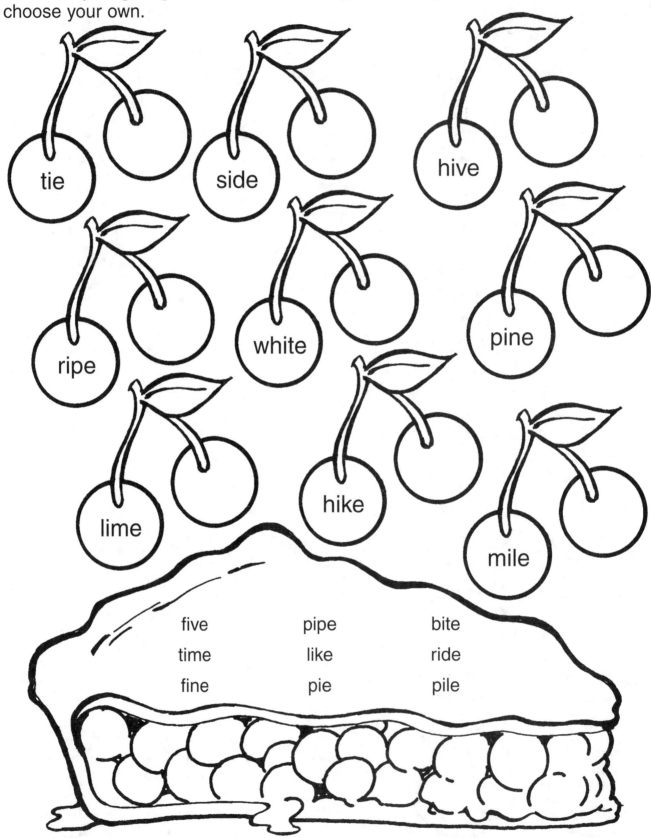

five   pipe   bite

time   like   ride

fine   pie   pile

Frozen Cone

Use a pink crayon to color the sections of the ice-cream cone that have a picture of long O words as in the word *cone*.

Scrambled Long O

The letters *oa* can make the long O sound. Unscramble the letters to spell long O words. Write the words on the lines.

1. _____

2. _____

3. _____

4. _____

5. _____

6. _____

7. _____

8. _____

9. _____

10. _____

11. _____

12. _____

1. dato

    7. kosa

2. taco

    8. drao

3. paso

    9. toba

4. dola

    10. laoc

5. toga

    11. famo

6. flato

    12. foal

Looking for Bones

Circle the long O word on each bone. Then find and circle each word in the puzzle below.

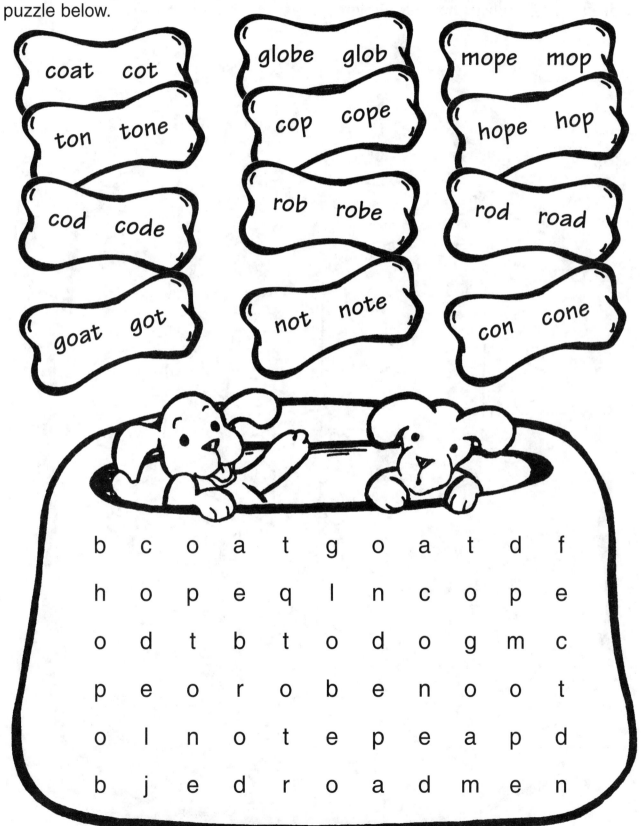

coat   cot

ton   tone

cod   code

goat   got

globe   glob

cop   cope

rob   robe

not   note

mope   mop

hope   hop

rod   road

con   cone

b	c	o	a	t	g	o	a	t	d	f
h	o	p	e	q	l	n	c	o	p	e
o	d	t	b	t	o	d	o	g	m	c
p	e	o	r	o	b	e	n	o	o	t
o	l	n	o	t	e	p	e	a	p	d
b	j	e	d	r	o	a	d	m	e	n

A Juicy Fruit

Use a yellow crayon to color the sections of the pineapple with pictures of long U words such as in *juicy* and *fruit*. Color the rest of the pineapple green.

Word Clouds

Some of the words below are not real. Use a yellow crayon to color the 12 clouds with real words. Notice that these long U words have the silent *e* at the end of the word.

use   fune   tube   huge

cute   hude   sube   rude

fuse   fume   tude   cube

mule   mute   mube   rule

fute   cuje   cuve   hule

ruke   hupe   tune   ruve

Tulip Clues

Use the words and picture clues given to complete the puzzle.

blue

cube

cucumber

Cupid

glue

juice

museum

pupa

pupil

tulip

tube

fuse

Across

2.   3.   5.   8.   9.   10.

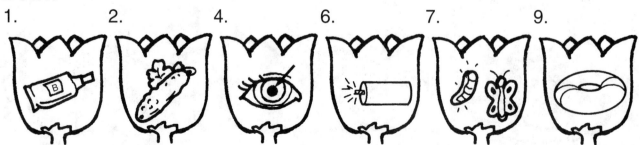

Down

1.   2.   4.   6.   7.   9.

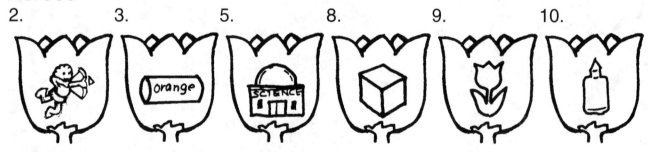

Park Garden

Color red the flowers with pictures of words with the *ar* sound as in *park*. Color the other flowers a different color.

Ornaments

The letters *or* usually sound like the *or* in ornament. Use a green crayon to color the ornaments that have pictures of words with the *or* sound. Color the ornaments that do not have the words with the *or* sound a different color.

Purple Shirts

The special vowel sounds of *ur*, *ir*, and *er* usually sound like the *ir* in *shirt*. Use a purple crayon to color the shirts with pictures of *ir* sounds. Color the shirts with pictures of words that do not have the *ir* sound a different color.

Mixed Signals

Use a red crayon to color the lights with pictures of *ar* words.

Use a yellow crayon to color the lights with pictures of *or* words.

Use a green crayon to color the lights with pictures of *ur* words.

Party Favors

Use a red crayon to color the parts with *ar* words.

Use an orange crayon to color the parts with *er* words.

Use a yellow crayon to color the parts with *ir* words.

Use a green crayon to color the parts with *or* words.

Use a blue crayon to color the parts with *ur* words.

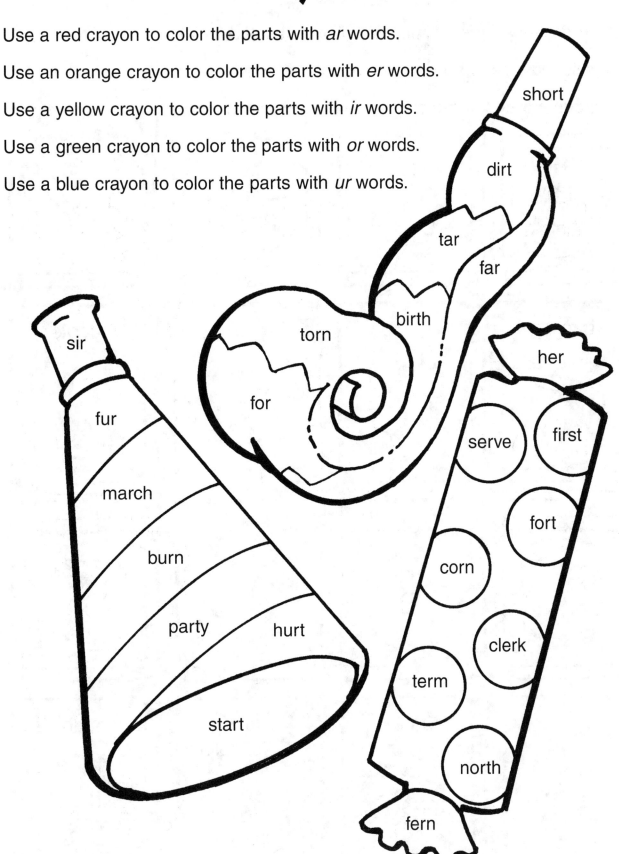

Hooked on Books

If the *oo* sounds like the *oo* in book, color the book blue.

If the *oo* sounds like the *oo* in moon, color the moon yellow.

Feathers

If the *ea* sounds like the *ea* sound in *feather*, color the feather blue.

If the *ea* makes the long E sound, color the feather green.

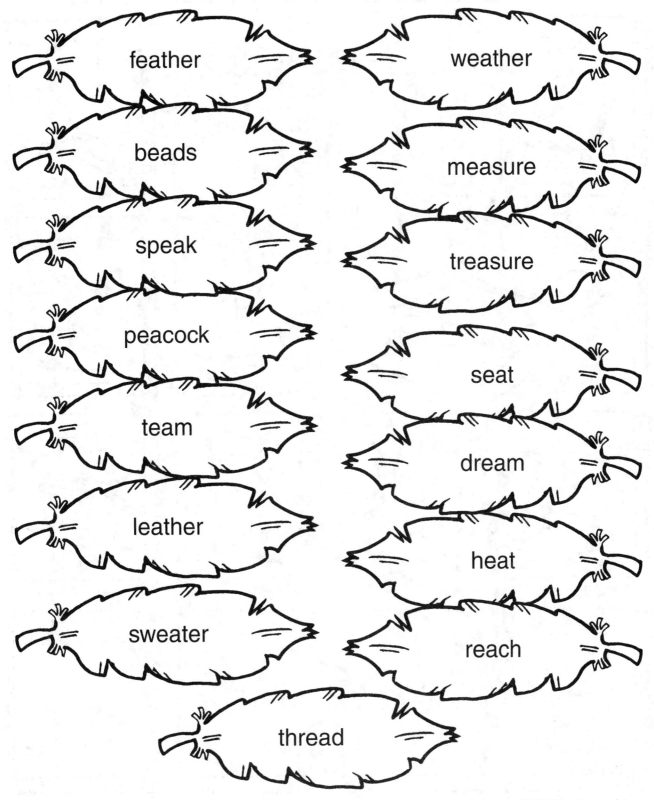

feather

weather

beads

measure

speak

treasure

peacock

seat

team

dream

leather

heat

sweater

reach

thread

Laundry Drawing

The letters *au* and *aw* do not follow the long vowel rule. Both have the sound of the *au* in laundry. Find and color the objects that have the *au* sound.

Crawling Caterpillar

Unscramble each *aw* word and write it on the lines.

calw

darw

wap

hakw

waj

carwl

AU Sound Puzzle

To complete this puzzle, use words that have the letters *au* in them.

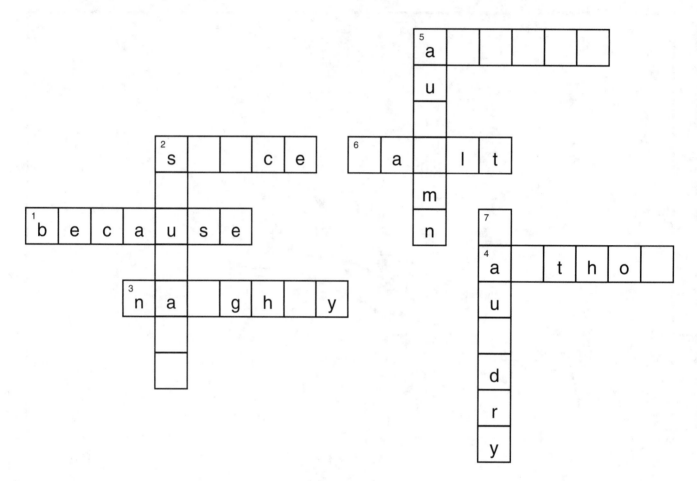

Across

1. My dog loves me _____ I am nice. (another word for *since*)

2. Apple _____ is made from mashed apples.

3. It is better to be nice than to act _____.

4. Someone who writes books is an _____.

5. The month after July is _____.

6. "I didn't do it; it's not my _____!"

Down

2. A kind of meat used on pizza is _____.

5. Another name for the fall season is _____.

7. A word that means clothing to be washed is _____.

Just Buzzing Around!

Look at the bees that have the words with the long O sound. Write the long O words two times on the hive.

Clown Show

If the *ow* in the word makes the sound like the *ow* in clown, color the spot on the clown's suit red. If the *ow* in the word makes the sound like the *ow* in show, color the spot on the clown's suit yellow.

Wise Owl

Look at the boxes that have the words with *ow* as in owl. Write the words in the owl.

| cow | owl | brown | how |

| down | crow | blow |

Mouse in the House

The letters *ou* usually sound like the *ou* in mouse. Find and circle 11 *ou* words that are hidden in the mouse house. Learn to spell all 11 words.

Noisy Toy

The letters *oi* and *oy* make the sound like the *oy* in toy. Color the sections of the box that have pictures that have the sound of *oy* as in toy.

A Zany Zebra

Write *oi* or *oy* in the blanks to finish each word. Use a dictionary if you need help. Read the words. Color the picture.

Candy House

If the *ou* sounds like the *ou* in **house**, color the section YELLOW.

If the *ea* sounds like the *ea* in **gingerbread**, color the section RED.

If the *oo* sounds like the *oo* in **cookie**, color the section GREEN.

If the *ew* sounds like the *ew* in **chew**, color the section ORANGE.

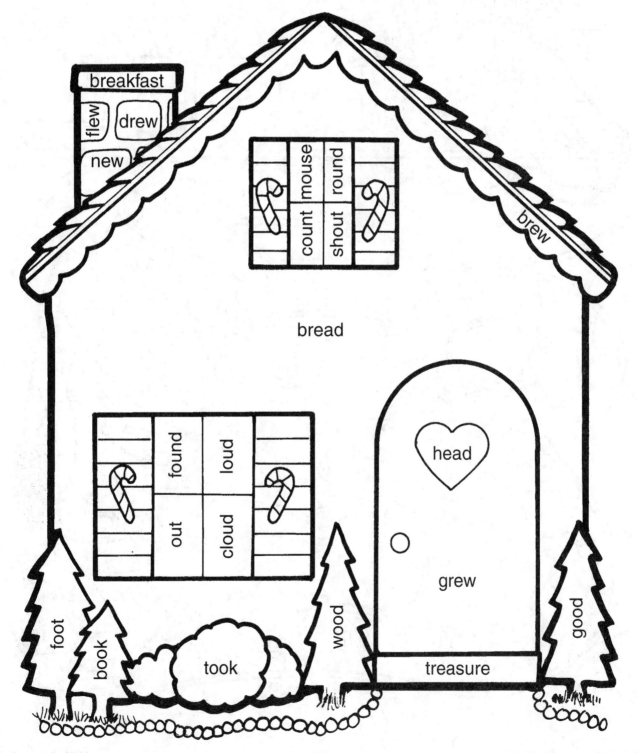

On the Right Track

Help the train get to the zoo. Draw a line to follow the track with words that start with *r* blends.

Color the L Blends

Color the pictures in each row that begin with the same blend as the first picture. These are *l* **blends**.

S Blends Parade

Write the **s blends** that begin these words.

___ ___ ile

___ ___ ool

___ ___ onge

___ ___ an

___ ___ ___ ing

___ ___ oon

___ ___ ing

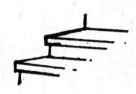

___ ___ airs

Answer Box				
sm	sp	st	sw	spr

Stick Out Your Neck!

Draw a line from each **s blend** to a picture whose name begins with that sound. Some pictures will not match.

Capture the Flag

The frogs and swans played a game. Only one team got to the flag and won.
Draw a line to show how that team got to the flag. Staying on a path of blends
will help you find the way.

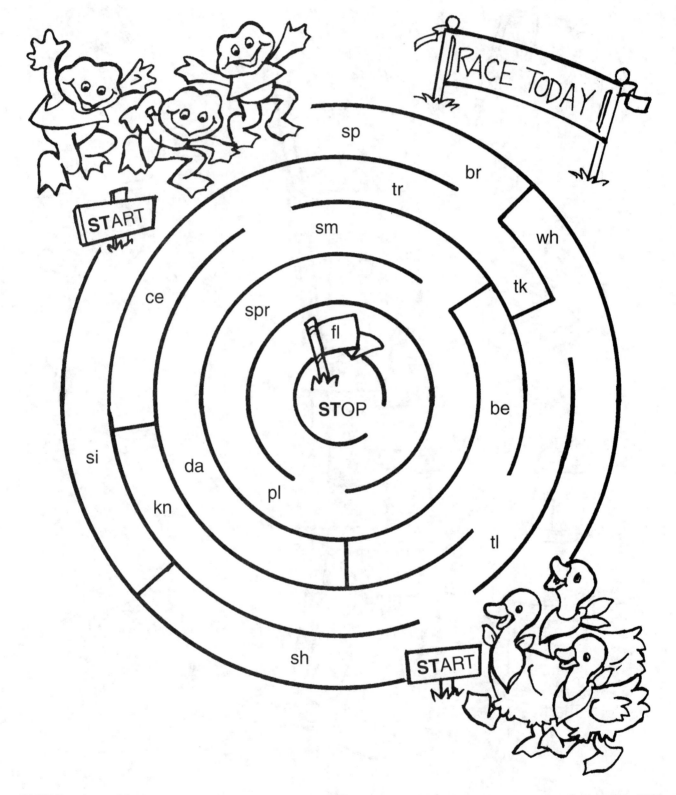

Find the Blends

Circle the blends in the sentences below. Then follow the directions to color the picture on the page 62.

1. Color the tree trunk brown.

2. Color the leaves green.

3. Color the small flowers yellow.

4. Color the stems on the flowers green.

5. Color the clouds gray.

6. Color the sky and the drops of rain blue.

7. Color Bret Bear black.

8. Color Brad Bear brown.

9. Color the frog green.

                                                 #6455 *Practice and Learn*

Find the Blends (cont.)

To complete this page, follow the directions found on page 61.

Write a sentence about this picture. Try to use some blend words.

A Good Catch

Which fish have pictures of *sh* words on them?　Draw a line from these fish to the fisherman's hook.

A Whale of a Good Time

Find and draw a ring around these *wh* words.

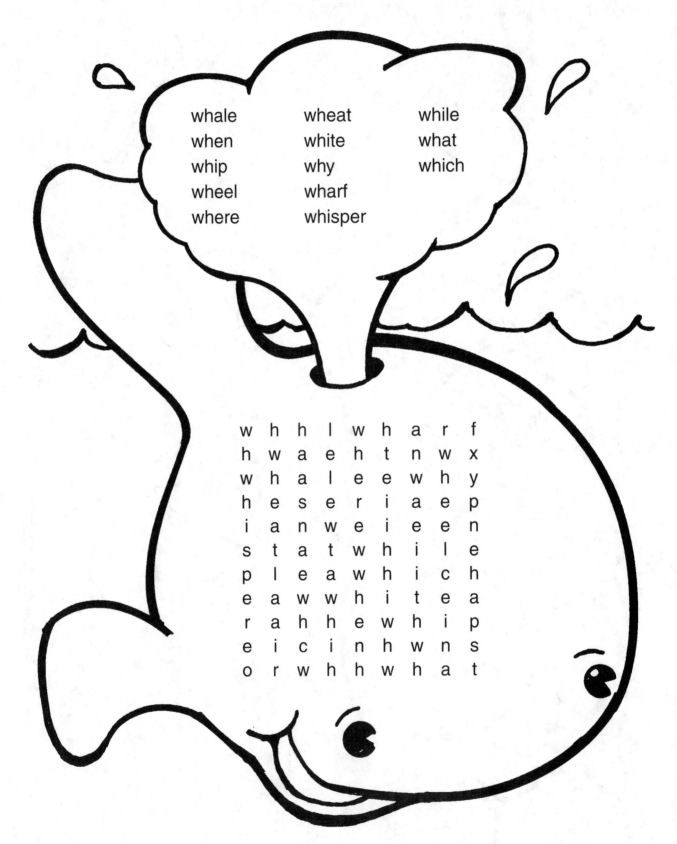

whale   wheat   while
when   white   what
whip   why   which
wheel   wharf
where   whisper

w h h l w h a r f
h w a e h t n w x
w h a l e e w h y
h e s e r i a e p
i a n w e i e e n
s t a t w h i l e
p l e a w h i c h
e a w w h i t e a
r a h h e w h i p
e i c i n h w n s
o r w h h w h a t

Dolphin Tricks

Use a **blue** crayon to color the dolphins that have pictures of *ch* words.

Gone Fishing

Which words begin with a quiet, or soft, *th*? Which words begin with a noisy, or hard, *th*? Draw a line from the fish to its correct fishing boat.

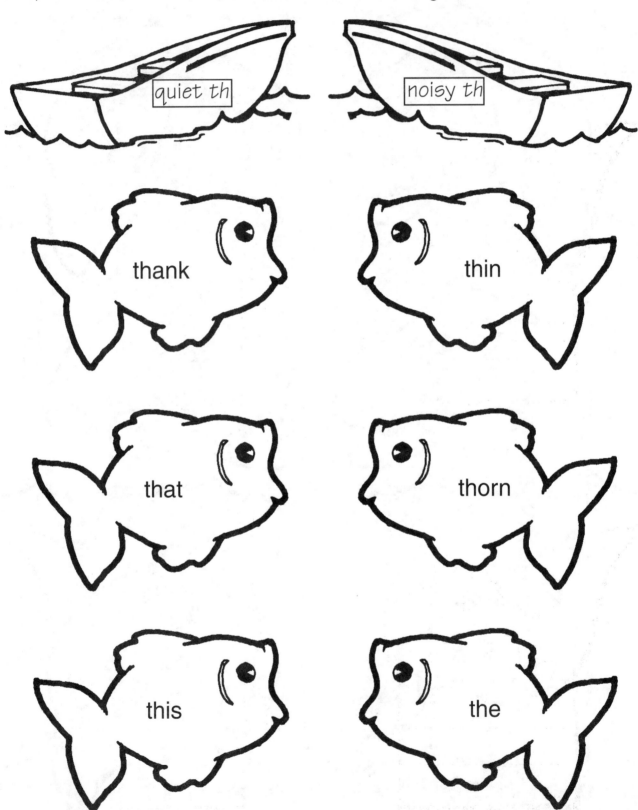

quiet th

noisy th

thank

thin

that

thorn

this

the

Silly Seals

Circle the correct beginning for each word. Then write the words on the lines.
Color the pictures.

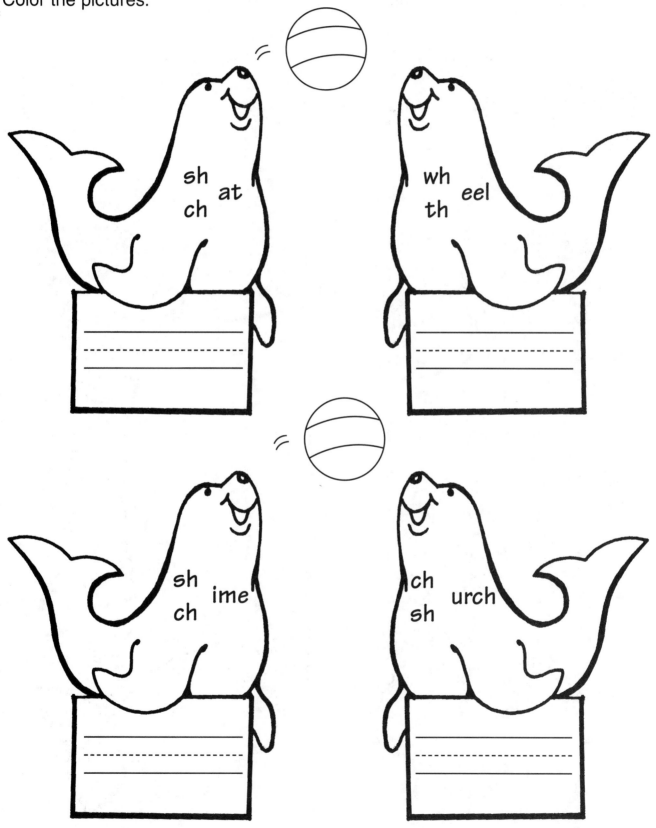

Knock, Knock, Who's There?

The letters *kn* at the beginning of a word sounds like *n*. The *k* is silent. Find and draw a ring around these *kn* words.

knock   knit   knob   knee   knot   knuckle
knight   knead   knife   know   kneel

k n n k o c k
k n u c k l e
n k n i g h t
k n e a d n p
n i e i u k m
o f i t c k h
w t k n o c k
j k b c k n e
k n o t o w o
n t k k w n k
e t k n i f e
e l n i k o w
l e o f b u c
f e b k n w e

A Full Birdhouse

Say the word *swallow*. Listen to the sound of the *sw* blend. It is the blend of the sound of the two letters *s* and *w*. Unscramble the *sw* words. Then write the words on the birds.

Reptile Rock

Use the consonants on the rock to write the correct beginning consonant for each animal word.

____ abbit

____ ird

____ at

b
c
p

z
s
r

____ ebra

____ ig

____ nake

Take It from the Turtles

Write the beginning consonant on each turtle to spell different turtle body parts.

1.

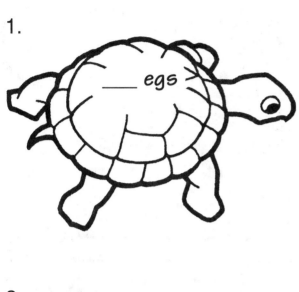

2.

3.

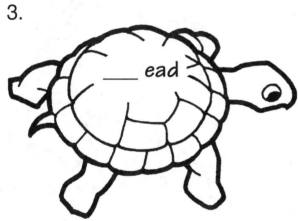

4.

5.

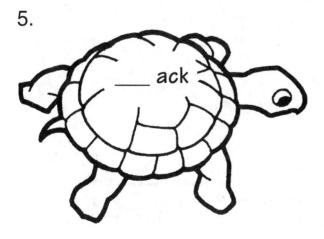

6.

                                                           #6455 Practice and Learn

Life in a Fishbowl

Say the word for each kind of pet. Circle the missing consonant sound you hear in the middle of each word. Then write in the missing letter.

r   m

f___og

k   t

b   d

tur___le

gol___fish

m   n

s___ail

Name That Pet!

Choose a consonant or pair of consonants to finish each pet's name. Then draw a picture to show how you think a pet with that name might look.

t dd	ff ck
Boo_____s	Mr. So_____s
Te_____y Bear	Miss Mu_____in

What Makes "Scents"

Choose a final consonant from the flower to complete each word on the skunk.

c l o u ○
s m e l ○
f l o w e ○
g a r d e ○
k i s ○
s k u n ○

d   k
r n l
r
s

Who's Behind That Mask?

Write *n* or *m* in each box to finish each word. Use a brown crayon to color the stripes with words that end with *n*. Use black to color the stripes with the *m* words. Then color the rest of the picture any colors you choose.

Porcupine Picks

Draw a line to match each porcupine on the left with a porcupine on the right so that the letter combinations spell a word. Then write each word.

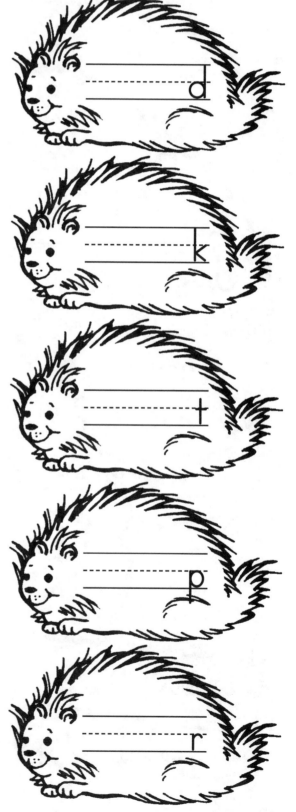

A Path for the Platypus

Find the path for the duckbill platypus to get to his friend. Fill in each box with a *p* or a *d* to spell a word. Then draw a line only on the path of words that end with *p*.

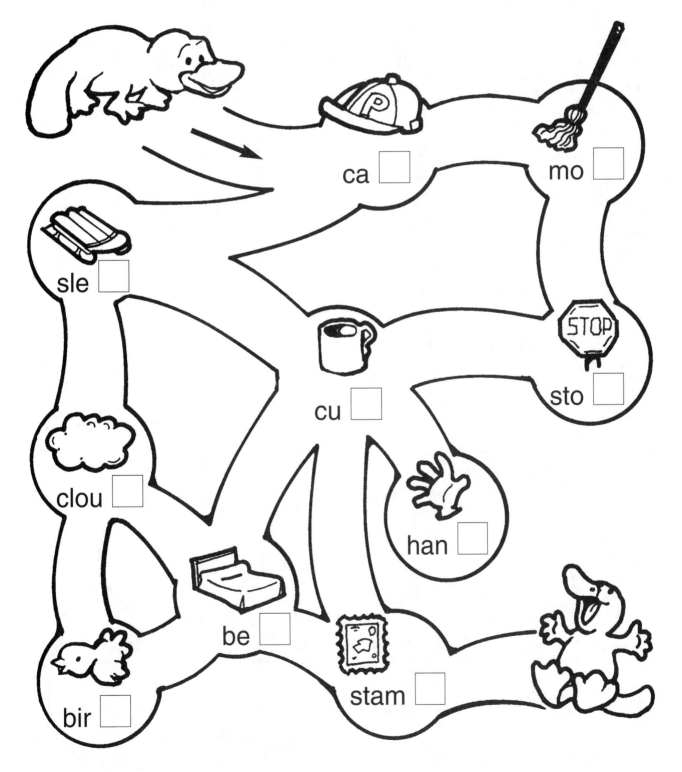

ca ☐

mo ☐

sle ☐

sto ☐

cu ☐

clou ☐

han ☐

be ☐

stam ☐

bir ☐

Hang in There!

Some *s* words make the *s* sound as in *miss*. Other *s* words make the sound like a *z* as in *his*. Read the words on the opossums. Then draw them hanging by their tails onto the correct side of the tree.

Chipmunk Chatter

Circle the correct letter on the chipmunk's shirt to spell a word. Color the picture after you finish making the words.

The Fox Family

The letter *x* at the end of a word makes the sound of the two letters *ks*. Say *fox* and listen for the two sounds that the *x* makes. Then unscramble these words that end with an *x*. Write each word on the line beneath it.

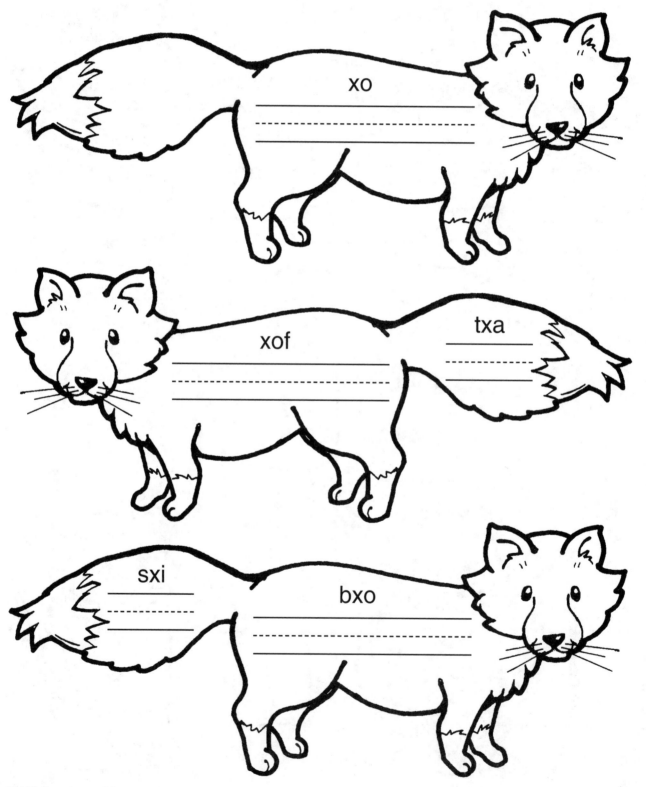

xo

xof

txa

sxi

bxo

The Climbing Cougar

Unscramble the *ld* words. Write them on the lines. Say each word and listen to the two sounds the *ld* blend makes. If you need help, check the words at the bottom of the page.

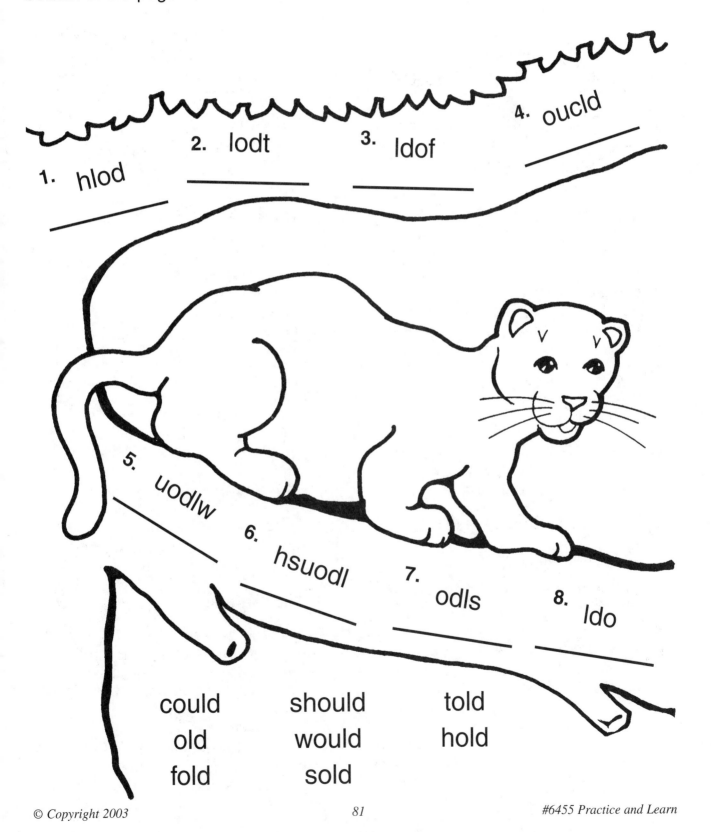

1. hlod

2. lodt

3. ldof

4. oucld

5. uodlw

6. hsuodl

7. odls

8. ldo

could   should   told

old   would   hold

fold   sold

NK Sound Puzzle

To complete the sections of this puzzle, use words that end with the letters *nk*.

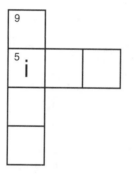
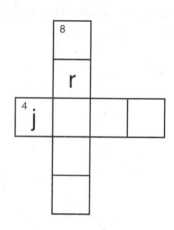

Across

1. Wash the dishes in the ____.

2. You put your money in the ____.

3. Your brain helps you _____.

4. Old stuff that is not worth much is called ____.

5. A pen has ___ inside it.

Down

1. The boat did not float. It ____!

3. When someone does something nice for you, you should say, "_____ you!"

6. You skate at a ____.

7. A black and white animal that can give off a bad odor is a _____.

8. An elephant can pick up peanuts with its _____.

9. A color made by mixing red and white is ____.

Where the Buffalo Roam

Find and draw a ring around the *nd* words on the bison (buffalo). As you circle the words, say them. Listen to the sounds the *nd* blend makes.

hand	land	sand	stand	lend
mend	send	friend	wind	pond
around	found	ground	pound	sound

```
f   w   e
f   r   i   e   n   d
d   p   e   n   n   w   i   e   n
n   o   d   d   d   m   n   d   d   l
d   u   n   s   s   e   i   e   n   a   p
o   n   s   l   e   n   d   s   a   n   d   f
s   d   t   n   n   d   p   o   n   d   o   o
o   h   a   n   d   i   p   i   e   n   d   u
u   s   n   d   n   e   r   t   o   u   n   n
n   n   d   i   n   a   r   o   u   n   d   d
d   d   g   r   o   u   n   d   e   n   i   e
e   i   n   d   n   d
```

Bear Tracks

Help the lost bear cubs find their way back to their mother. Unscramble and write the *nt* words on the circles to get them there. Say each word and listen to the sounds the *nt* blend makes.

1. uatn

2. ntte

3. awtn

4. estn

5. ihtn

6. bnet

7. wetn

The Big Bear Family

Draw a ring around the correct blend to finish each word. Write each word on the lines. Then use a black crayon to color the bears that have words ending with *mp*. Use a brown crayon to color the bears that have words ending with *nk*.

la | mp nt ld

dri | nk nt mp

bu | ld nd mp

ta | ld nk nt

"Moo"sical Cowbells

Circle the correct letter on each cow's bell to complete the *st* word. Then write each word written on the cow's spots. Then write the complete word on the cow's side. Color the pictures.

Piggy Pictures

Each pig has a picture of a word that ends with *ng*. Write the correct beginning for each word on the line below each picture.

How "Egg"citing!

Write *ch* at the end of each word. Then write the whole word inside an egg.

pea ___ ___

coa ___ ___

wat ___ ___

ben ___ ___

sandwi ___ ___

Little Duckies

Unscramble the *ck* words on the baby ducks. On each baby duck's back write the word you would use to finish the sentence.

1. A _____ says "_____."

2. A hen says "_____."

3. A chicken will _____ at its food.

4. A baby _____ hatches from an egg.

uqakc

clcku

hcick

uckd

ckpe

Llama Puzzle

Finish the sections of the puzzle, using words that end with *ll*.

Across:

1. Don't ___ ___ ___ ___ ___ your glass of water.

2. Jack and Jill went up the ___ ___ ___ ___.

3. Jack ___ ___ ___ ___ down and broke his crown.

4. ___ ___ ___ ___ the pail up from the well.

Down:

5. Please ___ ___ ___ ___ my glass with water.

6. The doctor said to swallow your ___ ___ ___ ___ with water.

7. Fill the pail with water from a ___ ___ ___ ___.

8. "Don't ___ ___ ___ ___ down again, Jack!" cried Jill.

The Sheep and the Goats

You do not hear the *b* in words such as lamb that end with *mb*. Write *mb* to finish the word on each sheep. Say each word aloud. Use a dictionary to look up any words you do not know. Then draw a line to match each word to its definition.

la ___ ___

nu ___ ___

thu ___ ___

li ___ ___

not feeling anything

a baby sheep

a tree branch

the shortest and fattest finger on a hand

First Words

Can you write a sentence? If you can, write a sentence about the picture below.

When you begin to write words to make sentences, you must know this very important capitalization rule.

Capitalize the first word in a sentence.

Change the lowercase letters to capitals where they are needed. Each time you make a capital letter, write that letter on the blank below that matches the sentence number. When you are finished, you will find out what present is in one of the birthday boxes!

1. is everyone walking to the park?

2. are we reading our library books now?

3. give me my crayons, please.

4. today is the day of the party.

5. robots are fun to watch.

6. under the rock is a snake.

_____ _____ _____ _____ _____ _____
  3   6   1   4   2   5

Capitalize and Punctuate

Every sentence ends with a period (.), a question mark (?), or an exclamation point (!). Rewrite the sentences found below. Be sure to begin each one with a capital letter. End each one with the correct punctuation mark.

1. my cousin spent the night at my house

   _____

   _____

2. john said I could look at his snake

   _____

   _____

3. jim entered the bicycle race

   _____

   _____

4. what a race it was

   _____

   _____

5. did he wear a helmet

   _____

   _____

6. who won the race

   _____

   _____

What's My Ending?

Add a period (.), a question mark (?), or an exclamation point (!) to the end of each sentence.

1. He can go with him ☐

2. Where are you ☐

3. Help ☐

4. Who made the bed ☐

5. Go to third base ☐

6. I like to eat cookies ☐

7. What a fine job ☐

8. The tools are in the shed ☐

9. How much do you want ☐

10. What is your name ☐

Sentence Hunt!

Can you find the sentences on this page? Write a capital letter for the first word in every sentence you find. Remember that all sentences must end with an end mark: a period (.), question mark (?), or exclamation point (!).

1. is this your first sentence hunt?

2. bread, cheese, lettuce, and a tomato

3. i packed a sandwich for lunch.

4. a lion and a tiger

5. the animals smelled food.

6. do not eat me!

7. the sandwich in my backpack

8. i fed the wild animals.

9. no more lunch

10. now, I am hungry!

How many sentences did you find?_____

Choose one of the numbers that was not a sentence. Make it into a sentence. Don't forget a capital letter and an end mark!

_____

_____

_____

_____

Scrambled Sentences

Unscramble the words to make a sentence. Be sure to add a capital letter at the beginning and punctuation at the end.

1. bird cat the chased the

   _____

   _____

2. letter friend I a wrote my to

   _____

   _____

3. puzzle the solved the family together

   _____

   _____

4. a baker cake baked the

   _____

   _____

5. sea jumped into penguin a the

   _____

   _____

6. frog the log over leaped the

   _____

   _____

Sentences About Me

Complete each sentence. Draw a picture of yourself in the box.

1. My name is _____

    _____.

2. I am_____years old.

3. I like to_____

_____.

4. I am best at _____.

5. My friends think that I am _____.

6. My parents think that I am _____.

7. I wish I had a _____ .

8. I wish I could _____.

9. My favorite thing about myself is _____

_____.

10. I am proud of _____.

What's a Noun?

Nouns are words that name a person, place, or thing. Write each word under the correct heading.

Adam	**farmer**	**motor**	**scientist**
attic	**football**	**museum**	**state**
comb	**hoe**	**rainbow**	**zookeeper**
Dr. Roberts	**London**	**room**	
door	**mother**	**Russia**	

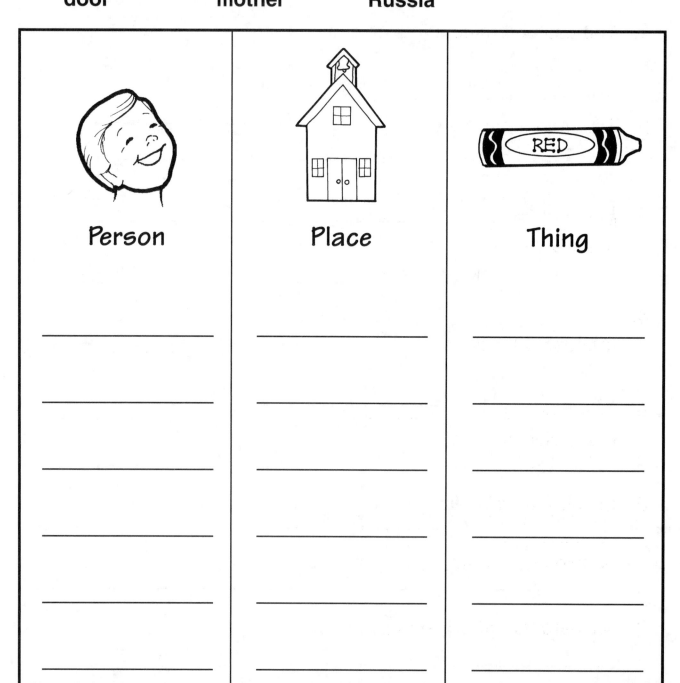

Person   Place   Thing

Person, Place, or Thing?

Complete each sentence with a noun from the word box. Then tell if the noun names a person, place, or thing.

dentist	sand	sister	truck
house	school	tire	

Person, Place, or Thing?

1. The ostrich buried its head in the
   _____.   _____

2. The man drove his
   _____ into town.   _____

3. My _____ had a cold so
   she stayed home.   _____

4. Our _____ reminded us
   to brush after eating.   _____

5. The new _____ has
   many classrooms.   _____

6. My bicycle got a flat
   _____ from the sharp
   pebble in the road.   _____

7. My parents are going to paint our
   _____.   _____

Name One!

A noun names

a person,   place,   or thing.

Complete each sentence by adding a noun of your own. Choose the kind of noun written before the sentence.

person   1. The _____ delivered the mail.

thing   2. I can not find my _____.

thing   3. The dog played with the _____.

person   4. Jeff and _____ played ball in the park.

place   5. I read my book at the _____.

person   6. _____ played the piano.

place   7. Can we go to the _____?

Naming More Than One

Add **s** or **es** to each word to make it more than one.

1. cane _____

2. brush _____

3. duck _____

4. bear _____

5. fox _____

6. dress _____

7. glass _____

8. bag _____

9. bucket _____

10. sled _____

More Naming More Than One

Make each word more than one by **crossing out the y** and **adding ies.**

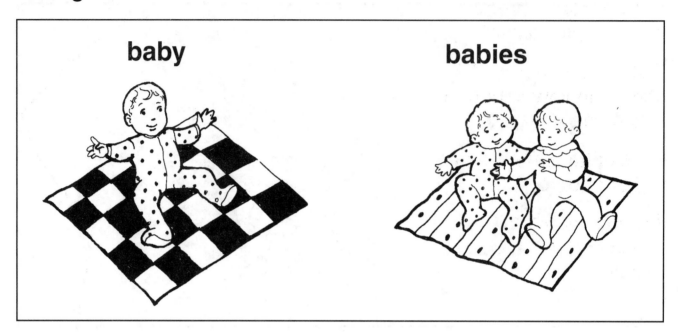

baby   **babies**

1. puppy _____   6. funny_____

2. lady_____   7. kitty _____

3. baby _____   8. daddy _____

4. candy _____   9. jelly _____

5. pony _____   10. ruby _____

That's My Name!

Write your first name on the shirt. Make a design on the shirt.

Did you start your name with a capital letter?

If you did, you already know one very important rule for capitalization:

Capitalize the names of people.

The names of people are capitalized—first, middle, and last.

name

Write your whole name here. Remember your capitals.

_____

Here are eight names that need capital letters. Write them correctly on the lines. The first one is done for you.

1. william   <u>   William   </u>

2. rachel   _____

3. laura   _____

4. michael   _____

5. carl garcia   _____

6. joey edwards   _____

7. barbara madison   _____

8. heather lee   _____

Pets

Do you have any pets at home? If you do, write the name(s) of your pet(s) here. _____

_____

Did you start your pet's name with a capital letter? If you did, you know a rule for capitalization:

Capitalize the names of pets.

The names of pets are always capitalized.

Here are some pets without names. Think of a name for each pet. Write the name under each pet. Color the pets if you would like to!

_____ _____ _____

_____ _____ _____

Did you remember to use capital letters?

Titles of People

Do you have an aunt or an uncle? If you do, write the name of your aunt or uncle here: _____

The word "aunt" or "uncle" is always capitalized when it is written with a name. It is called a title. Here are more titles:

| **Grandma** | **President** | **Mister (Mr.)** | **Miss** | **Cousin** |
| **Grandpa** | **Captain** | **Mistress (Mrs.)** | **Coach** | **Doctor (Dr.)** |

Sometimes titles are capitalized when they are written without a name, like Grandma or Grandpa. When titles are written with names, they are **always** capitalized.

Capitalize the titles of people when they are written with names.

Rewrite these names and titles with capitals where they are needed.

1. grandmother davis _____

2. mister hayes _____

3. captain jack _____

4. cousin jimmy _____

5. doctor morton _____

6. coach russell _____

J. R. for Short!

Capital letters are used with periods to make names shorter. These shortened names are called abbreviations and initials.

Mr. J. T. Oadie and
Mr. C. F. Roggles are
best friends.

Doctor Martin = Dr. Martin

Dr. is an abbreviation for doctor. It starts with a capital when it is used with a name. Here are some other abbreviations for titles:

Mister = Mr. Mistress = Mrs. or Ms. Captain = Capt. Junior = Jr.

Initials can be used to make names shorter, too.

Dr. James Robert Martin = Dr. J. R. Martin

J. R. are initials for James Robert. They need capital letters and periods.

Write abbreviations and initials for the underlined names. Don't forget capital letters and periods.

Mistress Emma Lou Hodges   Mistress Marissa Williams

_____   _____

Brian David Parker, Junior   Mister Anthony Charles Owens

_____   _____

Doctor Jessie Nevarrez   Captain Edward Thomas Lee

_____   _____

Write your name with abbreviations and initials here. Use the abbreviation for *mister* if you are a boy and use the word *miss* if you are a girl.

_____

Days of the Week

What day of the week is it today?_____

Did you use a capital letter to begin your answer? If you did, you know this capitalization rule:

Capitalize the days of the week.

Here are the days of the week. They are not in order, and they do not have capital letters. Write them in order with capitals on the lines inside the watch. Begin with Sunday.

friday   **sunday**

monday   **tuesday**

wednesday   **thursday**

saturday

When you have finished writing, color the strap. Cut it out, and cut out the slots marked A, B, and C. Put the strap around your wrist like a watch. Tuck the tab in the correct-fitting slot. Fold the tab over to hold the strap in place. You are wearing the days of the week now!

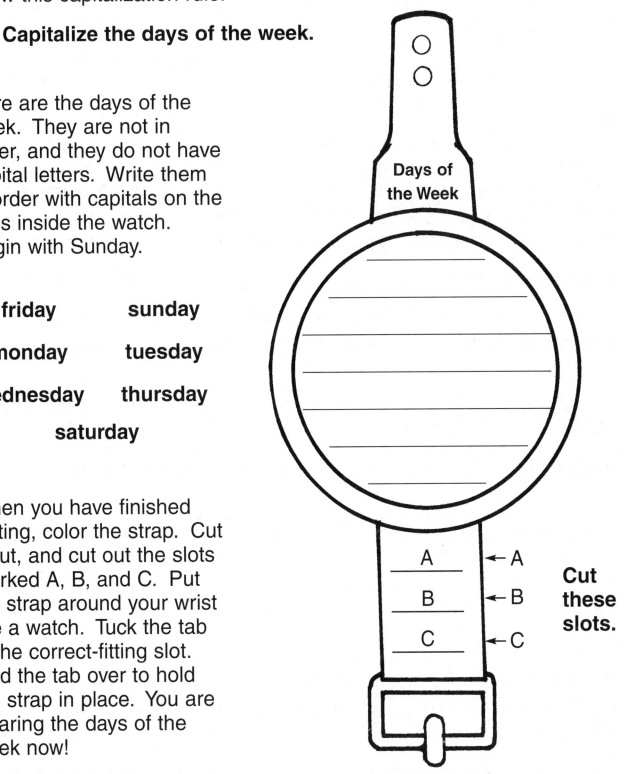

Cut these slots.

Months of the Year

What month of the year is it today? _____

Did you use a capital letter to begin your answer? If you did, you know this capitalization rule:

Capitalize the months of the year.

The months of the year are written in order below, but they do not have capital letters. Rewrite them in order with capitals. Next to each month, write something that you like about that month. It could be a special holiday, a pretty time of year, or even your birthday! On the back of this paper, draw a picture of what you like about one month.

january	**march**	**may**	**july**	**september**	**november**
february	**april**	**june**	**august**	**october**	**december**

1. _____   _____

2. _____   _____

3. _____   _____

4. _____   _____

5. _____   _____

6. _____   _____

7. _____   _____

8. _____   _____

9. _____   _____

10. _____   _____

11. _____   _____

12. _____

Holidays

What is your favorite holiday? _____

Did you start it with a capital letter? If you did, you know this capitalization rule:

Capitalize the names of holidays.

There are some names of holidays on this page. They are not capitalized correctly. Capitalize the holidays by changing a lowercase letter to a capital letter where it is needed. As you write each capital letter, color the same letter in the heart.

new year's Day

halloween

Fourth of july

hanukkah

father's day

mother's Day

easter

christmas

passover

valentine's Day

What letter did the colored hearts make? _____

Write the names of two holidays that begin with this letter.

1. _____

2. _____

Color the rest of the heart!

Vacation Time!

Do you like to go to museums, zoos, or parks?

Do you like to travel to a lake, ocean, river, or mountain?

These places and other places need capital letters when they are written with a name.

Capitalize the names of special places.

It is vacation time!

Here is a list of places that need capital letters. Correct the letters that need to be capitalized. Then choose three of the places you would like to visit!

1. pacific Ocean	5. san diego Zoo	9. disneyland
2. Grand canyon	6. hyde park	10. North pole
3. Mt. rushmore	7. sahara desert	11. rocky Mountains
4. amazon River	8. lake Louise	12. niagara falls

I would like to visit the following places:

1. _____

2. _____

3. _____

Name your favorite place to visit. Write something about this place.

_____

_____

_____

_____

Capital Thief

Mr. I. Stealem has taken most of the capitals on this page. Write capitals where they belong in his burglar bag.

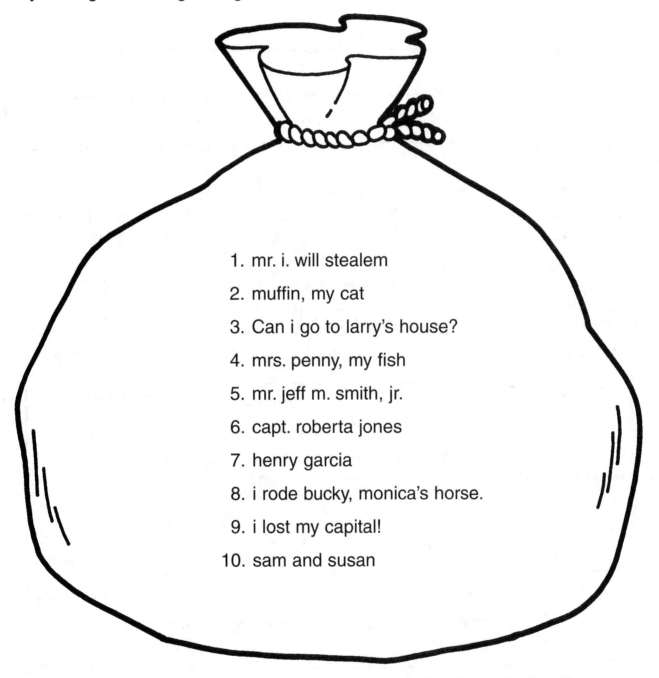

1. mr. i. will stealem

2. muffin, my cat

3. Can i go to larry's house?

4. mrs. penny, my fish

5. mr. jeff m. smith, jr.

6. capt. roberta jones

7. henry garcia

8. i rode bucky, monica's horse.

9. i lost my capital!

10. sam and susan

In the sentences above, what kinds of words needed to be capitalized?

_____

_____

_____

Central Park

Someone forgot to capitalize the name of the park in the park sign. Help the child reach this sign. Then capitalize all other words that need capitals.

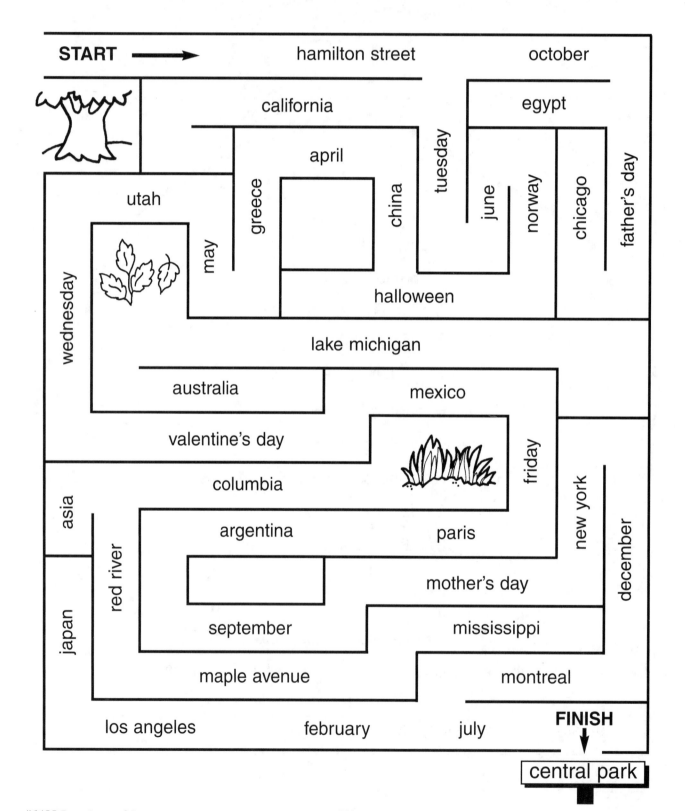

Action Word Fill-In

A **verb** shows the **action** of the sentence.

The train sped along the tracks.

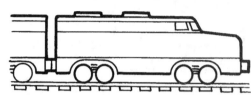

Write the word that shows what someone or something does.

1. The star twinkles in the sky. _____

2. The children watched the parade. _____

3. The dog chased the cat. _____

4. My brother set the table. _____

5. I swim like a fish. _____

6. The bird sings a pretty song. _____

7. You eat the last piece. _____

8. The player threw the ball. _____

"S" or No "S"?

Circle the correct verb form for each sentence.

The runner **races**
to the finish line.

The runners **race**
to the finish line.

Add "s" for
one person or thing.

Do not add "s" for more than
one person or thing.

1. John and Sue ___ the book.   **read**   **reads**

2. We ___ the kite.   **fly**   **flies**

3. Mary ___ across the pool.   **swim**   **swims**

4. Billy ___ the ball.   **chase**   **chases**

5. The monkey ___ the tree.   **climb**   **climbs**

6. I ___ a mile.   **run**   **runs**

7. We ___ up the mountain.   **hike**   **hikes**

8. They ___ to ten.   **count**   **counts**

9. He ___ the violin.   **play**   **plays**

10. We ___ the races.   **watch**   **watches**

More Action Word Fill-Ins

Write the word in the sentence. Add **s** or **es** if it is needed when the sentence is about one person or thing.

Jill **jumps** hurdles every day.

play   1. The cat _____ with the mouse.

win   2. The boxer _____ the match.

match   3. He _____ the opposites.

dance   4. We _____ to the music.

bark   5. My dog _____ at the birds.

eat   6. She _____ a hamburger.

like   7. Meg _____ to splash in the puddles.

shine   8. The sun _____ on the water.

watch   9. Jamie _____ the sunset.

walk   10. My uncle _____ five miles each day.

Present to Past

Draw a line to connect each action word from the present tense (today) to each word from the past tense (before today).

run	gave
see	brought
eat	saw
come	ate
make	built
build	ran
sleep	made
give	slept
take	took
bring	came
sing	sang

Describe It

Adjectives are words that describe.
Write an adjective for each word.

tall building

1. _____stairs

2. _____windows

3. _____stories

4. _____chimney

5. _____hallway

6. _____apartment

7. _____families

8. _____neighbor

9. _____room

10. _____street

11. _____door

12. _____friend

                                               #6455 Practice and Learn

Describing Word Fill-Ins

Write a describing word (adjective) in each blank.

1. The _____ man came to my house.

2. A _____ puppy ran through the yard.

3. I like the _____ bike.

4. We can play with this _____ toy.

5. I am wearing a _____ pair of shoes.

6. My mother is _____.

7. The nurse is _____.

8. I saw a _____ show on television.

9. The _____ pig rolled in the mud.

10. There was a _____ spider hanging from its web.

Describing with Your Senses

You have five senses. You can hear, see, feel, smell, and taste. Make a list of the things that you can sense: sounds you can hear, things you can see (the way things look), how things feel, how things smell, and how things taste.

hear	see	feel

_____   _____   _____

_____   _____   _____

_____   _____   _____

_____   _____   _____

_____   _____   _____

_____   _____   _____

_____   _____   _____

_____   _____   _____

smell	taste

_____   _____

_____   _____

_____   _____

_____   _____

_____   _____

_____   _____

_____   _____

What Is It? Name Something!

1. Name something round. _____

2. Name something rough. _____

3. Name something hot. _____

4. Name something cuddly. _____

5. Name something light. _____

6. Name something dark. _____

7. Name something loud. _____

8. Name something wet. _____

9. Name something funny. _____

10. Name something silly. _____

11. Name something small. _____

12. Name something square. _____

13. Name something orange. _____

14. Name something soft. _____

15. Name something big. _____

Pronouns

Read the sentences below. Decide who is the speaker. Write *he*, *she*, or *they* on the line after each statement.

1. "Wow, ice cream for dessert!" yelled the students in 2-B. _____

2. "Who wants to play soccer today?" asked Diana. _____

3. "That is my favorite song!" shouted Grandfather._____

4. "We're lost in the woods!" cried Hansel and Gretel. _____

5. "I wish I had a fairy godmother," sighed Cinderella._____

6. "Line up for recess," said Mrs. Johnson with a smile. _____

7. "You need to do your homework after supper," said Father. _____

8. "Let's order pizza for dinner," suggested Mother._____

"I"

When you write about yourself, you can use the word *I* instead of always writing your name. The word *I* is always capitalized.

Write capital letters where they belong in these rainbow sentences. Then lightly color each part of the rainbow the color each sentence is about.

Remember the rule: Always capitalize the word *I*.

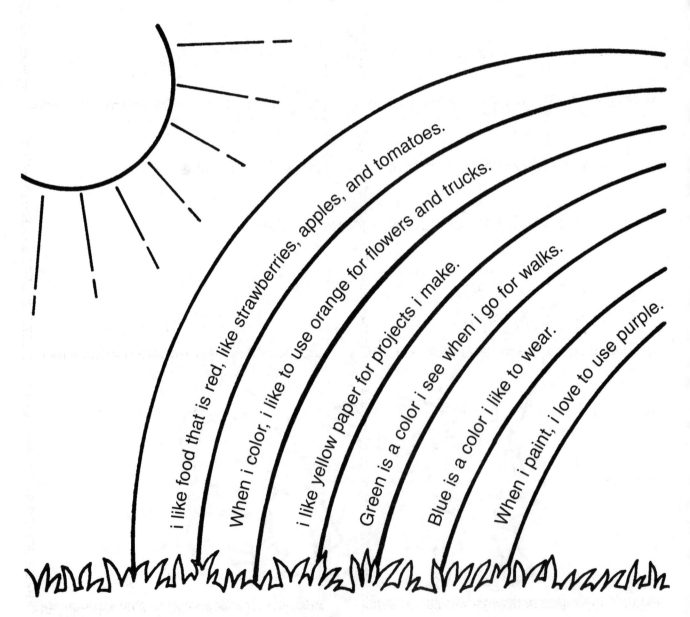

i like food that is red, like strawberries, apples, and tomatoes.

When i color, i like to use orange for flowers and trucks.

i like yellow paper for projects i make.

Green is a color i see when i go for walks.

Blue is a color i like to wear.

When i paint, i love to use purple.

What Are Synonyms?

Synonyms are words that have the same or almost the same meaning.

    Example: small, tiny

Illustrate each pair of synonyms.

smile, grin	wet, damp
bright, shiny	fast, quick
dirty, filthy	thin, skinny

The Synonym Connection

Draw a line to connect the synonym pairs. The first one is done for you.

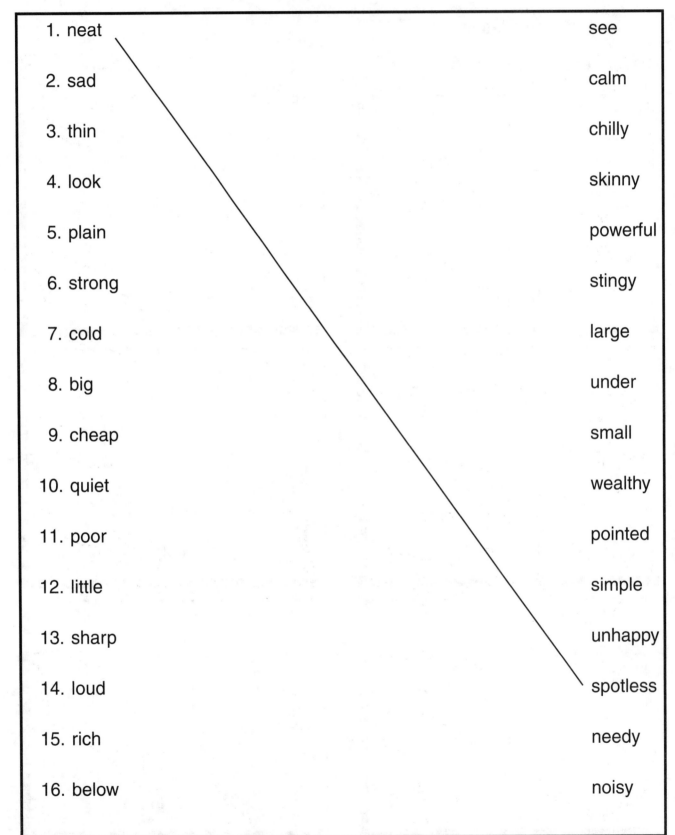

1. neat	see
2. sad	calm
3. thin	chilly
4. look	skinny
5. plain	powerful
6. strong	stingy
7. cold	large
8. big	under
9. cheap	small
10. quiet	wealthy
11. poor	pointed
12. little	simple
13. sharp	unhappy
14. loud	spotless
15. rich	needy
16. below	noisy

Synonym Blooms

Take a look at the flowers below. There are eight pairs of synonyms. Color the flowers with matching synonyms the same colors.

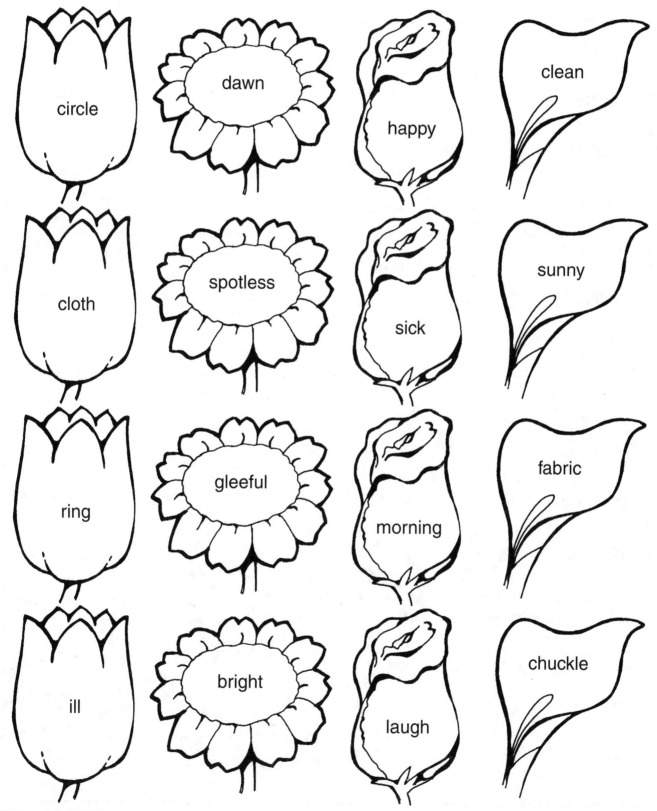

circle

dawn

happy

clean

cloth

spotless

sick

sunny

ring

gleeful

morning

fabric

ill

bright

laugh

chuckle

Synonym Search

Write two synonyms for each of the words below. You can use a dictionary or thesaurus to help you with this activity.

1. noise _____

2. kick _____

3. smart _____

4. funny _____

5. talk _____

6. eat _____

7. happy _____

What Are Antonyms?

Antonyms are words that have opposite meanings such as day and night. Draw two pictures to illustrate each antonym pair.

wet, dry

day, night

happy, sad

few, many

big, little

cry, laugh

The Antonym Connection

Draw a line to connect the antonym pairs. The first one has been done for you.

1. happy	young
2. brave	far
3. right	afraid
4. fast	weak
5. big	little
6. rude	tame
7. old	sad
8. strong	answer
9. crowded	ugly
10. smile	frown
11. close	slow
12. loud	wrong
13. ask	easy
14. wild	quiet
15. beautiful	empty
16. hard	polite

Antonym Fill-Ins

Complete each sentence with an antonym. You may choose to use a dictionary or thesaurus to help you find the best antonym. There are many correct answers.

1. A flower is soft, but a rock is _____.

2. Sugar is sweet, but a lemon is _____.

3. Fire is hot, but ice is _____.

4. Let's do the work now and not wait until _____.

5. Tell the truth. Don't _____.

6. Try to be kind and not _____.

7. The water is clear and not at all _____.

8. Keep moving forward. Don't go _____.

9. The sun rises in the east and sets in the _____.

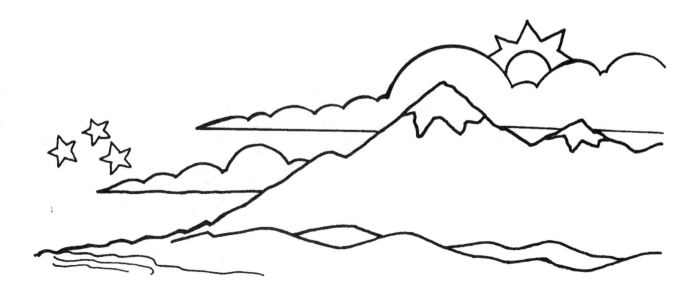

Synonyms/Antonyms Review

Synonyms are words that have the same or almost the same meaning.

Antonyms are words that have the opposite meaning.

Read the words below. Write "S" next to the synonyms and "A" next to the antonyms.

1. heat, warmth _____

2. litter, trash _____

3. happy, sad _____

4. speak, talk _____

5. hot, cold _____

6. hard, soft _____

7. fast, slow _____

8. wet, damp _____

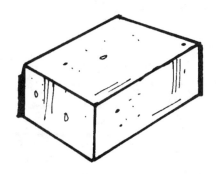

9. loud, noisy _____

10. hungry, starving _____

Synonym or Antonym?

Look at the word pairs. If they are synonyms, color the space red. If they are antonyms, color the space yellow.

Basic Sight Words

Basic sight words are an important part of reading. Sight words are those words that can be read without sounding out each letter. When you learn to read basic sight words, you will be able to read with speed and ease. Read the story below, and you will understand more about basic sight words.

"We're here!" shouted Carleigh. "We're finally at the zoo!"

"I'll go get the tickets," Mom said. "You wait here with Dad and Jeffrey."

As Mom walked to the gate, Carleigh and Jeffrey looked at the pictures of animals that were on the walls around the zoo. Jeffrey could read the words on the pictures, but Carleigh was too young to read much. "Some of the pictures have the same words on them," Carleigh noticed. "Why?"

Jeffrey smiled. "Those words are used over and over again when we talk and read. When you start school, your teacher will call them sight words."

"Why are they called sight words?" asked Carleigh.

"You will use those words so often that you won't want to take the time to sound them out. You just memorize the way the words look, and then you can read them quickly," Jeffrey answered. "Words such as *the*, *look*, and *said* are sight words."

"I'll be glad to learn to read," said Carleigh. "But right now, I would be happy just to go to the zoo. Look, there's Mom! Let's go!"

Practice Sight Words

Read the basic sight words to a parent or a friend. Put a check by the words that you do not know. You can make word cards to practice the words you do not know. If you learn these basic sight words, your reading speed will improve.

a	the	take	why
has	red	going	they
for	we	only	then
far	down	an	let
you	she	black	put
fast	good	eat	laugh
run	of	once	it
or	I	shall	cold
thank	his	these	him
done	blue	is	ask
went	at	made	when
and	found	hot	her
full	be	buy	ten
walk	drum	over	six
got	about	long	help
did	sit	where	please
if	read	he	have
saw	us	on	use
does	clean	around	funny
pick	go	wash	not

More Basic Sight Words

Here are more sight words to learn and know. They are a bit harder. Put a check by the words that you do not know. You can make word cards of those words and practice them. Try to learn all of these words.

came	show	every	wish
we're	pull	tell	into
own	find	may	by
been	green	five	my
soon	play	much	two
live	bear	water	box
garden	hand	time	cow
name	brother	sister	bed
chair	thing	watch	men
feet	home	nest	ate
very	light	pizza	could
new	because	cute	stop
say	your	knit	bring
ran	together	again	in
will	seven	round	all
under	white	first	yes
blue	orange	purple	tin
add	work	lucky	me
swam	mouse	knock	up
price	borrow	button	miss

More Basic Sight Words *(cont.)*

yellow	stop	jump	eight
cut	see	their	today
call	as	our	grow
old	no	better	ride
open	that	four	kind
like	try	never	this
now	just	can	write
to	had	must	get
which	do	make	but
with	said	what	fall
there	from	hold	how
was	am	off	best
warm	its	fly	some
so	big	think	any
drink	three	brown	carry
one	who	myself	sing
well	shall	little	come
pretty	don't	work	give
many	sleep	are	

How many sight words do you know? Keep practicing until you learn all the words!

Basic Sight Nouns

Here is a list of basic sight nouns. A noun can name a person or thing. Put a check by the words that you do not know. You can make word cards to practice those words. Reading will be a snap if you know these sight nouns.

baby	boat	wind	money
game	kitty	car	sun
paper	ball	dog	apple
girl	bell	song	eye
farm	tree	egg	father
boy	way	milk	doll
bird	rabbit	mother	toy
horse	cat	wood	table
leg	cake	seed	street
snow	ring	fire	coat
man	chicken	floor	farmer
hill	stock	shoe	house
back	robin	rain	cow
uncle	nest	duck	grandfather
window	bread	feet	cousin
grandmother	sister	watch	letter
birthday	corn	flower	night
home	thing	grass	head
men	party	house	chair
picture	brother	box	bear
name	time	day	frog
garden	fish	top	hand
aunt	sheep	store	orange

Alphabetical Order

When you put words in alphabetical order, you look at the first letter of each word. For example, the words car, airplane, and boat would be in this order: airplane, boat, car. Write these words in alphabetical order. Look carefully at the first letter of each word.

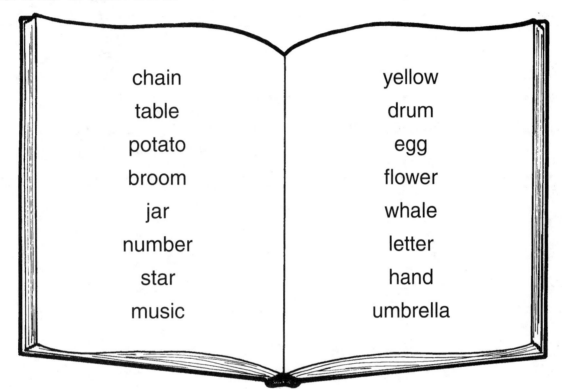

chain	yellow
table	drum
potato	egg
broom	flower
jar	whale
number	letter
star	hand
music	umbrella

1. _____

2. _____

3. _____

4. _____

5. _____

6. _____

7. _____

8. _____

9. _____

10. _____

11. _____

12. _____

13. _____

14. _____

15. _____

16. _____

ABC Animals

List the names of four of your favorite animals in alphabetical order.

1. _____

2. _____

3. _____

4. _____

Draw a picture of one of your animals and color it.

More Alphabetizing

When you put words in alphabetical order, you are alphabetizing. When you alphabetize, you usually look at the first letter of each word. But what do you do if you have more than one word that starts with the same letter? Look at the alphabetizing steps below.

1. Begin putting the words in alphabetical order. When you find two or more words that start with the same letter, put them in a neat stack.

   > dog
   > dad
   > doctor

2. Cross out or cover up the first letter of each of the words. Then you will see

   > og
   > ad
   > octor

3. Put these in alphabetical order. You know "ad" will be first because "a" comes before "o." Put the "d" back on the word and put "dad" first. That will leave these.

   > og
   > octor

4. Cross out or over the "o" because both words start with the same letter. That leaves:

   > g
   > ctor

5. "C" comes before "g" so "doctor" is before "dog" in alphabetical order. Here is the final list:

   > dad
   > doctor
   > dog

Circle the lists that are in alphabetical order.

bear	billy goat	bobcat	cougar
llama	cat	leopard	penguin
cheetah	parrot	parakeet	lion

ABC Review

A. List these words in alphabetical order.

river	friend	vest	jump
moon	house	silent	light
cart	ghost	tunnel	umbrella

_____   _____   _____

_____   _____   _____

_____   _____   _____

_____   _____   _____

B. List these words in alphabetical order. You will need to look at the second letters as well as the first.

dog	game	same	science
sort	lunch	grass	cell
loop	cane	lion	deer

_____   _____   _____

_____   _____   _____

_____   _____   _____

_____   _____   _____

Sequencing in Pictures

Arranging several pictures in sequence can seem like a hard job. Here are some hints for making it easier.

1. Look carefully for clues in each picture.

2. Think about what you already know about the sequence of events. Ask yourself what usually happens first.

3. Only look at two pictures at a time. Decide which of the two happened first. Put them in the correct sequence.

4. Pick a third picture to compare to the pictures you have already arranged. One at a time, compare the third picture to the others. Decide if the third picture comes before, between, or after the two pictures, and place it in the correct spot.

Write a number in each box to tell the order in which the events in each row happened.

More Pictures to Sequence

Indicate the correct order of the pictures in each row across by putting a 1, 2, or 3 in each circle.

Dessert in Sequence

Number the pictures in order. Color the pictures.

The Marching Band

Read the story. Then follow the directions below.

Marcus heard the music. "Listen!" he cried. "I hear it!" Marcus and his mother looked down the long street to their left. Only a moment later, they could see the band marching toward them. The bright red and blue uniforms sparkled almost as much as the shiny silver and gold instruments the musicians were playing.

As the band marched closer, Marcus looked at the instruments. He smiled when he saw the flutes. "Shawn should be coming by soon," he told his mother. After the flutes passed by, Marcus shouted, "There she is, Mom! There's Shawn!" He waved happily to his big sister.

When the parade was over, Marcus and his mother waited for Shawn to meet them. "You were great," he told Shawn.

"Thanks," Shawn answered. "I'm tired though. Let's go home!"

1. Circle the letter of the sentence that shows what happened first.

    A. Marcus saw the band.

    B. Marcus heard music.

    C. Shawn went home.

2. Circle the letter of the sentence that shows what happened after Marcus saw the flutes.

    A. He knew the trumpets would be next.

    B. He hugged his mother.

    C. He told his mother that he could see Shawn.

A Polar Bear's Day

Read the story. Then write the things that the polar bear does each day in order on the lines below.

The zookeeper at the Riverside Zoo was telling the children about the polar bear. "What does the polar bear do each day?" asked Paul.

"The polar bear swims, eats, plays, and sleeps," answered the zookeeper.

Paul thanked the zookeeper for his answer, but he was still curious. "When does the polar bear wake up? How many times does he eat each day? Does he take naps? Does he stay awake all night?" Paul's questions went on and on.

"Oh, I see. You want details about how the bear lives his day, right?" said the zookeeper. "Well, let me see. He gets up at dawn because the light and the heat wake him. He usually goes for a swim right away. He gets out of the water when we feed him, which is at about ten o'clock. He takes a nap after he eats. After his nap, he usually swims again. Then he plays until about six o'clock, when we feed him again. He swims and plays until bedtime, which is as soon as it gets dark. Now do you understand about a polar bear's day in the zoo?"

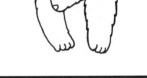

"Yes, thank you," answered Paul.   Then he turned to watch the polar bear with interest.

List the things the polar bear does each day. The first has been done for you.

1. He gets up at dawn.

2. _____

3. _____

4. _____

5. _____

6. _____

7. _____

8. _____

9. _____

Kelly's Puppet

Read the story. Then follow the directions below.

Kelly was cleaning her room. She found three buttons and an old sock that had a hole in it. She decided to use the things she had found to make a puppet. After she finished cleaning her room, she carried the sock and buttons to her mother. "May I make a puppet with these?" she asked.

Her mother smiled and said, "Yes, and you can also use the yarn in the sewing basket."

Kelly got the yarn and some glue. She carefully glued the buttons onto the sock so that they looked like two eyes and a nose. After that, she added yarn for hair. Finally, she put the puppet on her hand. What a great toy! Kelly rushed to show her mother her new puppet.

---

1. Circle what Kelly did after she finished cleaning her room.

    A. Kelly put the puppet on her hand.

    B. Kelly found some buttons.

    C. Kelly took the buttons and sock to show her mother.

2. Circle what Kelly did last.

    A. Kelly showed the puppet to her mother.

    B. Kelly put the sock puppet on her hand.

    C. Kelly glued yarn on her puppet to make it look like hair.

Trip to the Zoo

Read each story and then answer the questions.

Miles and Robin wanted to go to the zoo. Their mother said they could go after they finished their chores. First, they cleaned their rooms. Next they mopped the kitchen floor. After that, they washed the family's car. Finally, they got ready to go to the zoo.

1. What did Miles and Robin do first? _____

_____

2. What did the boys do after they mopped the floor?_____

_____

Miles and Robin were on an imaginary safari. First, their mother gave them a map of the zoo. Then, the boys went to the shark pool. Next, they found the way to the tiger cage. After that, they visited the wolf den. Finally, they met their mother at the alligator exhibit. Miles and Robin had a busy afternoon!

1. Where did the boys go after they saw the tiger?

_____

2. What did the boys see last?_____

_____

3. What did the boys do last? _____

_____

147

My Day

Think about some of the things you have done since you woke up this morning. Did you eat breakfast? Did you play? Did you go anywhere? If you wanted to tell a friend about your day, it would be easy. Just tell about your day in the order in which things happened.

Write five sentences telling about some of the things you did. Make sure the sentences are in the order in which they happened.

1. _____

2. _____

3. _____

4. _____

5. _____

Matching Pictures with Words

Underline the sentence that tells about each picture.

The lion roars.

Lions eat meat.

Lions sleep a lot.

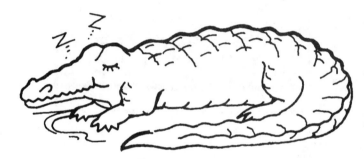

The alligator swims.

Two alligators rest.

The alligator sleeps.

The bear dives into the water.

The bear eats a fish.

The bear rolls in the grass.

Ice cream is a tasty treat.

Cupcakes are good.

I had spaghetti for lunch.

A Book by Its Cover

Sometimes, you can tell many things about a book by its cover. Look at the pictures on the covers below. Give each book a title that makes sense.

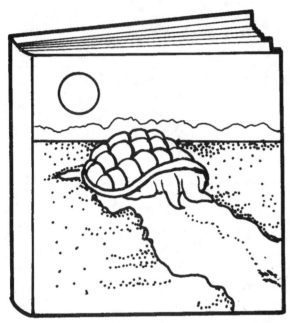

Title: _____

_____

Title: _____

_____

Title: _____

_____

Title: _____

_____

Title Mittens

If you read the title of a story, poem, or book, you will find a clue about the main idea. Read each title and description below. Draw a line to connect the pairs.

1. "The Snow Sunday"

2. "Ice Is Nice"

3. "Winter at the Pond"

4. "The Coldest Day of the Year"

5. "Disaster at the Ice Skating Party"

A. Animals and plants are still alive, even though the pond is frozen.

B. One very cold day, Sue learned that pets need special winter care.

C. Every Sunday, the aunts visited May Lie's house, except for the day that it snowed.

D. Ice has many important uses.

E. Skating on thin ice can be very dangerous.

A Hospital Career

Read the paragraph below. Color the doctor's bag that has the main idea.

Eric and Maria want to work in a hospital when they grow up. They read books about doctors, nurses, and the way the body works. Every time they see doctors or nurses, they ask many questions about their jobs and what they need to do in order to work in a hospital one day. They never get tired of asking, and fortunately their doctors are very patient! With so much research and interest, Eric and Maria are sure to make wonderful hospital employees one day.

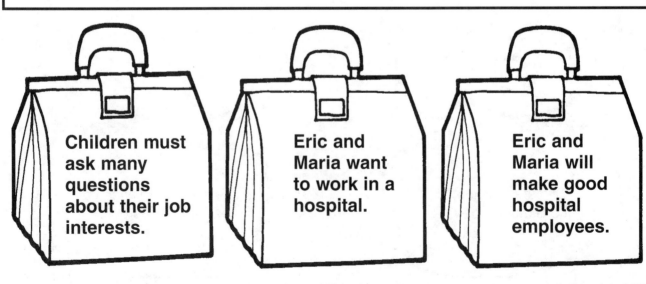

Children must ask many questions about their job interests.

Eric and Maria want to work in a hospital.

Eric and Maria will make good hospital employees.

Oops! No Homework!

Read the paragraph below. Color the girl who has the main idea.

Amy did not do her math homework. She was going to do it right after school, but a friend came over and they watched television. When Amy's friend left, she asked her mother if she could bake a pie for that night's dessert. She made an apple pie. After dinner, Amy went to her room to do her homework, but she discovered that she had left her math book at school. She was sleepy, so she turned out the light and went to bed early.

Amy forgot her math book at school.

Amy was too sleepy to do her math homework.

Amy did not do her math homework.

Picturing the Main Idea

Draw a picture that shows the main idea of each paragraph.

Kendra loves to read. She would keep her nose in a book every minute if she could. It is no wonder that she got her first library card when she was only three years old. Reading is her favorite thing to do!

The kitten crept up to the ball of yarn like a tiger stalking its prey. Moving first one paw and then the other, it kept its nose low to the ground and its eye on the ball. Every muscle was ready to jump.

Book Titles

Draw lines to match each book title to its main idea.

| No Television | A girl finds a dinosaur bone in her backyard. |

| George the Giraffe | An old key opens a secret door. |

| Follow the Star | A boy sets up an imaginary school for the neighborhood children. |

| The Mystery of the Broken Key | A lost girl finds her way by following the stars. |

| Saddles and Spurs | When the family television breaks, they all spend time together instead. |

| Fossils in the Neighborhood | Three children form a club to learn more about riding horses. |

| Sam's Summer Vacation | A make-believe giraffe has fun with his animal friends. |

| My Horse, Flash | A girl finally gets her wish, a horse. |

| Calvin Plays Teacher | A boy makes new friends at his summer camp. |

Inferences

When you use clues to draw conclusions about things, you are inferring. Read the paragraph below and make an inference.

"I could eat a horse! Lunch in the cafeteria wasn't very good today, so I didn't eat much," said Henry. "Do we have any cheese and crackers, or some apples?" asked Henry, as soon as he got home from school.

Henry was . . .

happy to be home.

hungry.

hurried.

If you said hungry, you are right. List three clues in the story that tell you that Henry is hungry.

1. _____

2. _____

3. _____

Making Inferences

Read the paragraphs and answer the questions that follow each paragraph.

"It sure is dark in here. Could we turn on some lights?" asked Wendy and Jack.

"The Fun House is too spooky!" said Jack, as he walked through it.

"I'm ready to go on the Ferris wheel," said Wendy.

1. What can you infer? _____

2. What clues did you find to prove you inferred correctly?

_____

_____

_____

_____

_____

_____

"I am not jealous of your new dress," said Mary. "I don't like that color on me anyway. My mother buys me more expensive things than that. I think the material looks like it would rip easily and not wash well. Where did you buy it? Was that the only one they had left?" asked Mary.

1. What can you infer? _____

2. What clues did you find to prove you inferred correctly?_____

_____

_____

Matching Inferences

Draw lines to match the sentence from the first column with the sentence that follows it in the second column.

1. The rabbit was too smart for the fox.	Now he can see much better.
2. We looked everywhere for our brother.	It hid in a hollow log and ran away when the fox passed by.
3. I like to play all kinds of games.	Stars twinkled all around.
4. The twins look exactly alike.	My favorite is hide-and-seek.
5. Emily saw a rainbow cross the entire sky.	We finally found him in the toy section of the department store.
6. The sky glowed in the moonlight.	Even their mother has a difficult time telling them apart.
7. The tiger crept through the tall grass and crouched in place.	Then it swiftly leapt at a nearby zebra.
8. Mr. Carter bought a new pair of glasses.	She thought she had never seen anything look so beautiful.

Drawing Conclusions

Finish the story below by drawing a picture and writing a conclusion.

"It was sure hot today!" said one of the children. They were in their bathing suits and ready to jump in the pool. Just then a swarm of buzzing bees flew near.

Conclusion:

_____

_____

Comprehension Fill-Ins

Complete each sentence with a word from the word box.

ate	knock
cough	laughed
cries	snore
delivers	wash
drove	wrote

1. Our mail carrier_____our mail early each morning.

2. I forgot to_____the dishes after dinner.

3. My cold made me _____and sneeze all day.

4. Did you see how fast he_____his race car?

5. I have never heard anyone _____as loudly as that!

6. The family_____pizza for dinner.

7. My neighbor_____a play for all of us to perform.

8. The doorbell is broken, so please_____.

9. The children_____at the circus clowns.

10. The puppy_____if we leave it alone.

Home Run!

Read the story. Then answer the questions.

Pow! Stacie stared in disbelief as the ball sailed over the pitcher, second base, and finally past the outfield fence. It was a home run, the first one she had ever hit! Dropping the bat at home plate, Stacie ran the bases one by one. Then she was home again, and the whole team rushed out to meet her.

1. What game is Stacie playing?

　　_____

2. How often does Stacie hit home runs?

　　_____

3. What does the team do when Stacie comes home?

　　_____

Draw a picture from the story.

Pounce!

Read the story. Then answer the questions.

Kenny woke up on Saturday morning and looked out the window. "It's raining!" he moaned and pulled the covers over his head. Just then, he felt a pounce on his feet and then on his stomach. He peeked out, and there was Buttons, purring and peeking back.

"Maybe it won't be such a bad morning, after all," Kenny thought, and, petting Buttons, he jumped out of bed.

1. What kind of animal is Buttons?

   _____

2. How does Kenny feel about the rain?

   _____

3. What happens to cheer up Kenny?

   _____

Draw a picture from the story.

Sing a Song of Sixpence

Read the poem. Then answer the questions.

Sing a song of sixpence, a pocket full of rye;

Four and twenty blackbirds baked in a pie.

When the pie was opened, the birds began to sing;

Now, was not that a dainty dish to
    set before the king?

The king was in his counting house,
    counting out his money;

The queen was in the parlor, eating
    bread and honey.

The maid was in the garden,
    hanging out the clothes

When down came a blackbird and
    pecked off her nose.

1. How many blackbirds are in the pie? _____

_____

2. What do the birds do when the pie is opened? _____

_____

3. What is the king doing? _____

_____

4. Where is the queen? _____

_____

5. What happens to the maid? _____

_____

There Was a Crooked Man

Read the poem. Then answer the questions.

There was a crooked man,

And he walked a crooked mile.

He found a crooked sixpence

Against a crooked stile.

He bought a crooked cat,

Which caught a crooked mouse.

And they all lived together

In a little crooked house.

1. Who walked a mile? _____

   _____

2. What did he find? _____

   _____

3. What did he buy? _____

   _____

4. What did the cat do? _____

   _____

5. What does everything in the poem have in common? _____

   _____

Old King Cole

Read the poem. Then answer the questions.

Old King Cole
Was a merry old soul,
And a merry old soul was he.
He called for his pipe,
And he called for his bowl,
And he called for his fiddlers three.
Every fiddler, he had a fiddle,
And a very fine fiddle had he.
Oh, there is none so rare
As can compare
With King Cole and his fiddlers three.

1. What sort of person is old King Cole? _____

_____

2. What is the second thing King Cole calls for? _____

_____

3. How many fiddlers are there? _____

_____

4. What kind of fiddles do the fiddlers have? _____

_____

5. List two pairs of rhyming words from the poem._____

_____

Lemonade for Sale!

Read the story. Then answer the questions.

Amy and Melanie wanted to earn some money to go to the movies. They tried washing dogs, but it was too messy. They tried babysitting, but it took too much time. So they decided to have a lemonade stand in front of their apartment building.

On a hot, dry, Saturday morning in June, the girls mixed the cold drinks in a plastic pitcher. They sold the lemonade drinks for one quarter each. Ten children and two adults bought the cold lemonade. Amy and Melanie each needed one dollar to get into the movies. Hooray! They were on their way!

1. Who is this story about?

_____

2. What two ways do they try to make money without any success?

_____

3. When do they open their lemonade stand?

_____

4. How much is a glass of lemonade?

_____

5. Do they get to go to the movies?

_____

Everything Counts

Count and write the number of space things in the picture. Then color the pictures.

 ☐   ☐   ☐

 ☐   ☐   ☐

 ☐   ☐   ☐

#6455 Practice and Learn

Coloring Fun

Color 3 stars yellow.

Color 2 balls red.

Color 1 bell blue.

Color 3 tops yellow.

Color 4 apples red.

Color 5 hats blue.

1. How many things are yellow? _____   ___stars + ___ tops = ___

2. How many things are red? _____   ___apples + ___ balls = ___

3. How many things are blue?_____   ___bell + ___ hats = ___

Circle the Number Words

Find the sum of the number pairs. Then circle the number words hidden in the word puzzle. The words can be found up, down, across, and backwards.

Example: 0 + 0 = 0

1. 3 + 2 = _____   8 + 3 = _____   5 + 4 = _____   4 + 3 = _____

2. 2 + 1 = _____   5 + 1 = _____   6 + 6 = _____   6 + 2 = _____

3. 1 + 0 = _____   9 + 1 = _____   1 + 1 = _____   3 + 1 = _____

Puzzle Words

zero
one
two
three
four
five
six
seven
eight
nine
ten
eleven
twelve

The puzzle grid:

f	o	u	r	e	z	e
t	w	e	l	v	e	i
x	t	l	o	i	r	g
i	c	e	n	f	o	h
s	e	v	e	n	e	t
r	e	e	r	h	t	x
p	c	n	i	n	e	z

Counting Dot to Dot

Draw a line to connect the dots from 0 to 100. Color the picture.

Gingerbread House

Write the numerals from 1 to 100.

1	2	3	4	5	6	7	8	9	10
11	12	13	14	15	16	17	18	19	20
21	22	23	24	25	26	27	28	29	30
31	32	33	34	35	36	37	38	39	40
41	42	43	44	45	46	47	48	49	50
51	52	53	54	55	56	57	58	59	60
61	62	63	64	65	66	67	68	69	70
71	72	73	74	75	76	77	78	79	80
81	82	83	84	85	86	87	88	89	90
91	92	93	94	95	96	97	98	99	100

Gumball Machine

Trace over the shaded numerals. Write the missing numerals in the blank gumballs. Count from 1 to 100. Color the picture.

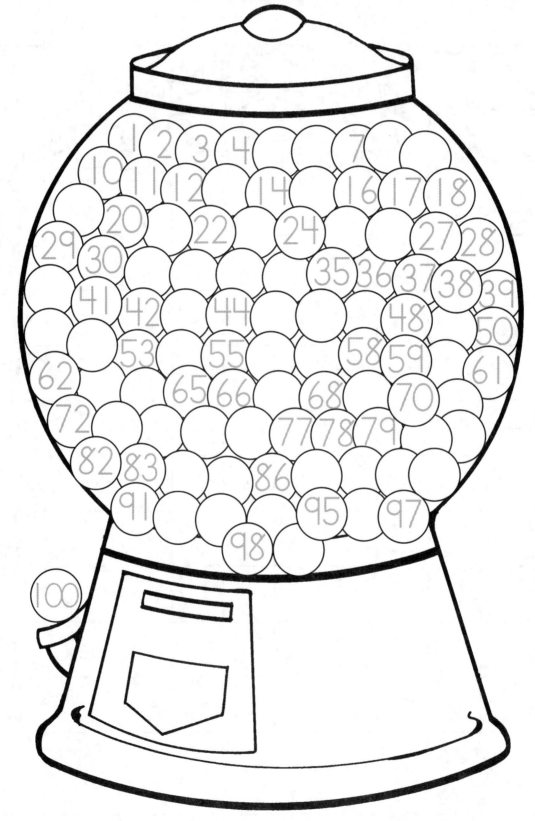

Making Sets

A set is a group of things with something in common, such as color, size, shape, or type of thing. Color the things that belong in each set.

Seasonal Sets

Color the things that belong in each set.

1. Autumn

2. Winter

3. Spring

4. Summer

Number Sets

Equivalent sets have the same number of members in both sets. Write the number in each set. Then color the two sets that have the same number of things.

1.

How many? _____

2.

How many? _____

3.

How many? _____

4.

How many? _____

Matching Sets

Draw a line to connect the matching things. Color each set of two matching things the same color.

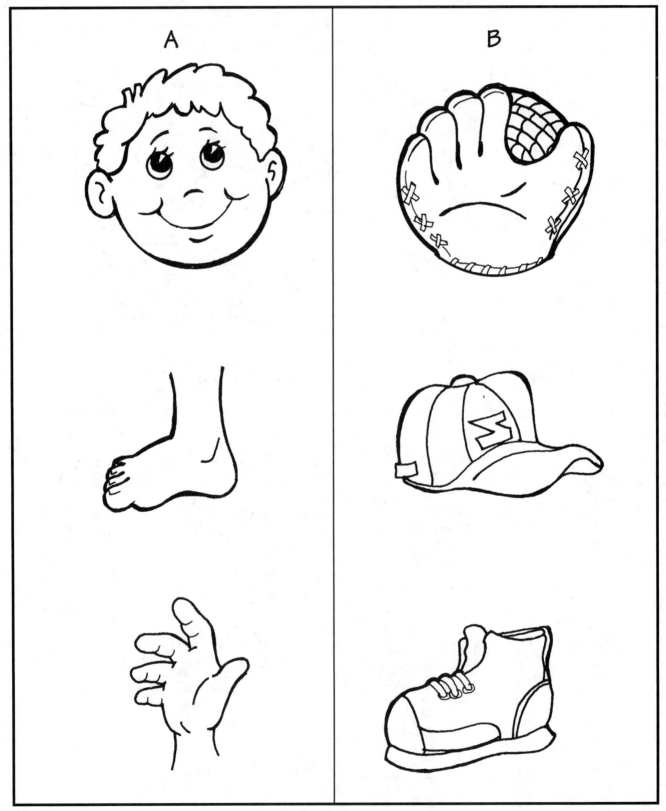

Which Is More? Which Is Less?

Write the numerals that show the number of things in each group or set. Color the group which is more in each row.

< is the symbol for less than

> is the symbol for greater than

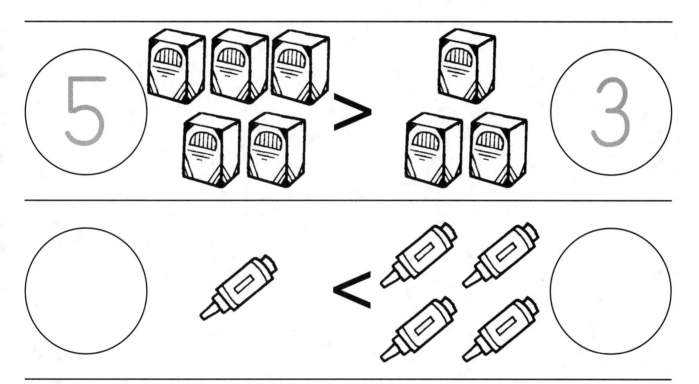

Write the correct less than (<) or greater than (>) symbol between the two numbers.

10	◯	8		2	◯	0		35	◯	14
64	◯	51		9	◯	11		79	◯	97
5	◯	6		21	◯	24		100	◯	12

Picking Lemons

"Pick" the lemons on the tree that have number pairs that equal 4. Color them each yellow. Color the lemons that have number pairs that do not equal 4 green. In each blank lemon, write and solve an addition problem.

Five Frolicking Frogs

Each number pair should equal 5. Write the missing numbers. Then follow the directions.

1. Use the green crayon to color the frog that had the missing number 0.

2. Use the red crayon to color the frog that had the missing number 4.

3. Use the blue crayon to color the frog that had the missing number 1.

4. Use the purple crayon to color the frog that had the missing number 3.

5. Use the orange crayon to color the frog that had the missing number 2.

$3 + \underline{\hspace{1cm}} = 5$

$5 + \underline{\hspace{1cm}} = 5$

$\underline{\hspace{1cm}} + 4 = 5$

$1 + \underline{\hspace{1cm}} = 5$

$2 + \underline{\hspace{1cm}} = 5$

Seeking Six

1. Color the fish that have number pairs that equal 6.

2 + 4   5 + 3   6 + 0   3 + 3

2. Color the gifts that have number pairs that equal 6.

1 + 5   2 + 2   2 + 1   4 + 2

3. Color the apples that have number pairs that equal 6.

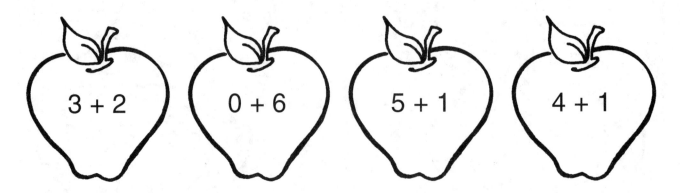

3 + 2   0 + 6   5 + 1   4 + 1

Trapeze Addition

Help the trapeze artist get caught by the right partner. Solve the problems. Draw a line from the trapeze artist to the partner with the sum of 8. Color the picture.

Jellybeans Add Up!

Color the jellybeans.

3 red	5 orange
2 brown	6 green
1 purple	8 black
4 pink	7 yellow

1. How many jellybeans are red or green?   _____ + _____ = _____

2. How many jellybeans are orange or pink?   _____ + _____ = _____

3. How many jellybeans are yellow or brown?   _____ + _____ = _____

4. How many jellybeans are purple or black?   _____ + _____ = _____

Books of Nine

Find the total of the number pair on each book. Color each book with a number pair that equals 9.

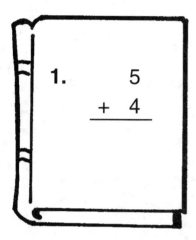

1.   5
   + 4

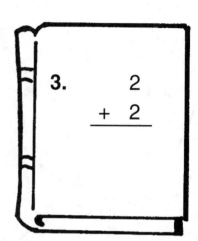

2.   6
   + 3

3.   2
   + 2

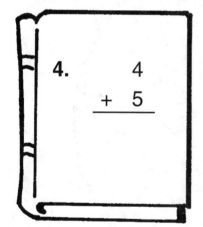

4.   4
   + 5

5.   5
   + 2

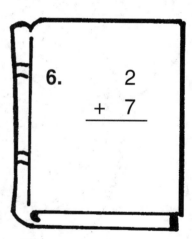

6.   2
   + 7

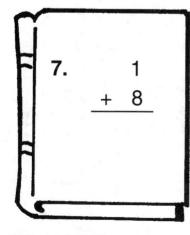

7.   1
   + 8

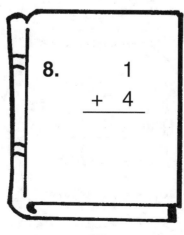

8.   1
   + 4

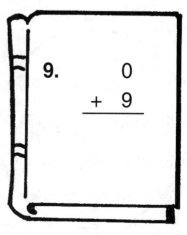

9.   0
   + 9

#6455 Practice and Learn

Add Tens

Each number pair should equal 10. Write the missing numbers.

8 + _____ = 10

7 + _____ = 10

9 + _____ = 10

10 + _____ = 10

6 + _____ = 10

4 + _____ = 10

2 + _____ = 10

5 + _____ = 10

1 + _____ = 10

3 + _____ = 10

0 + _____ = 10

Busy Bee Addition

Help the bee find the right flower. Solve the problems. Draw a line from the bee to the flower with the sum of 11.

Color the picture.

Math

Over the Wall

Harry built a wall. It protects his number trees. Solve the problems on the bricks. Right answers will make a strong wall!

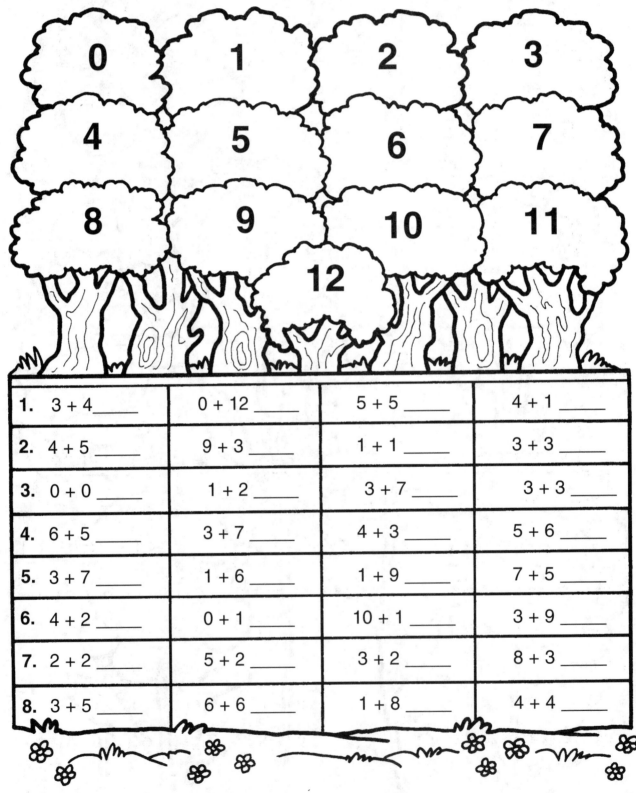

1. 3 + 4 _____	0 + 12 _____	5 + 5 _____	4 + 1 _____
2. 4 + 5 _____	9 + 3 _____	1 + 1 _____	3 + 3 _____
3. 0 + 0 _____	1 + 2 _____	3 + 7 _____	3 + 3 _____
4. 6 + 5 _____	3 + 7 _____	4 + 3 _____	5 + 6 _____
5. 3 + 7 _____	1 + 6 _____	1 + 9 _____	7 + 5 _____
6. 4 + 2 _____	0 + 1 _____	10 + 1 _____	3 + 9 _____
7. 2 + 2 _____	5 + 2 _____	3 + 2 _____	8 + 3 _____
8. 3 + 5 _____	6 + 6 _____	1 + 8 _____	4 + 4 _____

A Purse Full of Money

One of these purses is filled with money. To find the lucky purse, write the total of each number pair. Then follow the directions found below.

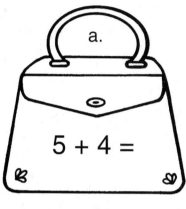

a.

5 + 4 =

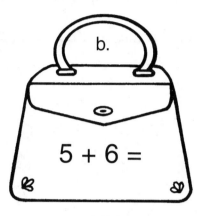

b.

5 + 6 =

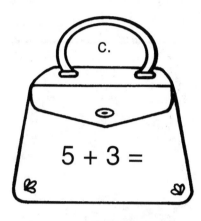

c.

5 + 3 =

d.

5 + 4 =

e.

1 + 2 =

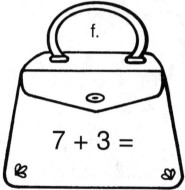

f.

7 + 3 =

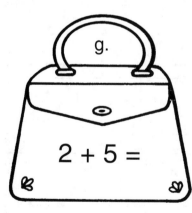

g.

2 + 5 =

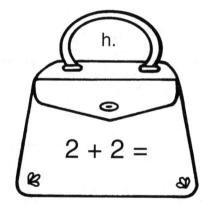

h.

2 + 2 =

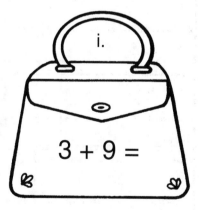

i.

3 + 9 =

It is not 11. Cross it out.

It is not 8. Cross it out.

It is not 9. Cross it out.

It is not 12. Cross it out.

It is not 4. Cross it out.

It is not 3. Cross it out.

It is not 6. Cross it out.

It is not 7. Cross it out.

What's in the Box? Addition

Guess what is in the box. Find the sums. Then write the letter in each box that matches each sum. Read the word you spell and draw a picture of it in the box.

5	6	7	8	9
r	g	a	o	f

3	4	1	6	2
+4	+5	+4	+2	+4
7				
a				

Getting the Eggs Home

To find the path through the maze, color and connect the number pairs that equal 12.

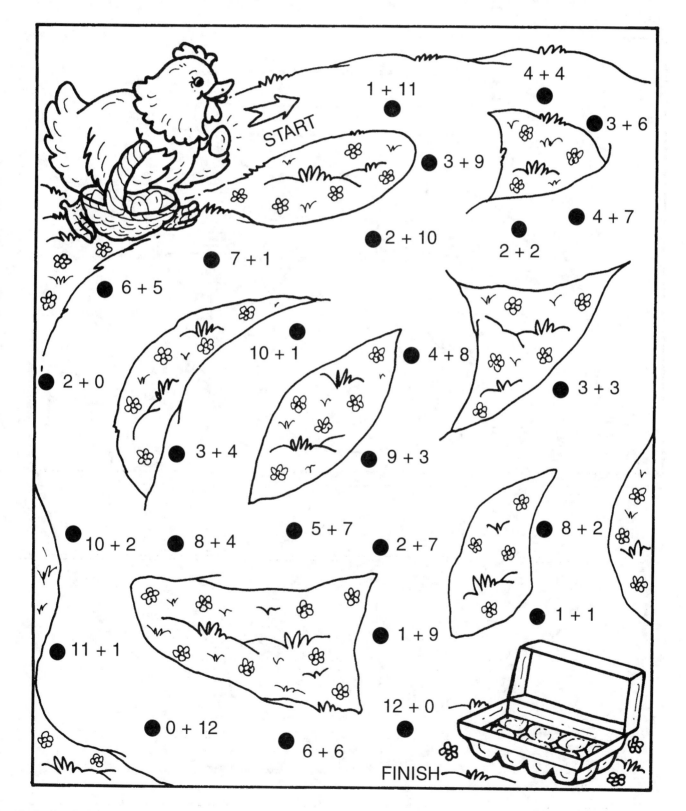

Fishbowl Addition

Find the sums. Color the picture.

9 = orange 10 = brown 11 = blue 12 = yellow

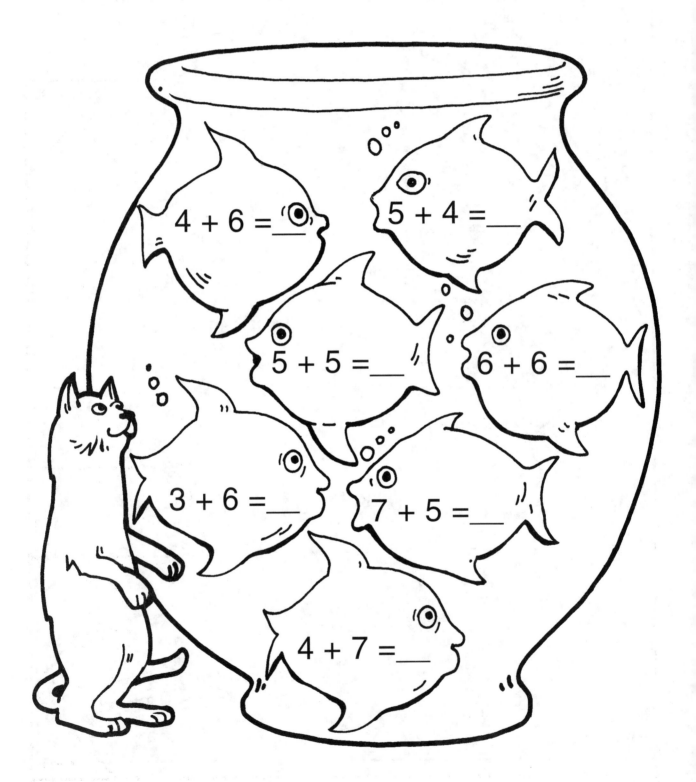

Butterfly Addition

Cross out each answer in the net as you solve the problems.

a
0 + 5 =

b
1 + 7 =

c
3 + 8 =

d
4 + 2 =

e
5 + 10 =

f
6 + 7 =

g
7 + 3 =

h
8 + 8 =

i
9 + 6 =

5 8 13 6 11
15 10 16 15

Adding Up in the Sky

Cross out each answer in the balloon as you solve the problems.

a
$0 + 6 =$

b
$1 + 10 =$

c
$2 + 3 =$

d
$3 + 5 =$

e
$4 + 7 =$

f
$5 + 9 =$

g
$6 + 8 =$

h
$7 + 4 =$

i
$8 + 2 =$

j
$9 + 5 =$

k
$10 + 9 =$

19 5 11 10 14 14

14 11 8 11 6

Money Addition

Use the prices to write addition problems. Find the sums.

a. | 🧸 + | 📗 =

$\underline{9} + \underline{5} = \underline{14}$ dollars

d. | 🧸 + | ◉ =

___ + ___ = ___

b. | 🐻 + | 🏎 =

___ + ___ = ___

e. | 📗 + | 🪀 + | 🏎 =

___ + ___ + ___ = ___

c. | 🧩 + | 🪀 =

___ + ___ = ___

f. | 🐻 + | 🧩 + | 🧸 =

___ + ___ + ___ = ___

Solving Word Problems

Read each word problem. In the box, write the number sentence it shows. Find the sum.

a

Kevin went for a walk and saw 1 frog, 3 cats, and 5 flowers. How many things did he see in all?

b

When Sally got on the school bus, there were 8 boys and 10 girls already there. How many children were there in all?

c

John ate a pizza with 7 mushrooms, 7 olives, and 5 pieces of pepperoni. How many toppings were on his pizza in all?

d

Today Jan saw 3 cats, 2 dogs, and 5 puppies in the park. How many animals did she see in all?

Adding Palm Trees

There are several ways to add numbers in a column. One way is to add the top two numbers first. Then add the bottom number to the sum of the first two numbers. Add the numbers on each tree.

1.
```
  2
  2
+ 2
———
```

2.
```
  4
  9
+ 1
———
```

3.
```
  9
  2
+ 1
———
```

4.
```
  4
  2
+ 1
———
```

5.
```
  3
  4
+ 1
———
```

6.
```
  6
  1
+ 4
———
```

7.
```
  8
  1
+ 1
———
```

8.
```
  3
  2
+ 3
———
```

          #6455 Practice and Learn

Skyscrapers Touch the Sky!

Skyscrapers stand very tall. Add the numbers on each one. Start by adding the top two numbers together and the bottom two numbers together. Then add the sums of each of those pairs to each other.

1. 3
    4
    3
  + 2

2. 4
    3
    2
  + 1

3. 2
    5
    2
  + 2

4. 4
    1
    2
  + 1

5. 1
    3
    1
  + 1

6. 2
    1
    3
  + 1

7. 3
    2
    1
  + 3

Our New Neckties

Find the sum of the numbers on the giraffe's tie. Remember to add the top two numbers and the bottom two numbers first. Then add their sums together. For numbers 4 through 6, remember to add the last digit.

1.
```
  2
  1
  4
+ 5
___
```

2.
```
  3
  2
  1
+ 2
___
```

3.
```
  6
  2
  1
+ 4
___
```

4.
```
  1
  2
  1
  3
+ 4
___
```

5.
```
  2
  2
  2
  1
+ 1
___
```

6.
```
  3
  2
  2
  1
+ 4
___
```

　　　　　　　　　　　　　　#6455 Practice and Learn

Playing on the Pipe Organ

Pipe organs make beautiful music. Each pipe makes a different sound. Add the numbers on the pipes of this organ.

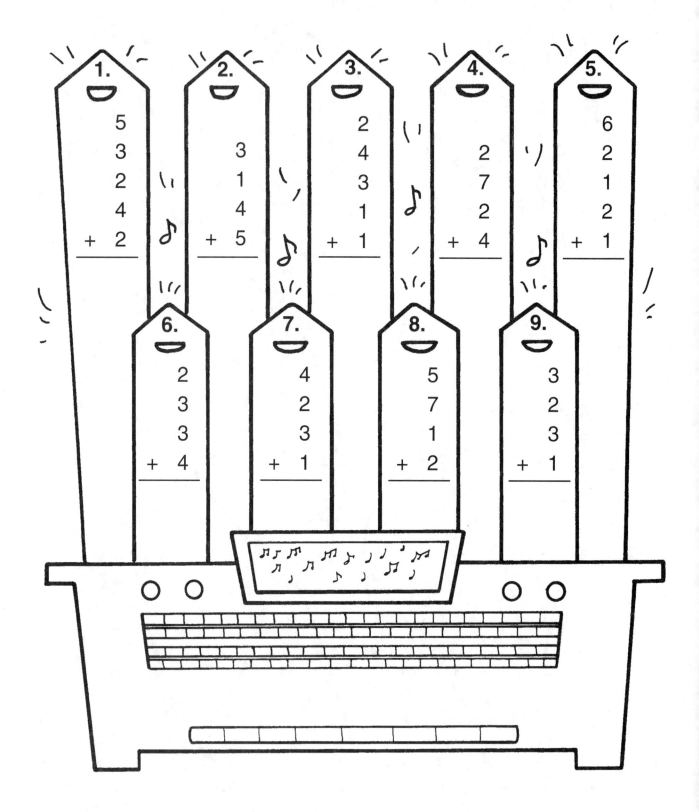

Adding Standing Up

See how well you do adding these columns of three, four, and five numbers.
Don't count on your fingers.

1.
```
    2
    4
+   2
―――
```

2.
```
    3
    5
+   1
―――
```

3.
```
    7
    2
+   1
―――
```

4.
```
    6
    2
+   3
―――
```

5.
```
    7
    4
+   1
―――
```

6.
```
    9
    2
    1
+   1
―――
```

7.
```
    8
    3
    2
    3
+   1
―――
```

8.
```
    7
    2
    3
    1
+   1
―――
```

9.
```
    3
    4
    3
+   2
―――
```

10.
```
    9
    1
    4
+   2
―――
```

Adding Larger Numbers

Marty and Karen collect stuffed bears. Marty has 4; Karen has 5. How many bears do they have? Simple!

You just add

The answer is

$$4$$
$$+\ 5$$
$$\overline{9}$$

If Marty and Karen continue to collect stuffed bears, and Marty has 40 and Karen has 50, how many bears will they have?

The numbers are larger, but you can add them just as simply.

First: Add the two numbers in the ones column.

$$\begin{array}{cc} \text{tens} & \text{ones} \\ 4 & 0 \\ +\ 5 & 0 \\ \hline & 0 \end{array}$$

Second: Add the two numbers in the tens column.

$$\begin{array}{cc} \text{tens} & \text{ones} \\ 4 & 0 \\ +\ 5 & 0 \\ \hline 9 & 0 \end{array}$$

You have your answer just like that!

Color the Quilt

Find the sums. Then follow the directions and color the picture.

Use a red crayon to color blocks with sums of 24.

Use a yellow crayon to color blocks with sums of 38.

Use a blue crayon to color blocks with sums of 41.

Use a green crayon to color blocks with sums of 57.

1. $\begin{array}{r} 20 \\ +\ 21 \\ \hline \end{array}$	**2.** $\begin{array}{r} 26 \\ +\ 12 \\ \hline \end{array}$	**3.** $\begin{array}{r} 12 \\ +\ 12 \\ \hline \end{array}$
4. $\begin{array}{r} 32 \\ +\ 25 \\ \hline \end{array}$	**5.** $\begin{array}{r} 14 \\ +\ 10 \\ \hline \end{array}$	**6.** $\begin{array}{r} 15 \\ +\ 42 \\ \hline \end{array}$
7. $\begin{array}{r} 11 \\ +\ 13 \\ \hline \end{array}$	**8.** $\begin{array}{r} 15 \\ +\ 23 \\ \hline \end{array}$	**9.** $\begin{array}{r} 11 \\ +\ 30 \\ \hline \end{array}$

Making the Baskets

Find the sum of the numbers on each "basketball" circle.

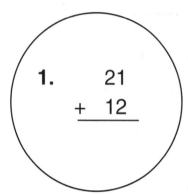

1. 21
+ 12
——

2. 16
+ 13
——

3. 32
+ 11
——

4. 10
+ 19
——

5. 21
+ 13
——

6. 31
+ 22
——

7. 40
+ 24
——

What Is the Secret Number?

To discover the secret number, find the sums and follow the directions.

1. 21 + 18	**2.** 31 + 16	**3.** 31 + 21
4. 41 + 31	**5.** 12 + 12	**6.** 10 + 17

1. It is not number 24. Cross it out.

2. It is not number 39. Cross it out.

3. It is not number 52. Cross it out.

4. It is not number 72. Cross it out.

5. It is not number 47. Cross it out.

What is the secret number?_____

Sailing into Addition

What a great day to go sailing! Solve the problems on each sailboat, and you will go far!

1.
$$\begin{array}{r} 10 \\ +\ 87 \\ \hline = \end{array}$$

2.
$$\begin{array}{r} 54 \\ +\ 22 \\ \hline = \end{array}$$

3.
$$\begin{array}{r} 21 \\ +\ 47 \\ \hline = \end{array}$$

4.
$$\begin{array}{r} 50 \\ +\ 28 \\ \hline = \end{array}$$

5.
$$\begin{array}{r} 85 \\ +\ 14 \\ \hline = \end{array}$$

6.
$$\begin{array}{r} 73 \\ +\ 13 \\ \hline = \end{array}$$

7.
$$\begin{array}{r} 24 \\ +\ 21 \\ \hline = \end{array}$$

The Shape of Things

Solve the problems on each shape. Can you name each one? Color the shapes that you can identify.

1.
$$\begin{array}{r} 17 \\ +\ \ 1 \\ \hline \end{array}$$

2.
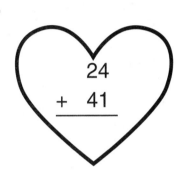
$$\begin{array}{r} 24 \\ +\ \ 41 \\ \hline \end{array}$$

3.
$$\begin{array}{r} 72 \\ +\ \ 11 \\ \hline \end{array}$$

4.
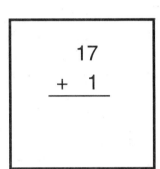
$$\begin{array}{r} 10 \\ +\ \ 10 \\ \hline \end{array}$$

5.
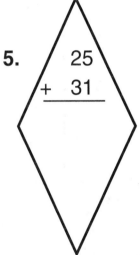
$$\begin{array}{r} 25 \\ +\ \ 31 \\ \hline \end{array}$$

6.
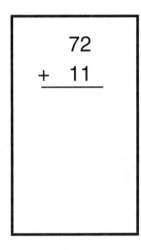
$$\begin{array}{r} 19 \\ +\ \ 40 \\ \hline \end{array}$$

7.
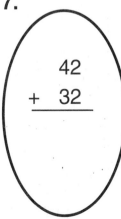
$$\begin{array}{r} 42 \\ +\ \ 32 \\ \hline \end{array}$$

8.
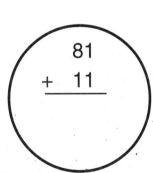
$$\begin{array}{r} 81 \\ +\ \ 11 \\ \hline \end{array}$$

9.
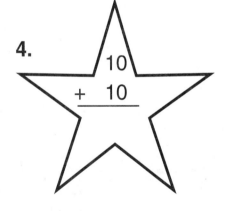
$$\begin{array}{r} 20 \\ +\ \ 40 \\ \hline \end{array}$$

10.
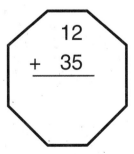
$$\begin{array}{r} 12 \\ +\ \ 35 \\ \hline \end{array}$$

What's in the Box? Addition

Guess what is in the box. Find the sums. Then write the letter in each box that matches each sum. Read the word you spell and draw it in the box.

25	26	27	28	29
k	c	a	o	l

$$\begin{array}{r} 13 \\ +14 \\ \hline 27 \end{array}$$

$$\begin{array}{r} 14 \\ +12 \\ \hline \end{array}$$

$$\begin{array}{r} 11 \\ +18 \\ \hline \end{array}$$

$$\begin{array}{r} 16 \\ +12 \\ \hline \end{array}$$

$$\begin{array}{r} 13 \\ +13 \\ \hline \end{array}$$

$$\begin{array}{r} 12 \\ +13 \\ \hline \end{array}$$

Add Them All Up!

To discover a secret message, find the sums. Then place each letter in the matching numbered space.

A.	B.	C.	D.	E.	G.
21 + 21	23 + 12	51 + 10	15 + 14	10 + 10	26 + 11

I.	L.	M.	N.	O.	R.
31 + 20	42 + 11	51 + 41	53 + 31	24 + 43	21 + 10

S.	T.	U.	W.	Y.
33 + 33	13 + 12	24 + 15	34 + 14	62 + 10

____ ____ ____ ____ ____ ____ ____ ____ ____ ____ ____ ____ ____ ____ ____!
61 67 84 37 31 42 25 39 53 42 25 51 67 84 66

____ ____ ____   ____ ____ ____   ____ ____ ____ ____ ____ ____
72 67 39   42 31 20   42 29 29 51 84 37

—

____ ____ ____   ____ ____ ____ ____ ____
25 48 67   29 51 37 51 25

____ ____ ____ ____ ____ ____ ____.
84 39 92 35 20 31 66

Learning to Regroup

You've come a long way. You can now add

$$11 + 5 \quad \text{or} \quad 10 + 15$$

Here's a problem for you: Sandy has 15 marbles. George also has 15 marbles. All together, how many marbles do Sandy and George have?

Simple! You just add.

<table>
<tr><td>tens</td><td>ones</td></tr>
<tr><td>1</td><td>5</td></tr>
<tr><td>+1</td><td>5</td></tr>
<tr><td>2</td><td>1 0</td></tr>
</table>

<table>
<tr><td>tens</td><td>ones</td></tr>
<tr><td>1 1</td><td>5</td></tr>
<tr><td>+1</td><td>5</td></tr>
<tr><td>3</td><td>0</td></tr>
</table>

Which answer do you think is correct? If you said 30, you are right.

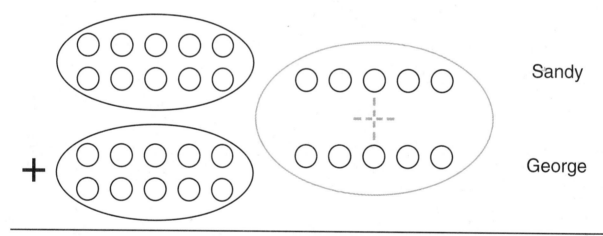

Sandy

George

+

2 tens + 1 more group = 3 tens, or 30 of tens

Adding in this way is called regrouping. When you add the two numbers in the ones column and your answer is 10, 11, 12, 13, 14, 15, 16, 17, 18, or 19, you must place the 1, which is in the tens column, on top of the two numbers in the tens column. Then you add those three numbers to find the correct answer.

The Champion Egg Layer

Gertie's chickens are the champion egg layers of Cameron County. Add the numbers on the eggs to learn how many eggs her chickens lay each day.

14 + 18	15 + 15	19 + 17
Sunday	Monday	Tuesday
15 + 19	19 + 12	16 + 17
Wednesday	Thursday	Friday
19 + 19		
Saturday		

211   #6455 Practice and Learn

The Balloon Clown

Solve the problems on the balloons. Use the code to color each balloon.

54 = yellow   75 = blue   52 = green   45 = pink

88 = orange   36 = red   63 = purple   96 = brown

1.
```
   49
+  39
```

2.
```
   57
+  18
```

3.
```
   18
+  18
```

4.
```
   38
+  58
```

5.
```
   16
+  36
```

6.
```
   47
+  16
```

7.
```
   27
+  27
```

8.
```
   27
+  18
```

Reveal the Message

To discover the special secret message, find the sums. Then place the letters in the correct spaces.

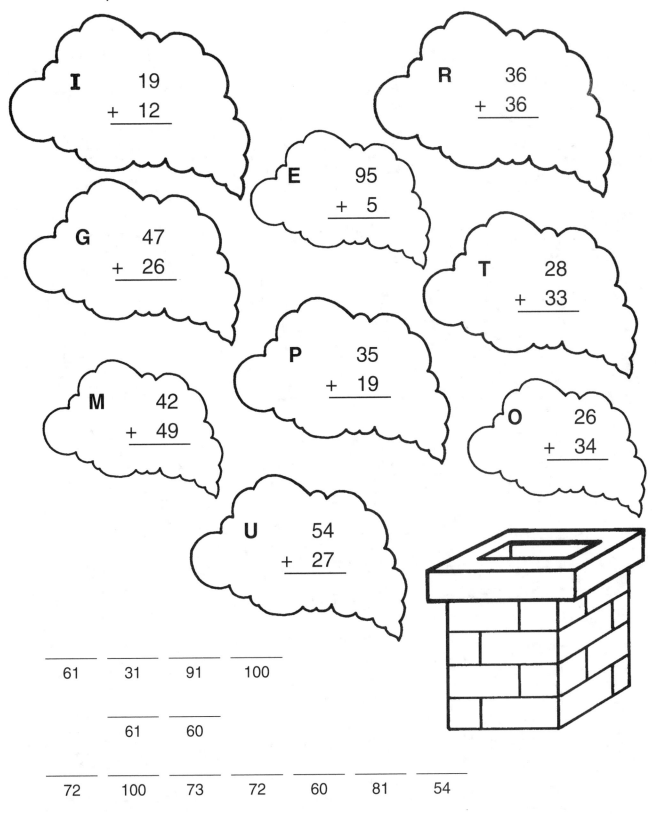

I 19
+ 12

R 36
+ 36

E 95
+ 5

G 47
+ 26

T 28
+ 33

P 35
+ 19

M 42
+ 49

O 26
+ 34

U 54
+ 27

___ ___ ___ ___
61   31   91   100

___ ___
61   60

___ ___ ___ ___ ___ ___ ___
72   100   73   72   60   81   54

Pick a Hat

Find each sum. Draw a circle around the hat with the smallest sum.

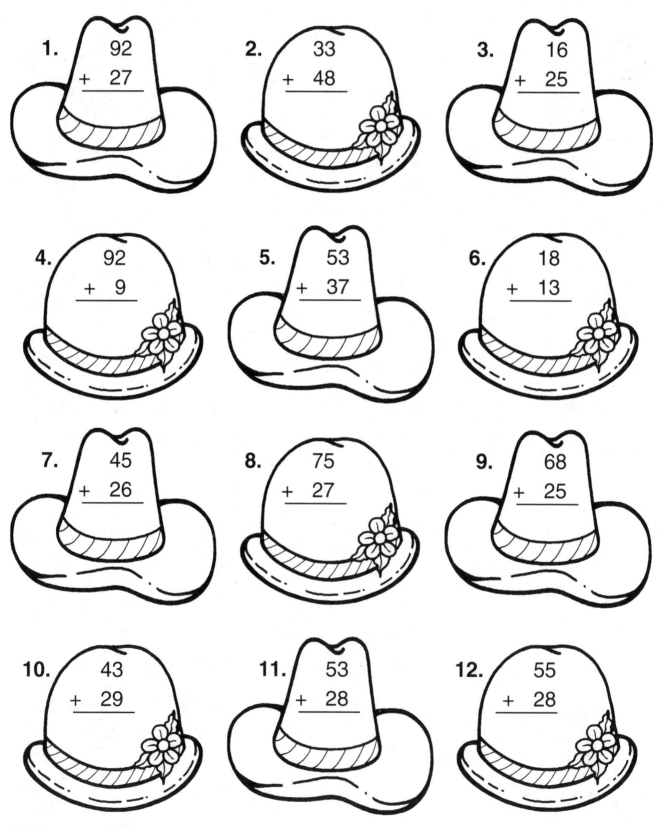

1. 92
    + 27

2. 33
    + 48

3. 16
    + 25

4. 92
    + 9

5. 53
    + 37

6. 18
    + 13

7. 45
    + 26

8. 75
    + 27

9. 68
    + 25

10. 43
     + 29

11. 53
     + 28

12. 55
     + 28

Right on Target

Find the sums of the numbers on the target. Where did Aaron's arrow land if he hit 60? Color that ring green.

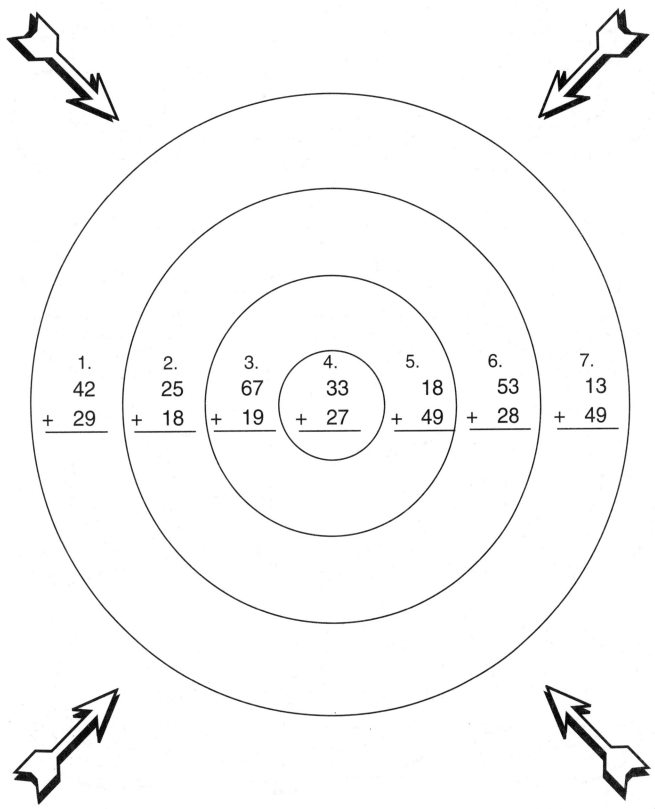

Search for the Missing Puppies

Peter's puppies have wandered away. Find the three missing puppies. Their tag numbers are 61, 48, and 27. Find the sums of the numbers on the tags. Use a brown crayon to color the tags from the missing puppies.

1.

$$\begin{array}{r} 19 \\ + \ 29 \\ \hline \end{array}$$

2.

$$\begin{array}{r} 15 \\ + \ 15 \\ \hline \end{array}$$

3.

$$\begin{array}{r} 24 \\ + \ 37 \\ \hline \end{array}$$

4.

$$\begin{array}{r} 26 \\ + \ 46 \\ \hline \end{array}$$

5.

$$\begin{array}{r} 19 \\ + \ 8 \\ \hline \end{array}$$

6.

$$\begin{array}{r} 18 \\ + \ 23 \\ \hline \end{array}$$

7.

$$\begin{array}{r} 92 \\ + \ 9 \\ \hline \end{array}$$

Foxy Addition

Help the fox find his den. Solve the problems. Draw a line from the fox to the den with the sum of 82. Color the fox.

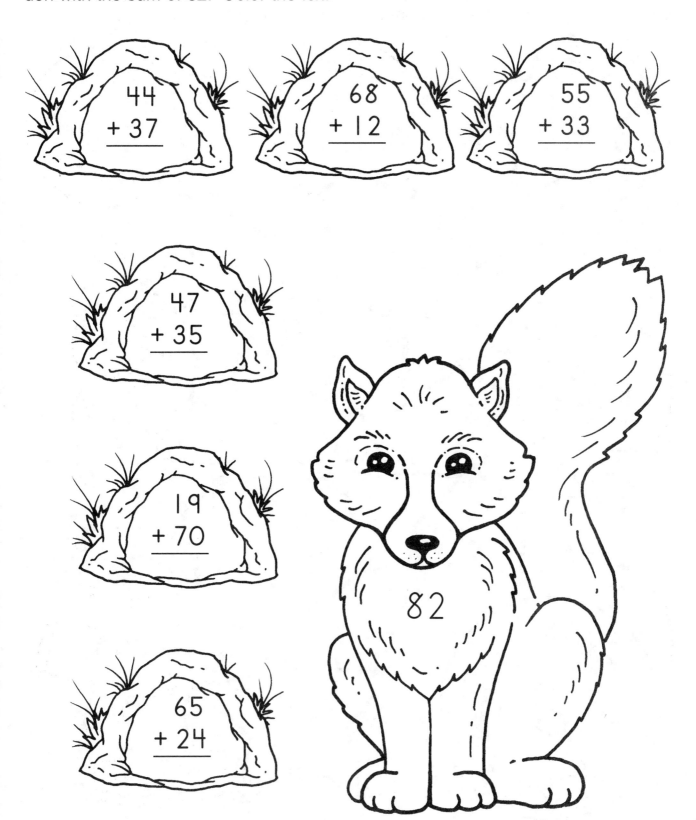

Addition in Space

Cross out each answer in the circle as you solve the problems.

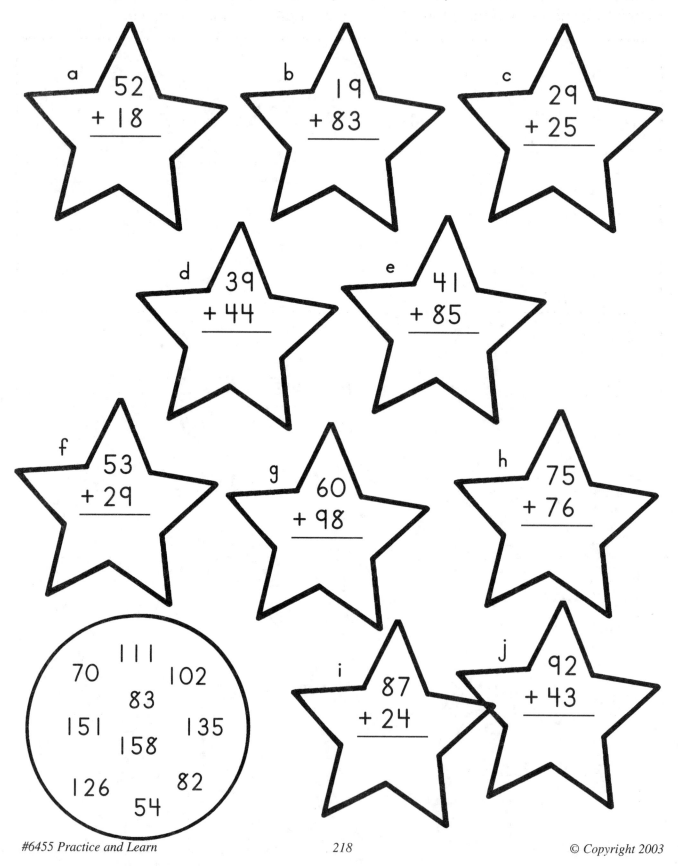

a
$$52$$
$$+ 18$$

b
$$19$$
$$+ 83$$

c
$$29$$
$$+ 25$$

d
$$39$$
$$+ 44$$

e
$$41$$
$$+ 85$$

f
$$53$$
$$+ 29$$

g
$$60$$
$$+ 98$$

h
$$75$$
$$+ 76$$

i
$$87$$
$$+ 24$$

j
$$92$$
$$+ 43$$

70   111   102

83

151   135

158

126   82

54

What's in the Box? Addition

Guess what is in the box. Find the sums. Then write the letter in each box that matches each sum. Read the word you spell and draw it in the box.

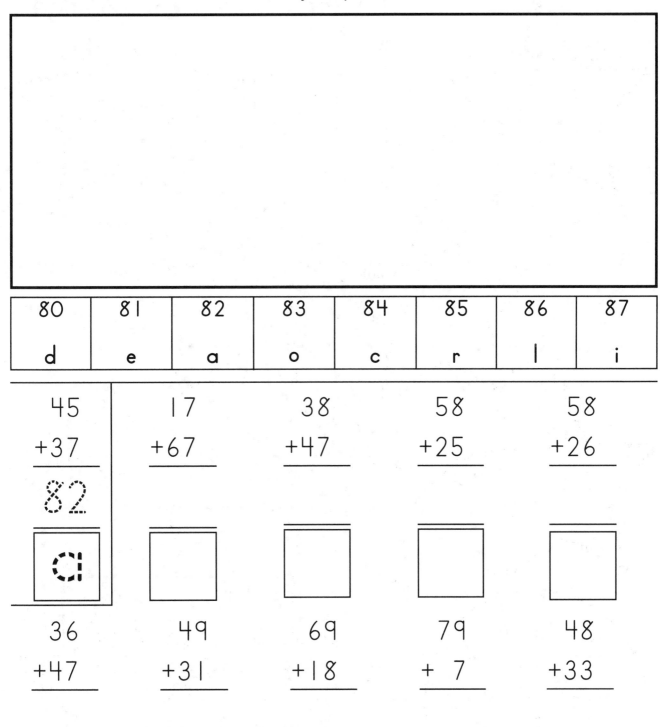

80	81	82	83	84	85	86	87
d	e	a	o	c	r	l	i

$$45 +37 = 82$$

a

$$17 +67$$

$$38 +47$$

$$58 +25$$

$$58 +26$$

$$36 +47$$

$$49 +31$$

$$69 +18$$

$$79 + 7$$

$$48 +33$$

Rainbow Addition

Find the sums. Color the picture.

45 = yellow	50 = red	55 = orange
60 = green		65 = brown

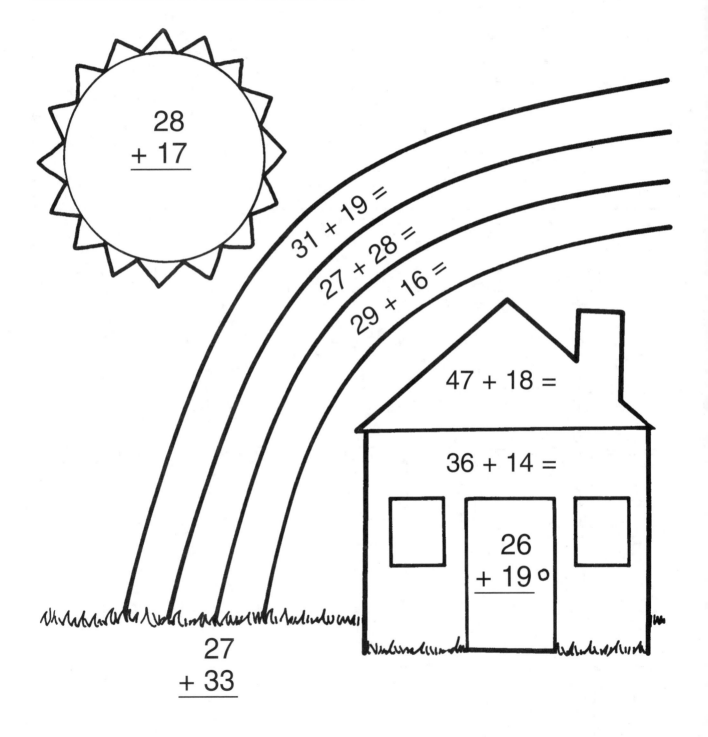

28
+ 17

31 + 19 =

27 + 28 =

29 + 16 =

47 + 18 =

36 + 14 =

26
+ 19 °

27
+ 33

Word Problems

Read each word problem. In the box, write the number sentence it shows. Find the sum.

a	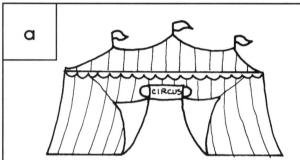

At the circus, Kenny saw 16 tigers, 14 horses, and 22 monkeys. How many animals did he see in all?

b	

When Sandra went to the tidepools, she counted 28 starfish, 32 fish, and 46 shells. How many things did she see in all?

c	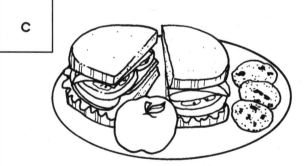

During one month, Jared ate 27 sandwiches, 23 apples, and 52 cookies. How many things did he eat in all?

d	

Emily did 19 addition problems and 33 subtraction problems at school. At home, her mother gave her 21 more. How many problems did she solve in all?

Subtraction Rainbow

Complete each subtraction problem. Then use the color code to color the rainbow. Add more detail to the bottom of the picture box.

6 = violet　　　　3 = green　　　　1 = orange

5 = purple　　　　2 = yellow　　　　0 = red

4 = blue

Ant Feelers

What do ants use to touch and smell? To discover the answer, first do the subtraction problems. Then use the number code and read the answer downwards.

Code: 1 = a
2 = e
3 = n
4 = t
5 = s

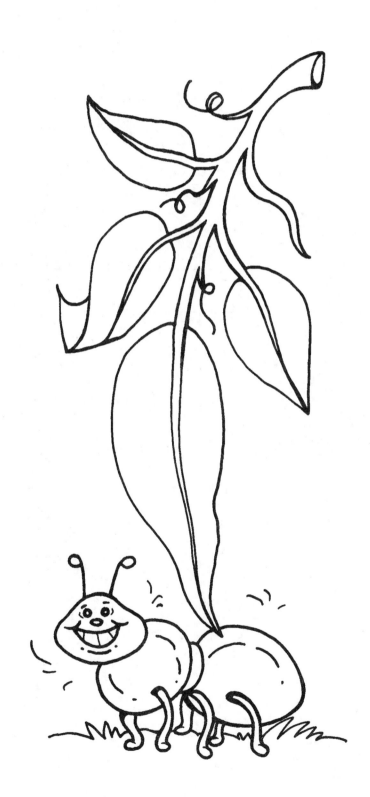

1. 6 − 5 = _____

2. 6 − 3 = _____

3. 6 − 2 = _____

4. 6 − 4 = _____

5. 6 − 3 = _____

6. 6 − 3 = _____

7. 6 − 5 = _____

8. 6 − 4 = _____

#6455 Practice and Learn

Ready to Paint

Find the differences. Use the answers to help you know where to put each color word in the puzzle.

Across

1. purple

2. orange

3. red

Down

1. blue

2. yellow

3. green

Hole in One

Find the answer to each problem. Draw a line connecting the pictures to show how the golfer can get from the flag with the answer 1 to the flag with the answer 9. Add other details to the golf course picture.

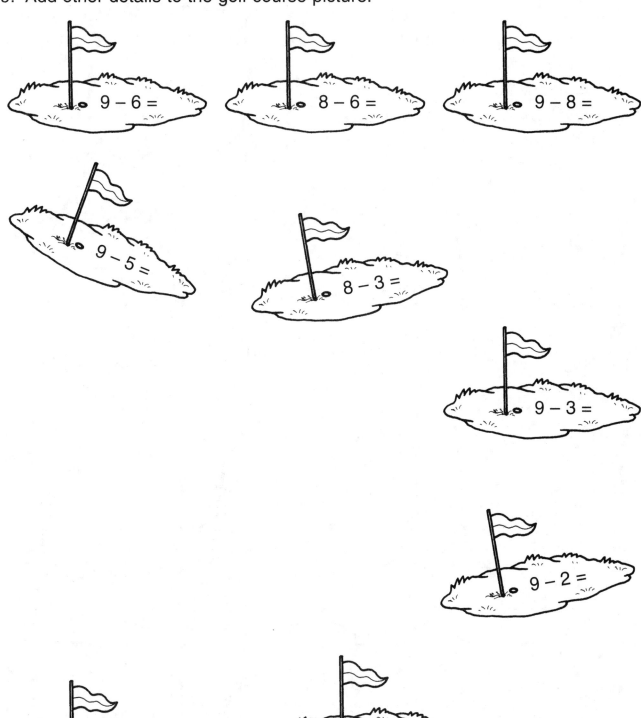

9 − 6 =

8 − 6 =

9 − 8 =

9 − 5 =

8 − 3 =

9 − 3 =

9 − 2 =

9 − 0 =

9 − 1 =

Subtraction Facts Garden

Solve each problem. Color each flower according to the color code.

0 = pink   5 = green
1 = blue   6 = purple
2 = red   7 = brown
3 = orange   8 = white
4 = yellow   9 = gray

1.

$9 - 9 =$ _____

2.
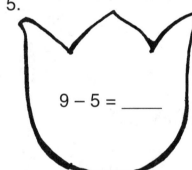
$9 - 6 =$ _____

3.
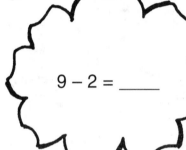
$9 - 2 =$ _____

4.

$9 - 8 =$ _____

5.
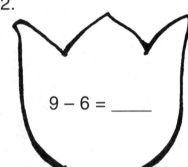
$9 - 5 =$ _____

6.
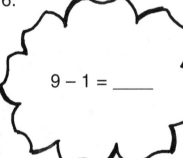
$9 - 1 =$ _____

7.

$9 - 7 =$ _____

8.
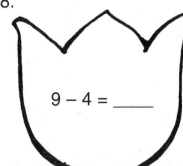
$9 - 4 =$ _____

9.
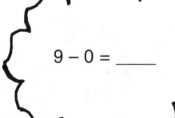
$9 - 0 =$ _____

10.

$9 - 3 =$ _____

Turtle Practice

Subtract each number in the middle ring from 10. Write the differences in the outside ring.

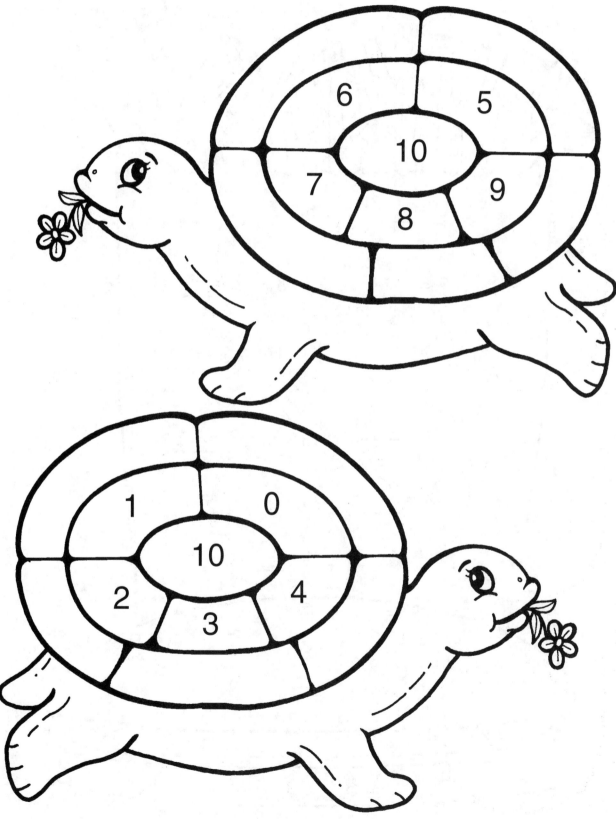

Fast Food Subtraction

Cross out each answer in the hamburger as you solve the problems.

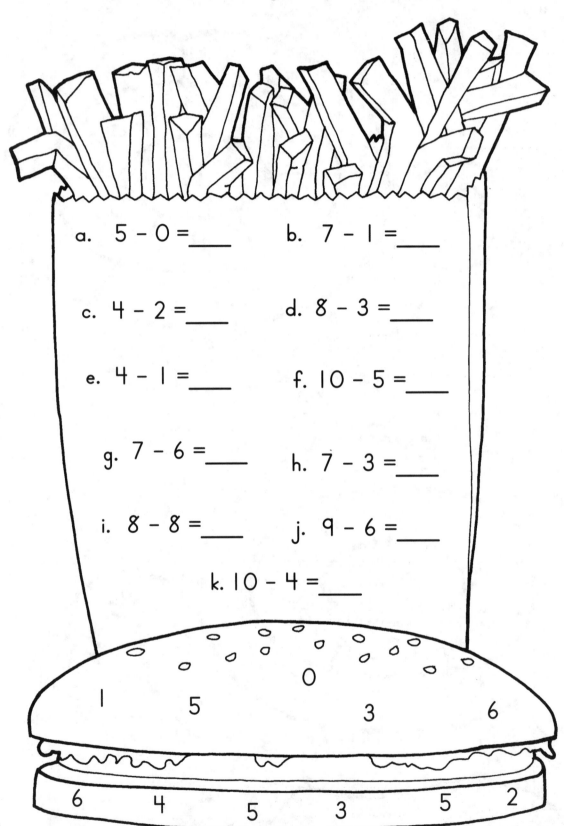

a. 5 – 0 = ____   b. 7 – 1 = ____

c. 4 – 2 = ____   d. 8 – 3 = ____

e. 4 – 1 = ____   f. 10 – 5 = ____

g. 7 – 6 = ____   h. 7 – 3 = ____

i. 8 – 8 = ____   j. 9 – 6 = ____

k. 10 – 4 = ____

Subtraction Crayons

Cross out each answer in the crayon box as you solve the problems.

a.
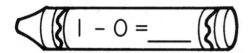
1 – 0 = ____

b.
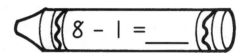
8 – 1 = ____

c.
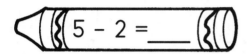
5 – 2 = ____

d.
4 – 3 = ____

e.
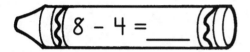
8 – 4 = ____

f.
5 – 4 = ____

g.
9 – 6 = ____

h.
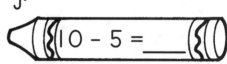
7 – 7 = ____

i.
8 – 7 = ____

j.
10 – 5 = ____

k.
9 – 3 = ____

My Crayons

| 7 | 3 | 1 | 1 | 4 |
| 3 | 1 | 0 | 6 | 5 | 1 |

Dog Bones!

Draw a line to match each equation to its answer.

a. $9 - 2 =$ _____

b. $7 - 4 =$ _____

c. $10 - 9 =$ _____

d. $6 - 6 =$ _____

e. $3 - 1 =$ _____

f. $8 - 4 =$ _____

1

2

7

0

4

3

What's in the Box? Subtraction

Guess what is in the box. Find the answers. Then write the letter in each box that matches each answer. Read the word you spell and draw it in the box.

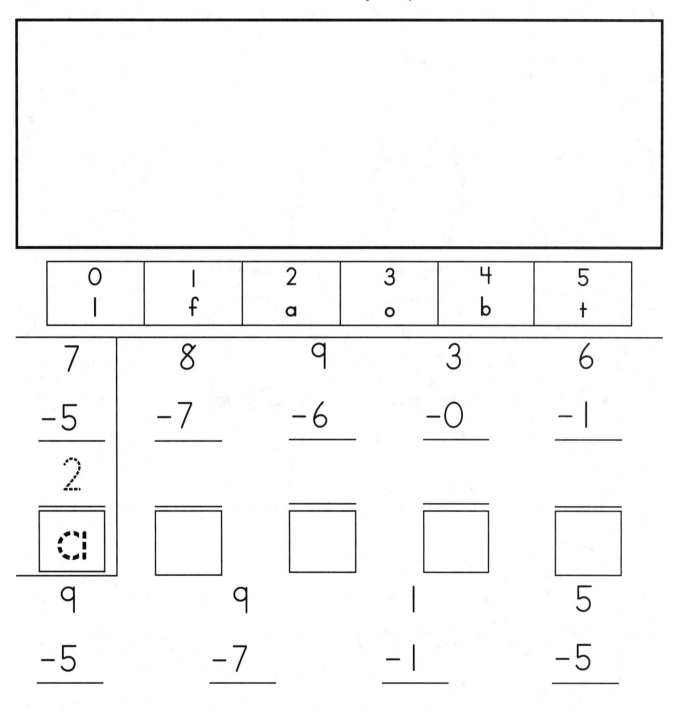

0	1	2	3	4	5
1	f	a	o	b	t

$$\begin{array}{r} 7 \\ -5 \\ \hline 2 \end{array} \quad \begin{array}{r} 8 \\ -7 \\ \hline \end{array} \quad \begin{array}{r} 9 \\ -6 \\ \hline \end{array} \quad \begin{array}{r} 3 \\ -0 \\ \hline \end{array} \quad \begin{array}{r} 6 \\ -1 \\ \hline \end{array}$$

$$\begin{array}{r} 9 \\ -5 \\ \hline \end{array} \quad \begin{array}{r} 9 \\ -7 \\ \hline \end{array} \quad \begin{array}{r} 1 \\ -1 \\ \hline \end{array} \quad \begin{array}{r} 5 \\ -5 \\ \hline \end{array}$$

Ice-Cream Yummies

Find the answers. Color the pictures.

| 0 = yellow | 1 = pink | 2 = brown | 3 = green | 4 = white |

To the Rescue

Solve each subtraction problem along the path. How fast can you get to the burning building?

11 − 11 =

11 − 10 =

11 − 8 =

11 − 7 =

11 − 9 =

11 − 2 =

11 − 3 =

11 − 6 =

11 − 5 =

11 − 4 =

11 − 1 =

11 − 0 =

A Dozen Eggs

Look at each egg carton. Count to see how many eggs there are in each one.
How many more are needed to make a dozen? Write a subtraction sentence for
each carton of eggs.

1.   12 – _____ = _____

2.   12 – _____ = _____

3.   12 – _____ = _____

4.   12 – _____ = _____

5.   12 – _____ = _____

6.   12 – _____ = _____

7.   12 – _____ = _____

Up and Away

Solve each subtraction problem. Then use the color code to color the picture.

1, 2 = blue   3, 4, 5, 6 = yellow   11, 12 = white

7, 8 = red   9, 10 = green

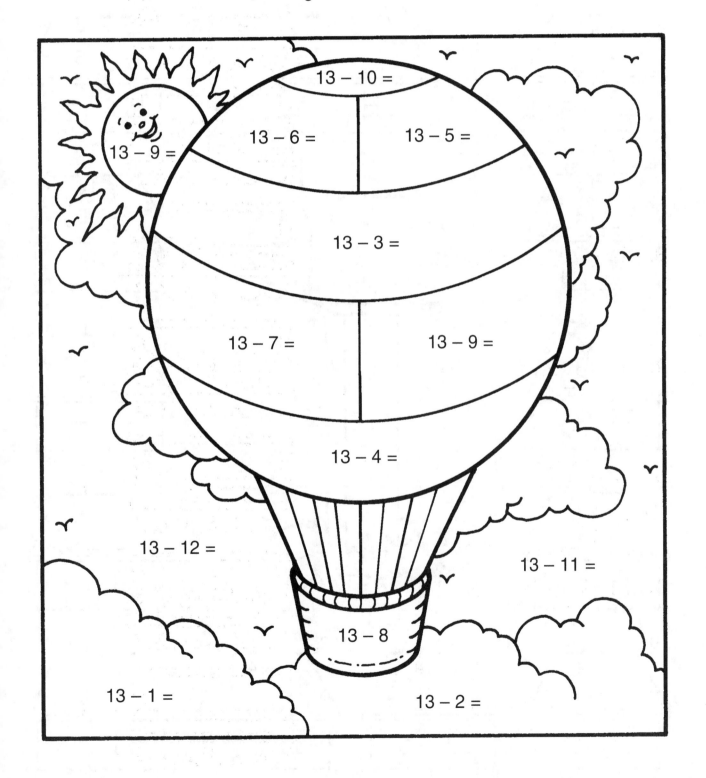

Subtraction Mail

Can you match the mailbox to the right house? Subtract to find the right house numbers. Draw a line from the mailbox to the correct house.

1. 14
    − 1

2. 14
    − 8

3. 14
    − 13

4. 14
    − 12

5. 14
    − 5

6. 14
    − 2

7. 14
    − 6

8. 14
    − 11

9. 14
    − 7

10. 14
    − 3

11. 14
    − 10

12. 14
    − 4

13. 14
    − 9

MAIL

8

In the Pet Store

How many pets are there in each tank? How many are shaded? Write a
subtraction number sentence on each line to show how many are not shaded.
Read the clues to find out. Then color the creatures that are not shaded.

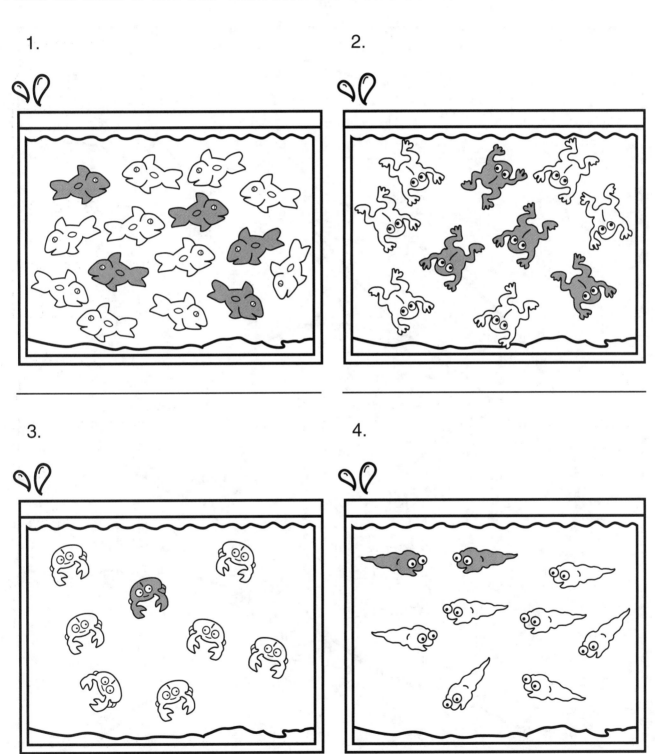

1.

2.

_____

3.

4.

_____

Food Fit for a What?

To discover what is hidden in the picture, use a blue crayon to color the areas with a difference more than 10. Use a gray crayon to color areas with a difference less than 10.

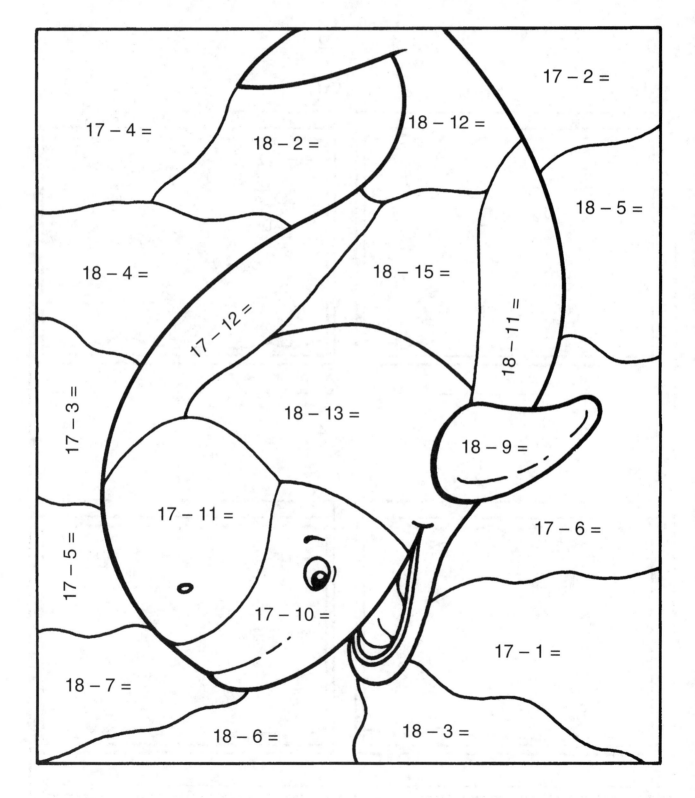

A Sneaky Snake

To find out what the sneaky snake has to say, subtract the problems. Then fill in the number code.

15 – 10 = G   17 – 6 = R

20 – 19 = A   13 – 6 = K

20 – 8 = S   14 – 11 = C

17 – 15 = B   17 – 9 = L

20 – 11 = N   12 – 6 = H

16 – 12 = E   13 – 3 = O

What a sneaky snake I am. I get my name from my hard, turned-up

____ ____ ____ ____. If I think someone might harm me, I flatten my
  9   10   12   4

head and hiss. Then I strike hard with my ____ ____ ____ ____, but I
                                            9   10   12   4

don't bite. Oh no! If that doesn't work, I ____ ____ ____ ____ over and
                                             11   10   8   8

play dead! If people pick me up, I ____ ____ ____ ____ limply. When
                                     6   1   9   5

they put me back down, I flip over on my ____ ____ ____ ____.
                                          2   1   3   7

I'm a ____ ____ ____ ____ ____ ____ ____ snake.
       6   10   5   9   10   12   4

Subtraction Word Problems

a. Count the apples. Cross out 4 apples. Write the numerals on the lines to show the subtraction problem and answer.

_____ − _____ = _____

b. Count the baskets. Cross out 2 baskets. Write the numerals on the lines to show the subtraction problem and answer.

_____ − _____ = _____

c. Count the pens. Cross out 3 pens. Write the numerals on the lines to show the subtraction problem and answer.

_____ − _____ = _____

d. Count the chicks. Cross out 4 chicks. Write the numerals on the lines to show the subtraction problem and answer.

_____ − _____ = _____

e. Count the snakes. Cross out 1 snake. Write the numerals on the lines to show the subtraction problem and answer.

_____ − _____ = _____

More Word Problems

Read each word problem. Write the number sentence it shows. Find the difference.

a

A dog was walking through his yard when he saw 7 cats on the fence. He barked, and 6 cats ran away. How many cats were left?

b

A woman grew a vegetable garden, and in it there were 9 ears of corn. She picked 3 ears on one day, 0 ears on the next, and 6 ears on the third day. How many ears of corn were left in her garden?

c

The monkey had 10 bananas. He ate 1 the first day and 6 the second. How many bananas were left?

d

A boy had 5 assignments for homework. He completed 3 before dinner and 1 after dinner. How many assignments were left?

Subtracting Two-Digit Numbers (No Regrouping)

When subtracting a two-digit number from another two-digit number, begin in the ones column. Subtract the ones from the ones. Then subtract the tens from the tens.

Problem: Max wants to subtract 12 from 23. He begins by subtracting 2 from 3 (the numbers in the ones column). Then he subtracts the 1 from 2 (the numbers in the tens column). The answer is 11.

tens	ones
2	3
−1	2
1	1

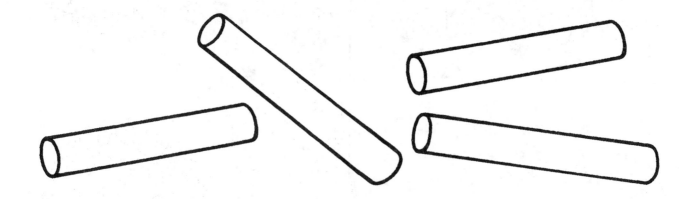

Busy Beaver Subtraction

Help the beaver find its dam. Solve the problems. Draw a line from the beaver to the dam with the answer of 22. Color the beaver.

49
− 26
_____

47
− 35
_____

68
− 47
_____

22

70
− 50
_____

55
− 33
_____

65
− 24
_____

Slow and Safe

What animal can live 150 years? Complete the subtraction problems and then use the code to find out.

27	59	36	48	73	82
− 10	− 30	− 10	− 10	− 30	− 60

   e   i   o   r   s   t

| 22 | 26 | 38 | 22 | 26 | 29 | 43 | 17 |

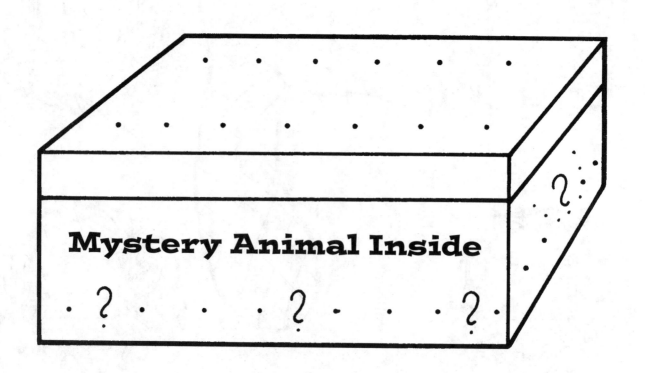

Mystery Animal Inside

Ocean Subtraction

Draw a line to match each problem to its answer.

a.  92 - 60 =____   25

b. 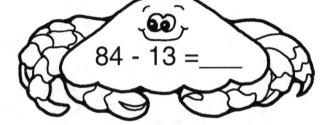 84 - 13 =____   32

c. 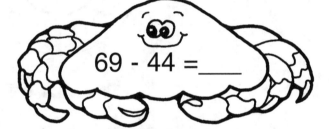 69 - 44 =____   1

d.  35 - 25 =____   15

e. 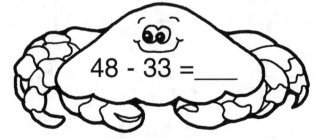 48 - 33 =____   71

f. 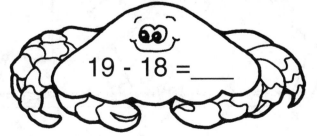 19 - 18 =____    10

                                       #6455 Practice and Learn

Target Practice

Begin with the number in the center. Subtract one of the numbers in the middle ring from the number in the center, and write the difference in the outer ring. The first one has been done for you. Repeat until you have filled every space in the outer rings.

1.

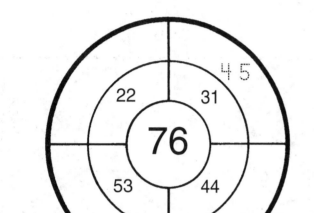

2.

3.

4.

Animal Buddies

Did you know that a crocodile lets birds sit on its back to eat insects? A crocodile will also let birds sit in its mouth to eat worms and insects from its teeth. What a toothbrush!

Complete each subtraction problem. Then use the color code to color the picture.

black = 21	blue = 12	green = 23
yellow = 31	gray = 26	red = 63

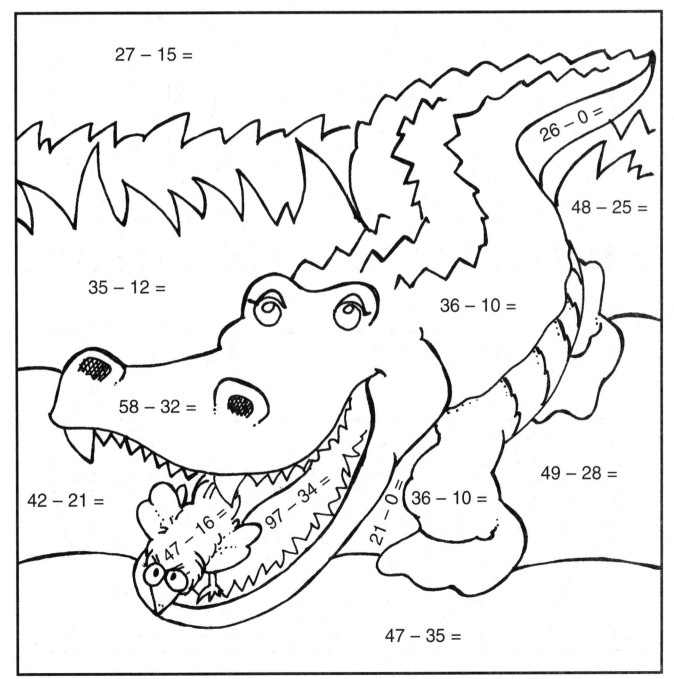

What's in the Box? Subtraction

Guess what is in the box. Find the answers. Then write the letter in each box that matches each answer. Read the word you spell and draw it in the box.

10	11	12	13	14
j	b	a	n	o

42	33	46	54	77	28
−30	−22	−34	−41	−67	−14

12

Subtracting Two-Digit Numbers (with Regrouping)

When regrouping to subtract, follow these directions:

1. Write the problem.

$$
\begin{array}{r}
53 \\
-\ 14 \\
\hline
\end{array}
$$

2. Subtract the ones. If there are not enough ones, take a ten from the tens column and add it as ten ones to the ones column (you now have 13 ones). Keep track of what you are doing above the problem so you can see your work.

$$
\begin{array}{r}
{}^{4\ 1}\cancel{5}3 \\
-\ \ 14 \\
\hline
\end{array}
$$

3. Now you can subtract the ones (13 − 4).

$$
\begin{array}{r}
{}^{4\ 1}\cancel{5}3 \\
-\ \ 14 \\
\hline
9
\end{array}
$$

4. Then subtract the tens (4 − 1).

$$
\begin{array}{r}
{}^{4\ 1}\cancel{5}3 \\
-\ \ 14 \\
\hline
39
\end{array}
$$

Color the Picture Frames

What color frame should each animal picture have? Solve the subtraction problem in each frame. Then use the code to color the frame the appropriate color.

22 = brown   25 = black   28 = red   29 = purple   51 = pink
74 = green   77 = blue   78 = orange 89 = yellow

1.

$$81$$
$$-\ \ 3$$

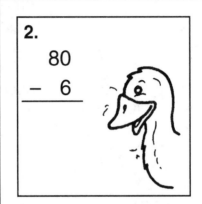

2.

$$80$$
$$-\ \ 6$$

3.

$$80$$
$$-\ \ 3$$

4.

$$30$$
$$-\ \ 8$$

5.

$$35$$
$$-\ \ 7$$

6.

$$60$$
$$-\ \ 9$$

7.

$$37$$
$$-\ \ 8$$

8.

$$97$$
$$-\ \ 8$$

9.

$$31$$
$$-\ \ 6$$

Three in a Row

Solve each subtraction problem. To win this tic-tac-toe game, draw a line through the three squares that have a 7 in their answers.

66 − 39	97 − 28	37 − 19
58 − 19	85 − 68	73 − 18
72 − 19	39 − 18	95 − 18

Who Took the Cookies?

To find out which bear ate the cookies, solve each subtraction problem. The bear with the numeral 6 in the difference took the cookies.

Who ate the cookies?

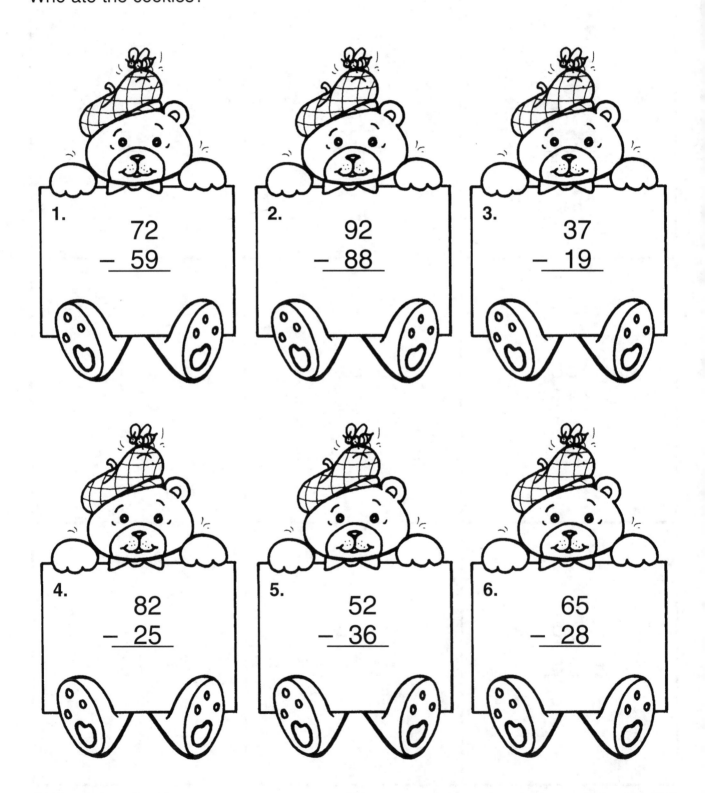

1.
$$\begin{array}{r} 72 \\ -\ 59 \\ \hline \end{array}$$

2.
$$\begin{array}{r} 92 \\ -\ 88 \\ \hline \end{array}$$

3.
$$\begin{array}{r} 37 \\ -\ 19 \\ \hline \end{array}$$

4.
$$\begin{array}{r} 82 \\ -\ 25 \\ \hline \end{array}$$

5.
$$\begin{array}{r} 52 \\ -\ 36 \\ \hline \end{array}$$

6.
$$\begin{array}{r} 65 \\ -\ 28 \\ \hline \end{array}$$

Catching Baseballs

Cross out each answer in the mitt as you solve the problems.

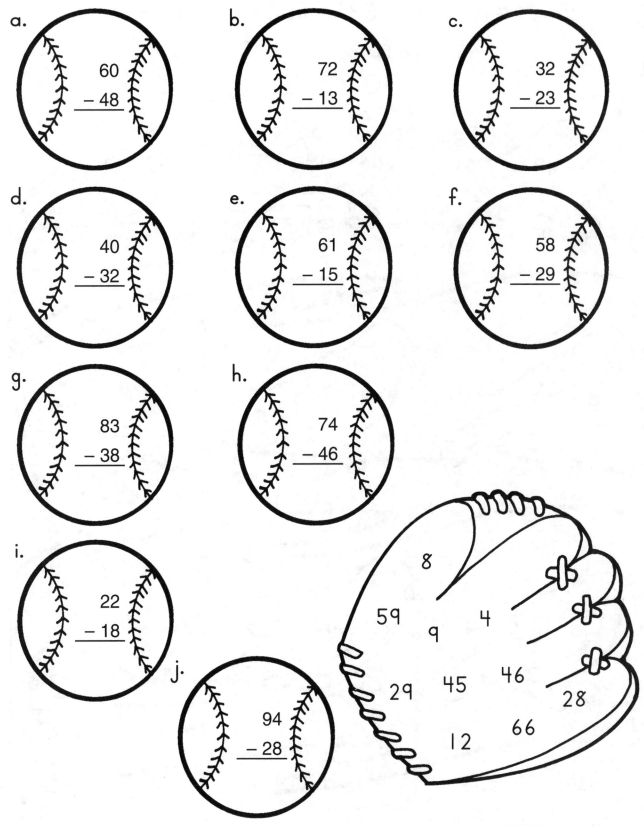

a.
$$\begin{array}{r} 60 \\ -\ 48 \\ \hline \end{array}$$

b.
$$\begin{array}{r} 72 \\ -\ 13 \\ \hline \end{array}$$

c.
$$\begin{array}{r} 32 \\ -\ 23 \\ \hline \end{array}$$

d.
$$\begin{array}{r} 40 \\ -\ 32 \\ \hline \end{array}$$

e.
$$\begin{array}{r} 61 \\ -\ 15 \\ \hline \end{array}$$

f.
$$\begin{array}{r} 58 \\ -\ 29 \\ \hline \end{array}$$

g.
$$\begin{array}{r} 83 \\ -\ 38 \\ \hline \end{array}$$

h.
$$\begin{array}{r} 74 \\ -\ 46 \\ \hline \end{array}$$

i.
$$\begin{array}{r} 22 \\ -\ 18 \\ \hline \end{array}$$

j.
$$\begin{array}{r} 94 \\ -\ 28 \\ \hline \end{array}$$

8

59   4

9

29   45   46

28

12   66

Colorful Birds

Find the answers. Color the pictures.

25 = orange	33 = green	35 = yellow
42 = purple	45 = blue	

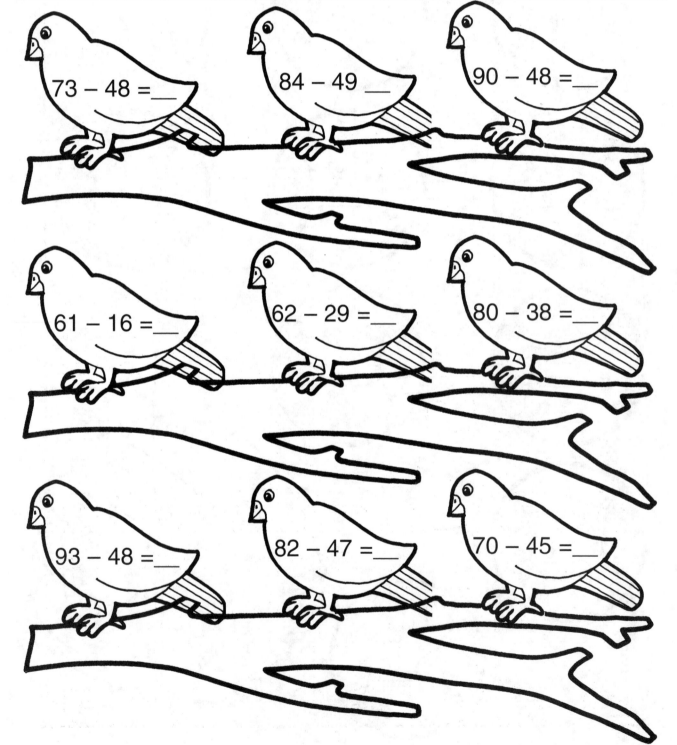

73 – 48 = __

84 – 49 = __

90 – 48 = __

61 – 16 = __

62 – 29 = __

80 – 38 = __

93 – 48 = __

82 – 47 = __

70 – 45 = __

The Number Train

Subtract the number on the second car from the number on the engine. Then subtract the number on the third car from the difference between those numbers. Continue subtracting until you get to the last car.

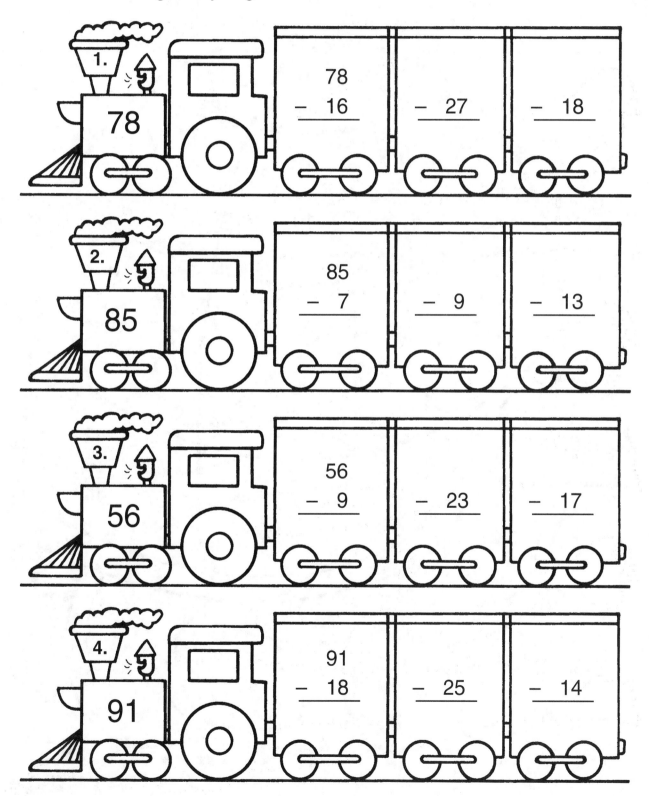

1.
78

78
− 16

− 27

− 18

2.
85

85
− 7

− 9

− 13

3.
56

56
− 9

− 23

− 17

4.
91

91
− 18

− 25

− 14

Turtle Talk

Check each subtraction problem below. Color sections of the shell with correct answers green. Color sections with incorrect answers brown.

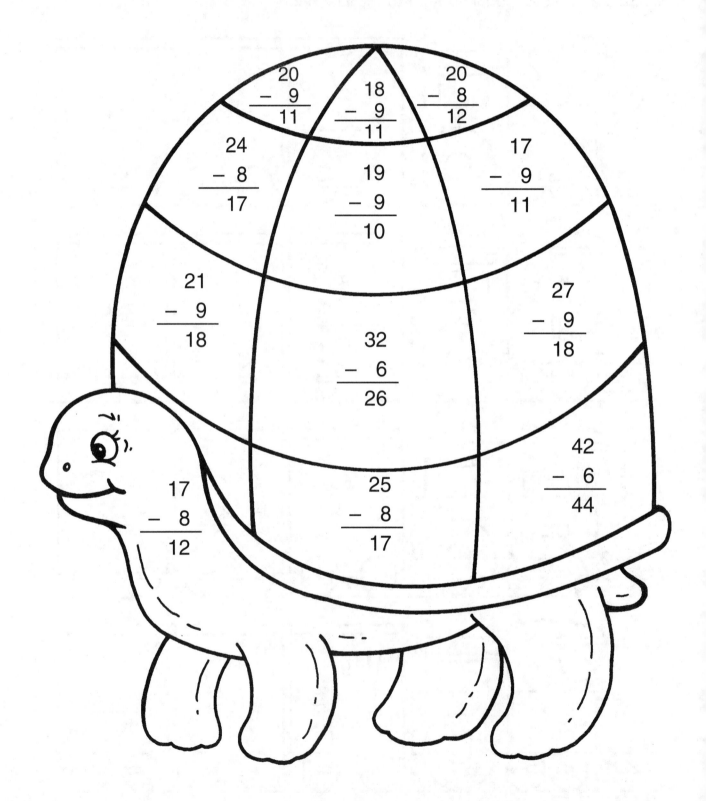

What's in the Box? Subtraction

Guess what is in the box. Find the answers. Then write the letter in each box that matches each answer. Read the word you spell and draw it in the box.

35	36	37	38	39	40
a	c	j	e	k	t

$$
\begin{array}{r} 80 \\ -45 \\ \hline 35 \end{array}
\qquad
\begin{array}{r} 75 \\ -38 \\ \hline \end{array}
\quad
\begin{array}{r} 92 \\ -57 \\ \hline \end{array}
\quad
\begin{array}{r} 52 \\ -16 \\ \hline \end{array}
\quad
\begin{array}{r} 72 \\ -33 \\ \hline \end{array}
\quad
\begin{array}{r} 92 \\ -54 \\ \hline \end{array}
\quad
\begin{array}{r} 107 \\ -67 \\ \hline \end{array}
$$

Subtraction Word Problems

Read each word problem. Write the number sentence it shows. Find the difference.

a

Farmer Cole raised 93 bushels of wheat. Farmer Dale raised 68 bushels. What is the difference in the number of bushels each raised?

b

Dennis scored 43 points in his basketball game. Claire scored 27. What is the difference in points each earned?

c

Jason bought a pair of shoes for 53 dollars. Clark bought a pair for 28 dollars. What is the difference paid?

d

Jill counted 83 ants near an ant hill. Jack counted 65. What is the difference in the ants counted?

What Is Multiplication?

Here is an easy way to learn how to multiply. You will need an egg carton and some dry cereal. We're going to use these to practice counting in groups.

Let's begin by putting 2 pieces of cereal in each section of the egg carton. Now count the dry cereal in 2 sections. How many did you count?

In addition, this is written like this:

$$2 + 2 = 4$$

In multiplication, it is written like this:

$$2 \times 2 = 4$$

Count the cereal in 5 sections. How many pieces did you count?

In addition, this is written like this:

$$2 + 2 + 2 + 2 + 2 = 10$$

In multiplication, it is written like this:

$$5 \times 2 = 10$$

Count the cereal in all 12 sections. How many pieces did you count?

In addition, this is written like this:

$$2 + 2 + 2 + 2 + 2 + 2 + 2 + 2 + 2 + 2 + 2 + 2 = 24$$

In multiplication, it is written like this:

$$12 \times 2 = 24$$

When you add by groups, it is the same as multiplying!

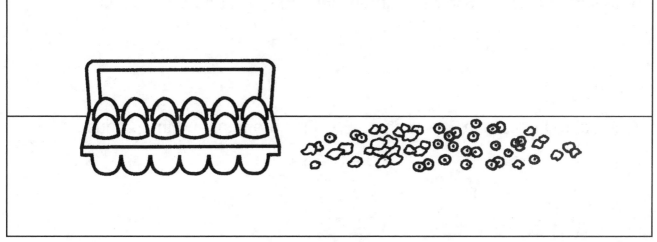

Practice Makes Perfect

Remember, multiplying is adding by groups. Counting in groups is faster than counting things one at a time. The answer to an addition problem is called the total. The answer to a multiplication problem is called the product.

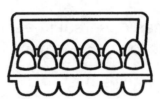 

Use an egg carton and cereal to complete these equations.

1. Make 3 groups of 4 by putting 4 pieces of cereal in each of 3 sections.

    Add 3 groups of 4.

    $$4 + 4 + 4 =$$

    Then multiply.

    $$3 \times 4 =$$

2. Make 5 groups with 2 in each group. Find the total and the product.

    $$2 + 2 + 2 + 2 + 2 =$$

    $$5 \times 2 =$$

3. Make 4 groups of 6 in each group. Find the total and the product.

    $$6 + 6 + 6 + 6 =$$

    $$4 \times 6 =$$

4. Make 5 groups with 3 in each group. Find the total and the product.

    $$3 + 3 + 3 + 3 + 3 =$$

    $$5 \times 3 =$$

Multiplication Is Easy!

When you add by groups, it is the same as multiplying. Look at the bags of marbles, and answer these questions.

1. How many bags?_____

   How many marbles in each bag?_____

   All together, how many marbles in all of the bags?_____

   We can write this as an addition equation like this:

   $$2 + 2 + 2 = 6$$

   Or, we can write it as a multiplication equation like this:

   $$3 \times 2 = 6$$

2. Let's try another problem.

   How many bags?_____

   How many marbles in each bag?_____

   All together, how many marbles in all of the bags?_____

   Write an addition equation for this problem.

   _____ + _____ = _____

   Write a multiplication equation for this problem.

   _____ x _____ = _____

Multiplication Marbles

Let's practice adding by groups and solving multiplication equations. Use the bags of marbles to help you complete each equation.

1.

$2 + 2 + 2 + 2 = $ _____

$4 \times 2 = $ _____

2.

$1 + 1 + 1 + 1 + 1 = $ _____

$5 \times 1 = $ _____

3.

$1 + 1 + 1 = $ _____

$3 \times 1 = $ _____

4.

$0 + 0 + 0 = $ _____

$3 \times 0 = $ _____

Multiplying by Zero

Here is a hint for you to use when you multiply by 0. Anytime you multiply by 0, the answer will always be 0. Use the bags of marbles to help you solve these multiplication problems.

1. 1 x 0 = _____

2. 3 x 0 = _____

3. 7 x 0 = _____

4. 12 x 0 = _____

     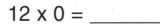

5. 10 x 0 = _____

Multiplying by One

Multiplying by 1 is simple! When you multiply by 1, it is like looking in a mirror.
The number being multiplied always sees itself. Use the bags of marbles to help
you fill in the blanks correctly.

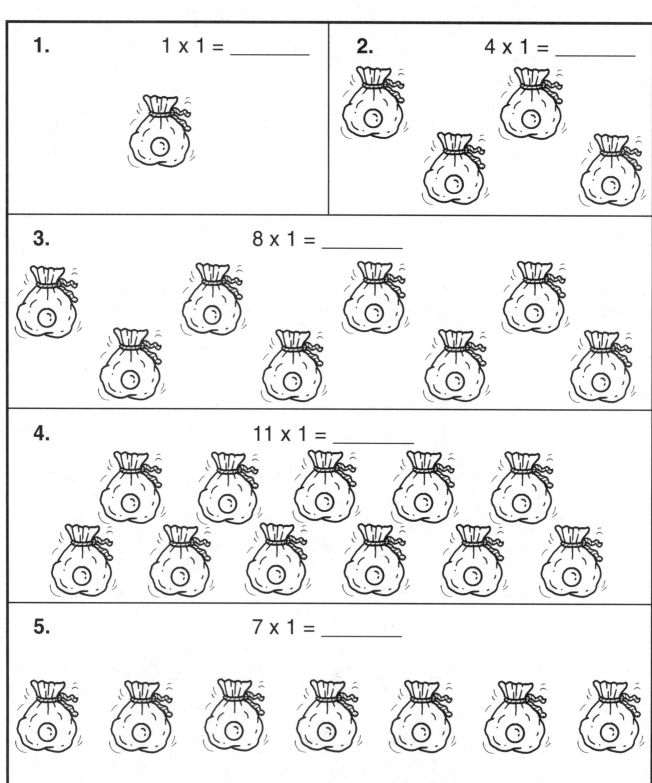

1.   1 x 1 = _____

2.   4 x 1 = _____

3.   8 x 1 = _____

4.   11 x 1 = _____

5.   7 x 1 = _____

Multiplying by Two

Multiplying by 2 is like adding a number to itself.

$$3 \times 2 = 6 \text{ or } 3 + 3 = 6$$

$$8 \times 2 = 16 \text{ or } 8 + 8 = 16$$

Multiply by 2 to find the answers to these equations and then add the first number to itself to check your answer.

1. $1 \times 2 =$ _____

$1 + 1 =$ _____

2. $2 \times 2 =$ _____

$2 + 2 =$ _____

3. $3 \times 2 =$ _____

$3 + 3 =$ _____

4. $4 \times 2 =$ _____

$4 + 4 =$ _____

5. $5 \times 2 =$ _____

$5 + 5 =$ _____

6. $6 \times 2 =$ _____

$6 + 6 =$ _____

7. $7 \times 2 =$ _____

$7 + 7 =$ _____

8. $8 \times 2 =$ _____

$8 + 8 =$ _____

9. $9 \times 2 =$ _____

$9 + 9 =$ _____

10. $10 \times 2 =$ _____

$10 + 10 =$ _____

11. $11 \times 2 =$ _____

$11 + 11 =$ _____

12. $12 \times 2 =$ _____

$12 + 12 =$ _____

The Answers Are the Same

Sometimes multiplication equations are written this way: $2 \times 2 = 4$

Sometimes multiplication equations are written this way:

$$\begin{array}{r} 2 \\ \times\ 2 \\ \hline 4 \end{array}$$

The answer will be the same either way it is written.

Complete the multiplication equations:

1. $2 \times 1 =$ _____

2. $6 \times 2 =$ _____

3. $9 \times 1 =$ _____

4. $3 \times 0 =$ _____

5. $1 \times 1 =$ _____

6. $10 \times 1 =$ _____

7. $11 \times 1 =$ _____

8. $5 \times 2 =$ _____

9. $8 \times 0 =$ _____

10. $6 \times 1 =$ _____

11.
$$\begin{array}{r} 8 \\ \times\ 1 \\ \hline \end{array}$$

12.
$$\begin{array}{r} 4 \\ \times\ 1 \\ \hline \end{array}$$

13.
$$\begin{array}{r} 5 \\ \times\ 0 \\ \hline \end{array}$$

14.
$$\begin{array}{r} 1 \\ \times\ 0 \\ \hline \end{array}$$

15.
$$\begin{array}{r} 9 \\ \times\ 2 \\ \hline \end{array}$$

16.
$$\begin{array}{r} 7 \\ \times\ 1 \\ \hline \end{array}$$

17.
$$\begin{array}{r} 8 \\ \times\ 2 \\ \hline \end{array}$$

18.
$$\begin{array}{r} 3 \\ \times\ 1 \\ \hline \end{array}$$

19.
$$\begin{array}{r} 2 \\ \times\ 2 \\ \hline \end{array}$$

20.
$$\begin{array}{r} 6 \\ \times\ 0 \\ \hline \end{array}$$

Mixed Practice

1. $\begin{array}{r} 5 \\ \times\ 1 \\ \hline \end{array}$	**2.** $\begin{array}{r} 6 \\ \times\ 1 \\ \hline \end{array}$	**3.** $\begin{array}{r} 1 \\ \times\ 1 \\ \hline \end{array}$
4. $\begin{array}{r} 11 \\ \times\ 2 \\ \hline \end{array}$	**5.** $\begin{array}{r} 4 \\ \times\ 1 \\ \hline \end{array}$	**6.** $12 \times 0 = \underline{\hspace{2cm}}$
7. $\begin{array}{r} 7 \\ \times\ 0 \\ \hline \end{array}$	**8.** $10 \times 1 = \underline{\hspace{2cm}}$	**9.** $9 \times 2 = \underline{\hspace{2cm}}$
10. $3 \times 0 = \underline{\hspace{2cm}}$	**11.** $8 \times 2 = \underline{\hspace{2cm}}$	**12.** $2 \times 2 = \underline{\hspace{2cm}}$

Multiplying by Three

Circle the number of triangles that match the equation. Then count the dots inside each triangle to solve the equations.

The first one has been done for you.

1. 4 groups of 3 = 12

4 x 3 = _____12_____

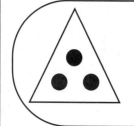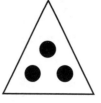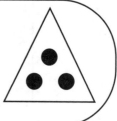

2. 6 groups of 3 =

6 x 3 = _____

3. 9 groups of 3 =

9 x 3 = _____

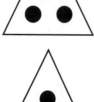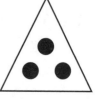

Multiplying by Three Is E-Z!

When you multiply, another word for the answer is *product*. Use the triangles on page 268, if you need help finding these products.

1.
 	
   1
x 3
‾‾‾
	2.
	
	   2
	x 3
	‾‾‾
		3.
		
		   3
		x 3
		‾‾‾

4.
 	
   4
x 3
‾‾‾
	5.
	
	   5
	x 3
	‾‾‾
		6.
		
		   6
		x 3
		‾‾‾

7.
 	
   7
x 3
‾‾‾
	8.
	
	   8
	x 3
	‾‾‾
		9.
		
		   9
		x 3
		‾‾‾

10.
 	
  10
x 3
‾‾‾
	11.
	
	  11
	x 3
	‾‾‾
		12.
		
		  12
		x 3
		‾‾‾

Multiplying by Four

There is a pretty green plant called a four-leaf clover. Some people say it will bring you luck if you find one. Maybe these four-leaf clovers will bring you luck while you learn to multiply by four. Use the leaves on the clovers to help you complete these equations.

1.   1 x 4 = _____

2.   7 x 4 = _____

3.   2 x 4 = _____

4.   8 x 4 = _____

5.   3 x 4 = _____

6.   9 x 4 = _____

7.   4 x 4 = _____

8.   10 x 4 = _____

9.   5 x 4 = _____

10.   11 x 4 = _____

11.   6 x 4 = _____

12.   12 x 4 = _____

Counting by Five

Can you count by five? It goes like this: 5, 10, 15, 20, 25, 30, 35, 40, 45, 50, etc. If you can, then you already know the five times table. Use the fingers on these hands to help you complete the equations.

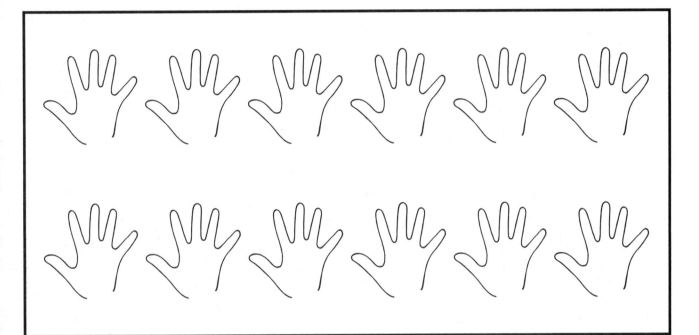

1. 1 x 5 = _____

2. 7 x 5 = _____

3. 2 x 5 = _____

4. 8 x 5 = _____

5. 3 x 5 = _____

6. 9 x 5 = _____

7. 4 x 5 = _____

8. 10 x 5 = _____

9. 5 x 5 = _____

10. 11 x 5 = _____

11. 6 x 5 = _____

12. 12 x 5 = _____

Practice Multiplying by Five

Circle the number that will complete each equation.

1. 6 x 5 = 30 25 40	**2.** 2 x 5 = 5 10 25	**3.** 5 x 5 = 10 25 5
4. 12 x 5 = 30 50 60	**5.** 9 x 5 = 10 60 45	**6.** 7 x 5 = 40 35 60
7. 1 x 5 = 5 10 25	**8.** 9 x 5 = 45 40 35	**9.** 3 x 5 = 5 10 15
10. 8 x 5 = 15 40 60	**11.** 10 x 5 = 50 15 60	**12.** 4 x 5 = 10 20 5
13. 11 x 5 = 70 55 50	**14.** 5 x 5 = 5 10 25	**15.** 8 x 5 = 50 40 45

Parts of a Whole

What part of each shape is shaded? Draw a line to the correct fractional part.
Hint: The top number of a fraction stands for the number parts that are colored.
The bottom number of a fraction stands for the total number of parts, colored
and not colored.

1. 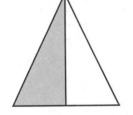 $\dfrac{1}{2}$

2. 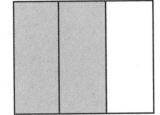 $\dfrac{2}{5}$

3. 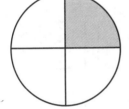 $\dfrac{3}{5}$

4. 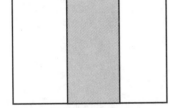 $\dfrac{2}{3}$

5. 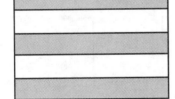 $\dfrac{1}{3}$

6. 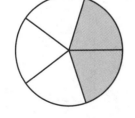 $\dfrac{1}{4}$

                                       #6455 Practice and Learn

Coloring Fractions

Color the part or parts or each shape or set of shapes to match the fractional number.

1.
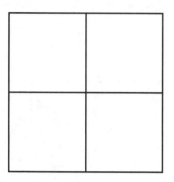
$\dfrac{1}{4}$

2.
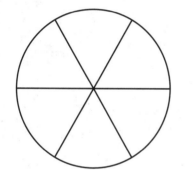
$\dfrac{3}{6}$

3.
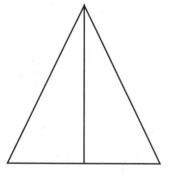
$\dfrac{1}{2}$

4.
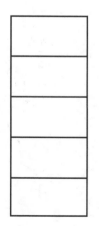
$\dfrac{2}{5}$

5.
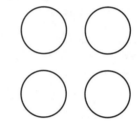
$\dfrac{3}{4}$

6.
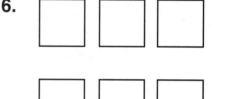
$\dfrac{1}{6}$

7.
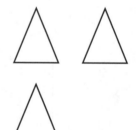
$\dfrac{2}{3}$

8.
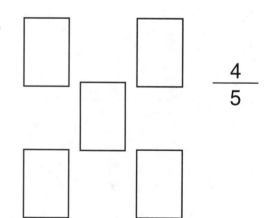
$\dfrac{4}{5}$

Fraction Fish

Color some fish in each bowl. Then write a fraction for the amount of fish you colored. For example, if you color 3 fish in the first bowl, you will write the fractional part ³/₅.

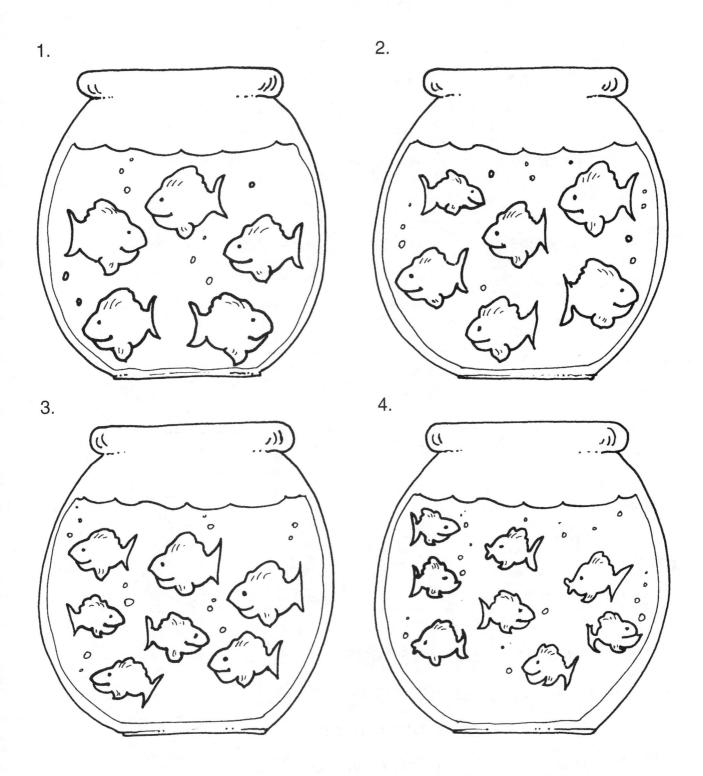

1.

2.

3.

4.

Coloring and Counting Shapes

Color the following shapes. Then count each shape and write in how many you found.

Color the ⬜ squares red.

Color the ⭕ circles blue.

Color the △ triangles green.

Color the ▭ rectangles yellow.

There are _____ red squares.

There are _____ blue circles.

There are _____ green triangles.

There are _____ yellow rectangles.

Shape Pictures

You see shapes every day. Use these four basic shapes (square, circle, triangle, and rectangle) to make a picture. Use as many shapes as you can.

Three-Dimensional Shapes

Here are some three-dimensional shapes.

cube
sphere
cone
cylinder

triangular prism

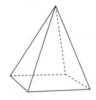

Write the name of the shape that matches the following objects.

_____

_____

_____

_____

_____

What Color, Please?

Make your own color chart for this picture. Then color the picture in the colors you chose for the chart.

number	color to use
1	
2	
3	
4	
5	
6	
7	

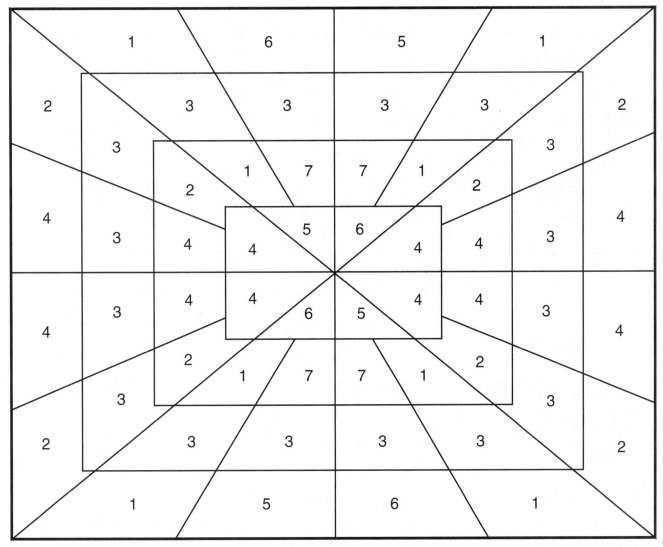

Graphing Fun

The graph tells how many of each animal there are. Use the graph to complete the addition problems below.

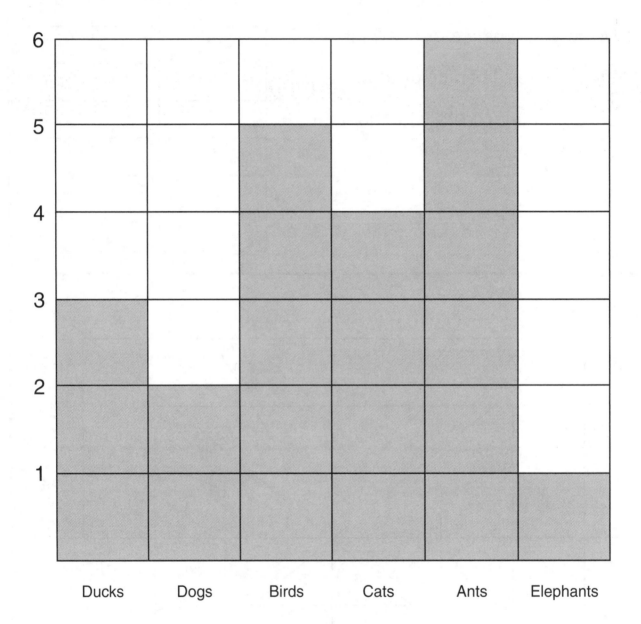

1. How many ducks and cats are there?   _____ + _____ = _____

2. How many birds and dogs are there?   _____ + _____ = _____

3. How many elephants and ants are there?   _____ + _____ = _____

Favorite Subject

The students in Mr. Lockwood's class took a class vote to find out what subject was liked most by class members. Mr. Lockwood kept a record of the votes for each subject on a tally chart.

Read the chart. Then answer the questions.

Our Favorite Subjects	
Subject	**Tally of Votes**
mathematics	|||
art	||||
history		
science	ЖЖ
music	||
reading	ЖЖ	
writing	|||
physical education	ЖЖ
health		

1. What subject is liked the most? _____

2. How many people liked it the most? _____

3. What subjects tied for second place? _____

4. Which subjects tied with writing? _____

5. How many liked mathematics more than history? _____

Pictographs

One type of graph that gives us information is called a pictograph. In a pictograph, pictures are used instead of numbers.

Here is a pictograph that shows the number of fish caught each day at Canyon Lake.

Daily Fish Catch at Canyon Lake	
Sunday	🐟 🐟 🐟 🐟 🐟 🐟 🐟
Monday	🐟 🐟
Tuesday	🐟
Wednesday	🐟 🐟 🐟
Thursday	🐟 🐟
Friday	🐟 🐟 🐟 🐟 🐟
Saturday	🐟 🐟 🐟 🐟 🐟 🐟
KEY: 🐟 = 10 fish	

1. On what day were the most fish caught? _____

2. How many fish were caught on this day? _____

3. On what day were 50 fish caught? _____

4. On what day were the fewest fish caught? _____

5. Were the same number of fish caught on Monday and Thursday? _____

6. How many fish were caught on both Saturday and Sunday? _____

Circle Graphs

One type of graph that gives us information is called a circle graph. In a circle graph, you can show how things are divided into the parts of a whole.

Read this circle graph about where Derek spends the hours in one day.

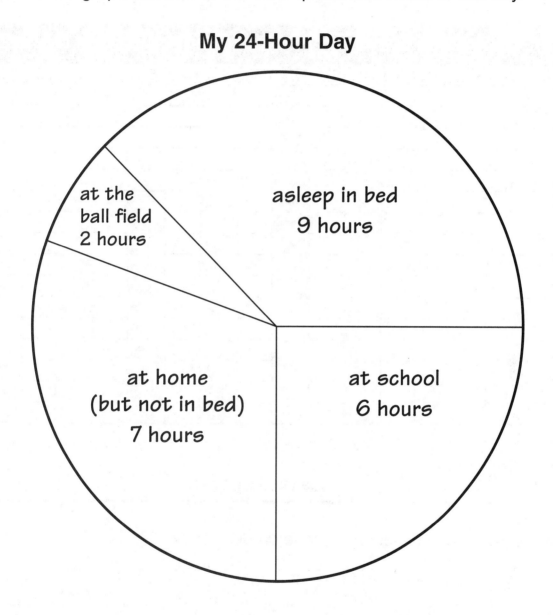

My 24-Hour Day

at the ball field 2 hours

asleep in bed 9 hours

at home (but not in bed) 7 hours

at school 6 hours

Use a red crayon to color the place Derek spends six hours a day.

Use a blue crayon to color Derek's sleeping time.

Use a green crayon to color the time Derek spends on the ball field.

Use a yellow crayon to color Derek's nonsleep time at home.

#6455 Practice and Learn

Which Class?

The classes at Barnsdale Elementary School kept a bar graph of the number of books each grade read for a week.

Study this bar graph of their reading and answer the questions below.

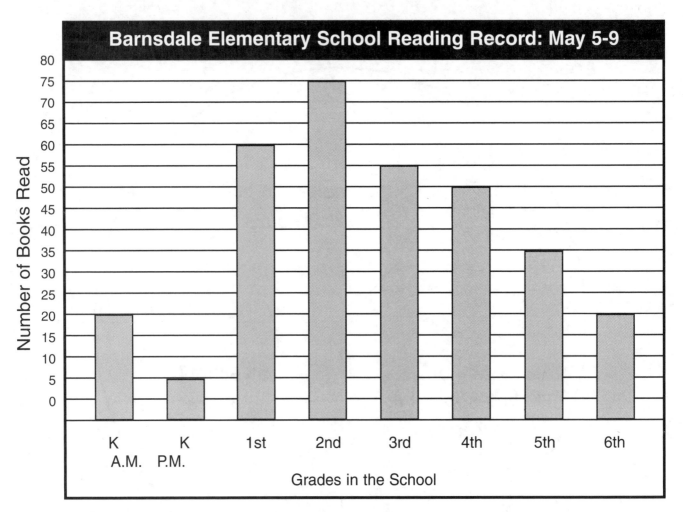

1. How many books did each of these grades read?

   K A.M. _____   1st _____   3rd _____   5th _____

   K P.M. _____   2nd _____   4th _____   6th _____

2. Which grade read the most books?

3. What two grades read the same number of books?

4. Which books do you think are longer: the books kindergartners read or the books sixth graders read?

5. How many books can you read in a week? Try it!

Venn Diagrams

A Venn diagram is a type of diagram that uses circles to show how things are related to each other. The overlapping parts of the circles show what things the circles have in common.

Look at this diagram of the activities of two kindergarten classes that share the same room.

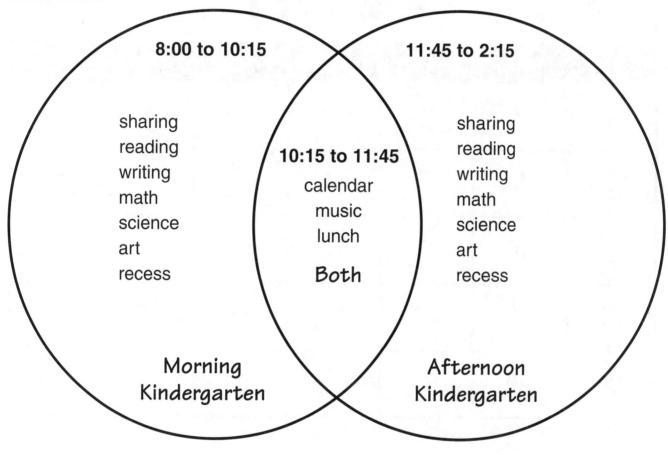

1. By reading this diagram, can you tell what time of day the two classes are together in the same room? _____ What time? _____

2. What activities do both classes do together? _____

   _____

3. What activities do the classes each do by themselves?

   _____

   _____

   _____

Birthdays!

A calendar helps us get organized. A calendar will show us what month it is and what the date is. Use this calendar to answer the following questions.

August

Sunday	Monday	Tuesday	Wednesday	Thursday	Friday	Saturday
1	2	3 Christopher	4	5	6	7 Karen
8	9	10	11	12 Alyssa	13	14
15 Billy	16	17	18	19	20	21
22	23	24	25 Alexander	26	27	28
29	30	31 Feather				

1. On what day is Christopher's birthday? _____

2. What date (month and day) is Alyssa's birthday? _____

3. Alexander's birthday is on August 25. What day is that? _____

4. How many birthdays are on Tuesdays? _____

5. Which days have no birthdays at all? _____

What Comes Next?

Draw the next thing in each series.

1.	○ □ □ ○ □ □ ○ □	
2.	♡ △ △ ♡ △ △ ♡ △	
3.	○ ☆ ○ ☆ ○ ☆ ○ ☆	
4.	□ □ □ ◗ ◗ ◗ ♡ ♡	
5.	○ △ ○ ▽ ○ △ ○ ▽	
6.	≡ ☆ □ ≡ ☆ □ ≡ ☆	
7.	□ △ △ ♡ ♡ ♡ ◗ ◗ ◗	
8.	△ △ ○ ○ △ △ □ □ △	
9.	♡ ♡ ☆ ♡ ♡ □ ♡ ♡ ☆ ♡	
10.	□ ▭ □ ▬ □ ▭ □ ▬	

Number Series

Write the next number in each series.

a. 1 2 3 4 5 6 7 8   _____

b. 2 4 6 8 10 12 14 16   _____

c. 5 10 15 20 25 30   _____

d. 2 3 4 6 7 8 10 11   _____

e. 2 2 3 3 4 4 5 5   _____

f. 1 3 1 4 1 5 1 6 1   _____

g. 8 7 6 5 4 3 2   _____

h. 3 2 6 4 9 6 12 8   _____

i. 1 5 9 13 17 21 25   _____

j. 10 20 30 40 50 60 70 80   _____

k. 20 18 16 14 12 10 8   _____

l. 0 1 0 2 0 3 0 4   _____

m. 6 5 4 3 2 1 6 5 4   _____

n. 3 6 9 12 9 6 3 6   _____

My Own Patterns

Make your own patterns using the following objects. Use any number of objects.
You can make the patterns easy or hard. The challenge is up to you.

and
different shapes
letters of the alphabet
different flowers
numbers
favorite fruits
animals
favorite toys

For a special challenge, use colors, too!

289

Answer Key

Page 11
1. alligator
2. an, albatross, accidentally
3. Ahh, albatross, shall
4. that
5. alligator, A-a-a-choo
6. that, albatross

Page 12

Across	Down
1. calf	1. clam
3. crab	2. bass
4. lamb	3. cat
6. ant	5. bat
7. stag	8. gnat
9. rat	
10. yak	

Page 13
1. exit, yelled, elk
2. Ehhh, Eskimo
3. exit, yelled, elk
4. Ehhh, Eskimo
5. exit, yelled, elk
6. end, Eskimo

Page 14

pen
bell
men
vest
shell
ten
dress
cent
jet
tent
bed
net
web
desk
nest
sled
hen

Page 15
1. iguana, insect
2. Ick, iguana
3. iguana, fish, swimming
4. sick
5. iguana
6. inviting, iguana, beginning

Page 16

pin
chin
zipper
fish
chimney
hill
mitt
witch
bib
bridge
lip
lid
list
gift

Page 17
1. frog, log
2. log, job, frog
3. rot
4. frog, spot
5. fox, frog, hop, trot, jog
6. on, log

Page 18

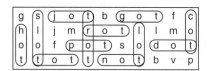

Page 19
1. bug, bug, mug
2. Uh, bug, shrug
3. bug, bug, jug
4. Uh, bug, shrug
5. bug, bug, rug
6. rug, bug, hug

Page 20

1. bud	7. cut
2. mud	8. gun
3. dug	9. rub
4. rug	10. tug
5. bug	11. bus
6. cub	12. tub

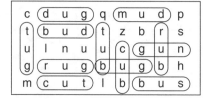

Page 21

red: fan, mask,
green: wig, ship
orange: cot
blue: bus, cup
yellow: bell, desk

Page 22

1. e		9. u
2. e		10. u
3. u		11. a
4. u		12. o
5. a		13. i
6. a		14. o
7. a		15. a
8. i		16. u

Page 23

gate *yellow*
rake
cave
cake
vase
cage
safe
cane
game
tape
wave

Page 25

bay, hay, day, lay, may, pay, ray,
say, way, stay, play, tray

Page 26

mane, vane, tape, cane, plane, rate,
cape, pane, made, fade, paste, tame

Page 27

bee
feet
knee
wreath
leaf
eagle
peas
squeeze
zebra
cheese
tree
three
queen
ear
key

Answer Key *(cont.)*

Page 28

Across:
1. see
2. tweet
3. tweeze
4. breeze
5. tree
7. three

Down:
1. street
2. teeth
6. freezer
8. feet
9. week

Page 29
1. peach
2. sea
3. leaf
4. bean
5. tea
6. beak
7. seal
8. peas
9. meat
10. leap
11. bead
12. beach

Page 30
bike
slide
spider
knife
nine
pipe
pie
lion

Page 31

The following words are not crossed out:
spike
nine
strike
slide
rise
dine
drive
bite
ride
hide
dive
time

Page 32

Answers may vary.
hive-five
white-bite
ripe-pipe
side-ride
lime-time
mile-pile
tie-pie
pine-fine
hike-like

Page 33
boat
toe
coat
hole
soap
nose
note
comb
rose
doughnut
hoe

Page 34
1. toad
2. coat
3. soap
4. load
5. goat
6. float
7. soak
8. road
9. boat
10. coal
11. foam
12. loaf

Page 35

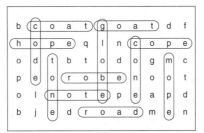

Page 36
tube *yellow*
tulip
cube
June
fruit
mule
glue
cupid
suit
ruler
flute

Page 37

The following words should be colored *yellow*:
use
tube
huge
cute
rude
fuse
fume
cube
mule
mute
rule
tune

Page 38

Across:
2. Cupid
3. juice
5. museum
8. cube
9. tulip
10. glue

Down:
1. blue
2. cucumber
4. pupil
6. fuse
7. pupa
9. tube

Page 39
star
jar
barn
target
dart
arm
car
harp

Page 40
corn
horn
fork
horse
sword
horse
acorn
ornament

Page 41
bird
girl
church
circle
flower
feather

Answer Key *(cont.)*

Page 42

red:
car
yarn
dart
jar
star
scarf
yellow:
horn
fork
horse
stork
corn
cork
green:
church
purse
nurse
turkey
turtle
curl

Page 43

red:
party
march
tar
start
far
orange:
her
term
fern
serve
clerk
yellow:
first
dirt
birth
sir
green:
short
corn
fort
for
torn
north
blue:
burn
hurt
fur

Page 44

blue:
book
cookies
wood
foot
hook
brook
woodpecker
yellow:
moon
spoon
goose
tooth
boots
rooster
food
hoop
moose

Page 45

blue:
feather
weather
leather
measure
sweater
thread
treasure
green:
team
dream
beads
heat
speak
reach
peacock
seat

Page 46

claw
saw
laundry
faucet
pawprint
sausage
hawk
strawberry

Page 47

claw
draw
paw
hawk
jaw
crawl

Page 48

Across:
1. because
2. sauce
3. naughty
4. author
5. August
6. fault
Down:
2. sausage
5. autumn
7. laundry

Page 49

snow
own
slow
know
yellow

Page 50

red:
frown
owl
brown
cow
towel
crowd
down
town
how
now
gown
yellow:
low
snow
blow
grow
crow
show
glow
flow
throw
own
slow

Page 51

owl
brown
how
down
cow

Answer Key *(cont.)*

Page 52

house
south
sound
loud
found
mouse
round
out
shout
mouth
pouch

Page 53

coins
poison
oil
boy
toys

Page 54

boy
joy
oil
join
voice
royal
moist
noise
choice
enjoy
point
spoil
soil
boil
coin
toy

Page 55

yellow:
mouse
round
count
cloud
shout
found
loud
out
red:
bread
treasure
head
breakfast

green:
wood
book
took
foot
good
orange:
flew
blew
grew
drew
brew
new

Page 56

crab
broom
drum
frog
grapes
tree

Page 57

block: blow, blouse
clown: clock, cloud
flower: flag, flute
gloves: glass, glue, globe

Page 58

smile
stool
sponge
swan
spring
spoon
swing
stairs

Page 59

sl: sleep
sm: smoke
sp: spool
st: stamp
sw: swing
spr: spray

Page 60

sp, br, tr, sm, spr, pl

Page 61

1. tree, trunk, brown
2. green
3. small, flowers
4. stems, flowers, green
5. grass, green
6. clouds, gray
7. sky, drops, blue
8. Brad, black
9. Bret, brown
10. frog, green

Page 63

sheep
shell
shovel
shoe

Page 64

Page 65

chain
cheese
church
chicken

Page 66

quiet *th*: thin, thank, thorn
noisy *th*: that, this, the

Page 67

chat
church
wheel
chime

Answer Key *(cont.)*

Page 68

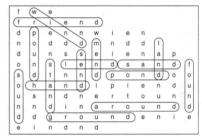

Page 69

swing
switch
sweep
swell

Page 70

bird
snake
rabbit
zebra
pig
cat, rat, or bat

Page 71

legs
tail
head
neck
back
toes

Page 72

frog
turtle
goldfish
snail

Page 73

Boots
Mr. Socks
Teddy Bear
Miss Muffin

Page 74

cloud
smell
flower
garden
kiss
skunk

Page 75

brown:
in
ten
brown
raccoon
black:
him
ham
mom

Page 76

gift
stop
had
kick
her

Page 77

cap
mop
stop
cup
stamp

Page 78

s sound: kiss, yes
z sound: stars, trees

Page 79

duck
heel
bus
room
sad

Page 80

ox
fox
tax
six
box

Page 81

1. hold
2. told
3. fold
4. could
5. would
6. should
7. sold
8. old

Page 82

Across:
1. sink
2. bank
3. think
4. junk
5. ink
Down:
1. sank
3. thank
6. rink
7. skunk
8. trunk
9. pink

Page 83

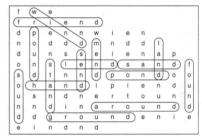

Page 84

1. aunt
2. tent
3. want
4. sent
5. hint
6. bent
7. went

Page 85

black: lamp, bump
brown: drink, tank

Page 86

fast
nest
list
most

Page 87

king
ring
swing
string

Page 88

peach
coach
watch
bench
sandwich

Answer Key *(cont.)*

Page 89
1. duck, quack
2. cluck
3. peck
4. chick

Page 90
Across:
1. spill
2. hill
3. fell
4. pull
Down:
5. fill
6. pill
7. well
8. fall

Page 91
lamb, a baby sheep
numb, not feeling anything
thumb, the shortest and fattest
  finger on a hand
limb, a tree branch

Page 92
All sentence beginnings are capitalized. Answer to puzzle: guitar

Page 93
1. My cousin spent the night at my house.
2. John said I could look at his snake.
3. Jim entered the bicycle race.
4. What a race it was!
5. Did he wear a helmet?
6. Who won the race?

Page 94
1. .
2. ?
3. !
4. ?
5. .
6. .
7. !
8. .
9. ?
10. ?

Page 95
Sentences 1, 3, 5, 6, 8, 10 (There are six sentences.)

Page 96
1. The cat chased the bird, or, The bird chased the cat.
2. I wrote a letter to my friend.
3. The family solved the puzzle together.
4. The baker baked a cake.
5. A penguin jumped into the sea.
6. The frog leaped over the log.

Page 97
Answers will vary.

Page 98
Person: Adam, Dr. Roberts, farmer, mother, scientist, zookeeper
Place: attic, London, museum, room, Russia, state
Thing: comb, door, football, hoe, motor, rainbow
(Accept attic, museum, room, and state as things, also.)

Page 99
1. sand; thing
2. truck; thing
3. sister; person
4. dentist; person
5. school; place
6. tire; thing
7. house; place

Page 100
Answers will vary.

Page 101
1. canes
2. brushes
3. ducks
4. bears
5. foxes
6. dresses
7. glasses
8. bags
9. buckets
10. sleds

Page 102
1. puppies
2. ladies
3. babies
4. candies
5. ponies
6. funnies
7. kitties
8. daddies
9. jellies
10. rubies

Page 103
1. William
2. Rachel
3. Laura
4. Michael
5. Carl Garcia
6. Joey Edwards
7. Barbara Madison
8. Heather Lee

Page 104
Answers will vary.

Page 105
1. Grandmother Davis
2. Mister Hayes
3. Captain Jack
4. Cousin Jimmy
5. Doctor Morton
6. Coach Russell

Page 106
Mrs. E. L. Hodges
B. D. Parker, Jr.
Dr. J. Nevarrez
Mrs. Marissa Williams
Mr. A. C. Owens
Capt. E. T. Lee

Page 107
Sunday
Monday
Tuesday
Wednesday
Thursday
Friday
Saturday

Page 108
1. January
2. February
3. March
4. April
5. May
6. June
7. July
8. August
9. September
10. October
11. November
12. December

Page 109
The colored hearts made the letter H. Two holidays that begin with this letter are Hanukkah and Halloween.

Answer Key *(cont.)*

Page 110
1. Pacific Ocean
2. Grand Canyon
3. Mt. Rushmore
4. Amazon River
5. San Diego Zoo
6. Hyde Park
7. Sahara Desert
8. Lake Louise
9. Disneyland
10. North Pole
11. Rocky Mountains
12. Niagara Falls

Page 111
1. Mr. I. Will Stealem
2. Muffin, my cat
3. Can I go to Larry's house?
4. Mrs. Penny, my fish
5. Mr. Jeff M. Smith, Jr.
6. Capt. Roberta Jones
7. Henry Garcia
8. I rode Bucky, Monica's horse.
9. I lost my capital.
10. Sam and Susan

Page 112
Hamilton Street, Tuesday, June, Norway, Halloween, China, April, Greece, May, Utah, Wednesday, Valentine's Day, Mexico, Friday, Paris, Argentina, September, Mother's Day, New York, December, Montreal, July, Central Park

Page 113
1. twinkles
2. watched
3. chased
4. set
5. swim
6. sings
7. eat
8. threw

Page 114
1. read
2. fly
3. swims
4. chases
5. climbs
6. run
7. hike
8. count
9. plays
10. watch

Page 115
1. plays
2. wins
3. matches
4. dance
5. barks
6. eats
7. likes
8. shines
9. watches
10. walks

Page 116
run, ran
see, saw
eat, ate
come, came
make, made
build, built
sleep, slept
give, gave
take, took
bring, brought
sing, sang

Page 117
Answers will vary. Students may choose adjective/noun combinations such as steep stairs, large windows, five stories, etc.

Page 118
Answers will vary.

Page 119
Answers will vary.

Page 120
Answers will vary.

Page 121
1. they
2. she
3. he
4. they
5. she
6. she
7. he
8. she

Page 122
I like food that is red, like strawberries, apples, and tomatoes. When I color, I like to use orange for flowers and trucks. I like yellow paper for projects I make. Green is a color I see when I go for walks. Blue is a color I like to wear. When I paint, I love to use purple.

Page 124
1. neat, spotless
2. sad, unhappy
3. thin, skinny
4. look, see
5. plain, simple
6. strong, powerful
7. cold, chilly
8. big, large
9. cheap, stingy
10. quiet, calm
11. poor, needy
12. little, small
13. sharp, pointed
14. loud, noisy
15. rich, wealthy
16. below, under

Page 125
circle/ring
happy/gleeful
cloth/fabric
sunny/bright
dawn/morning
clean/spotless
sick/ill
laugh/chuckle

Page 126
Answers may vary.

page 128
1. happy, sad
2. brave, afraid
3. right, wrong
4. fast, slow
5. big, little
6. rude, polite
7. old, young
8. strong, weak
9. crowded, empty
10. smile, frown
11. close, far
12. loud, quiet
13. ask, answer
14. wild, tame
15. beautiful, ugly
16. hard, easy

Answer Key *(cont.)*

Page 129

Answers may vary.

1. hard
2. sour
3. cold
4. later
5. lie
6. mean
7. murky
8. backward
9. west

Page 130

1. S
2. S
3. A
4. S
5. A
6. A
7. A
8. S
9. S
10. S

Page 131

red:
happy, joyful
tender, gentle
huge, big
tiny, small
cold, icy
loud, noisy
yellow:
black, white
fast, slow
in, out
up, down
big, little
day, night
good, bad
sad, happy

Page 137

1. broom
2. chain
3. drum
4. egg
5. flower
6. hand
7. jar
8. letter
9. music
10. number
11. potato
12. star
13. table
14. umbrella
15. whale
16. yellow

Page 139

billy goat
cat
parrot
bobcat
leopard
parakeet

Page 140

List A
cart
friend
ghost
house
jump
light
moon
river
silent
tunnel
umbrella
vest

List B
cane
cell
deer
dog
game
grass
lion
loop
lunch
same
science
sort

Page 141

3, 2, 1
2, 1, 3

Page 142

1, 2, 3
2, 1, 3
2, 3, 1
1, 3, 2

Page 143

Page 144

1. B
2. C

Page 145

1. He gets up at dawn.
2. He goes for a swim.
3. At ten o'clock he gets out of the water to eat.
4. He takes a nap.
5. He swims.
6. He plays.
7. At six o'clock, he eats again.
8. He swims and plays.
9. When it becomes dark, he goes to bed for the night.

Page 146

1. C
2. A

Page 147

1. They cleaned their rooms.
2. They washed the family's car.
1. They visited the wolf den.
2. They saw alligators.
3. They met their mother.

Page 149

The lion roars.
The alligator sleeps.
The bear eats fish.
Ice cream is a tasty treat.

Page 150

Titles will vary, but all should correspond directly with the pictures.

page 151

1. C
2. D
3. A
4. B
5. E

Page 152

Eric and Maria want to work in a hospital.

Page 153

Amy did not do her math homework.

Answer Key *(cont.)*

Page 154

The first picture should show a girl reading a book. The second should show a kitten ready to pounce on a ball of yarn.

Page 155

No Television
When the family television breaks, they all spend time together instead.
George the Giraffe
A make-believe giraffe has fun with his animal friends.
Follow the Star
A lost girl finds her way by following the stars.
The Mystery of the Broken Key
An old key opens a secret door.
Saddles and Spurs
Three children form a club to learn more about riding horses.
Fossils in the Neighborhood
A girl finds a dinosaur bone in her backyard.
Sam's Summer Vacation
A boy makes new friends at his summer camp.
My Horse, Flash
A girl finally gets her wish, a horse.
Calvin Plays Teacher
A boy sets up an imaginary school for the neighborhood children.

Page 156

Answers may vary.
1. He said he could eat a horse.
2. He didn't eat much at lunch.
3. He asked if there were any cheese and crackers or apples.

Page 157

1. The children are afraid.
2. Jack said it is spooky. Wendy wanted to leave.
1. Mary is jealous.
2. She asked where she could buy one and if there were any more like it.

Page 158

1. The rabbit was too smart for the fox. It hid in a hollow log and ran away when the fox passed by.
2. We looked everywhere for our brother. We finally found him in the toy section of the department store.
3. I like to play all kinds of games. My favorite is hide-and-seek.
4. The twins look exactly alike. Even their mother has a difficult time telling them apart.
5. Emily saw a rainbow cross the entire sky. She thought she had never seen anything look so beautiful.
6. The sky glowed in the moonlight. Stars twinkled all around.
7. The tiger crept through the tall grass and crouched in place. Then it swiftly leapt at a nearby zebra.
8. Mr. Carter bought a new pair of glasses. Now he can see much better.

Page 160

1. delivers
2. wash
3. cough
4. drove
5. snore
6. ate
7. wrote
8. knock
9. laughed
10. cries

Page 161

1. Stacie is playing baseball or softball.
2. This is Stacie's first home run. She does not hit them often.
3. The team rushes to meet Stacie at the plate.

Page 162

1. Buttons is a cat.
2. Kenny, does not like the rain. He is disappointed.
3. Buttons wants to play with Kenny and that cheers him up.

Page 163

1. There are four and twenty (24) blackbirds.
2. The birds begin to sing.
3. The king is counting his money.
4. The queen is in the parlor.
5. A blackbird pecks off the maid's nose.

Page 164

1. The crooked man walked a mile.
2. He found a crooked sixpence.
3. He bought a crooked cat.
4. It caught a crooked mouse.
5. Some answers may vary, but the best answer is that they are all crooked.

Page 165

1. King Cole is a merry old soul.
2. King Cole calls for his bowl.
3. There are three fiddlers.
4. The fiddlers have very fine fiddles.
5. List any two of the following pairs: Cole/soul; he/three; Cole/bowl; soul/bowl; rare/compare.

Page 166

1. The story is about Amy and Melanie.
2. They try washing dogs and babysitting.
3. They open their stand on a Saturday morning in June.
4. A glass of lemonade costs one quarter.
5. Yes, they can go to the movies.

Page 167

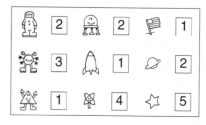

Page 168

1. yellow: $3 + 3 = 6$
2. red: $4 + 2 = 6$
3. blue: $1 + 5 = 6$

Answer Key *(cont.)*

Page 169

1. 5, 11, 9, 7
2. 3, 6, 12, 8
3. 1, 10, 2, 4

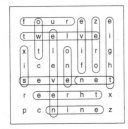

Page 173

1. The spoon, rolling pin, measuring cup, and mixing bowl should be colored.
2. All the triangles should be colored.
3. All the circles should be colored.
4. The strawberry, cherries, and grapes should be colored.

Page 174

Autumn: The leaf, rake, sweater, and football should be colored.
Winter: The tree without leaves, snowman, and sled should be colored.
Spring: The two flowers and bird in the nest should be colored.
Summer: The inner tube, sun, and swimming goggles and flippers should be colored.

Page 175

1. 5
2. 4
3. 4
4. 3
Numbers 2 and 3 should be colored.

Page 176

head and hat
foot and shoe
hand and glove

Page 177

5 > 3
1 < 4
10 > 8
64 > 51
5 < 6
2 > 0
9 < 11
21 < 24
35 > 14
79 < 97
100 > 12

Page 178

yellow: 0 + 4 = 4, 3 + 1 = 4,
1 + 3 = 4, 4 + 0 = 4, 2 + 2 = 4
green: 1 + 2 = 3, 0 + 0 = 0,
2 + 1 = 3, 1 + 1 = 2, 3 + 0 = 3,
2 + 3 = 5, 3 + 2 = 5

Page 179

orange: 3 + 2 = 5
green: 5 + 0 = 5
blue: 1 + 4 = 5
red: 1 + 4 = 5
purple: 2 + 3 = 5

Page 180

1. 2 + 4 = 6, 6 + 0 = 6, 3 + 3 = 6
2. 1 + 5 = 6, 4 + 2 = 6
3. 0 + 6 = 6, 5 + 1 = 6

Page 181

2 + 3 = 5
6 + 4 = 10
7 + 2 = 9
4 + 4 = 8
5 + 2 = 7
6 + 3 = 9

Page 182

1. 3 + 6 = 9
2. 5 + 4 = 9
3. 7 + 2 = 9
4. 1 + 8 = 9

Page 183

1. 5 + 4 = 9
2. 6 + 3 = 9
3. 2 + 2 = 4
4. 4 + 5 = 9
5. 5 + 2 = 7
6. 2 + 7 = 9
7. 1 + 8 = 9
8. 1 + 4 = 5
9. 0 + 9 = 9

Page 184

8 + 2 = 10, 7 + 3 = 10, 9 + 1 = 10,
10 + 0 = 10, 6 + 4 = 10, 4 + 6 = 10,
2 + 8 = 10, 5 + 5 = 10, 1 + 9 = 10,
3 + 7 = 10, 0 + 10 = 10

Page 185

2 + 6 = 8
9 + 1 = 10
4 + 10 = 14
8 + 3 = 11
4 + 8 = 12
5 + 7 = 12

Page 186

1. 7, 12, 10, 5
2. 9, 12, 2, 6
3. 0, 3, 10, 6
4. 11, 10, 7, 11
5. 10, 7, 10, 12
6. 6, 1, 11, 12
7. 4, 7, 5, 11
8. 8, 12, 9, 8

Page 187

a. 5 + 4 = 9
b. 5 + 6 = 11
c. 5 + 3 = 8
d. 5 + 4 = 9
e. 1 + 2 = 3
f. 7 + 3 = 10
g. 2 + 5 = 7
h. 2 + 2 = 4
i. 3 + 9 = 12
Lucky purse: 10

Page 188

3 + 4 = 7 (a)
4 + 5 = 9 (f)
1 + 4 = 5 (r)
6 + 2 = 8 (o)
2 + 4 = 6 (g)
a frog

Page 189

correct path: 1 + 11 = 12, 3 + 9 = 12, 2 + 10 = 12, 4 + 8 = 12, 9 + 3 = 12, 5 + 7 = 12, 8 + 4 = 12, 10 + 2 = 12, 11 + 1 = 12, 0 + 12 = 12, 6 + 6 = 12, 12 + 0 = 12

Page 190

4 + 6 = 10 (brown)
5 + 4 = 9 (orange)
5 + 5 = 10 (brown)
6 + 6 = 12 (yellow)
3 + 6 = 9 (orange)
7 + 5 = 12 (yellow)
4 + 7 = 11 (blue)

Answer Key *(cont.)*

Page 191

brown: 9 + 3 = 12, 6 + 6 = 12, 8 + 4 + 12

purple: 5 + 1 = 6, 4 + 2 = 6, 3 + 3 = 6, 6 + 0 = 6

blue: 1 + 7 = 8, 3 + 5 = 8, 7 + 1 = 8, 4 + 4 = 8, 6 + 2 = 8, 5 + 3 = 8,

green: 8 + 3 = 11, 7 + 4 = 11, 2 + 9 = 11

black: 2 + 3 = 5, 1 + 4 = 5, 5 + 0 = 5, 4 + 1 = 5

yellow: 3 + 6 = 9, 6 + 3 = 9, 4 + 5 = 9, 5 + 4 = 9, 8 + 1 = 9, 9 + 0 = 9, 7 + 2 = 9

red: 4 + 6 = 10, 5 + 5 = 10

Page 192

The peanuts are in the lion's den.

Page 193

a. 5	f. 13
b. 8	g. 10
c. 11	h. 16
d. 6	i. 15
e. 15	

Page 194

a. 6	g. 14
b. 11	h. 11
c. 5	i. 10
d. 8	j. 14
e. 11	k. 19
f. 14	

Page 195

a. 9 + 5 = 14 dollars
b. 7 + 2 = 9 dollars
c. 4 + 1 = 5 dollars
d. 9 + 3 = 12 dollars
e. 5 + 1 + 2 = 8 dollars
f. 7 + 4 + 9 = 20 dollars

Page 196

a. 1 + 3 + 5 = 9
b. 1 + 8 + 10- = 19
c. 7 + 7 + 5 = 19
d. 3 + 2 + 5 = 10

Page 197

1. 6
2. 14
3. 12
4. 7
5. 8
6. 11
7. 10
8. 8

Page 198

1. 12
2. 10
3. 11
4. 8
5. 6
6. 7
7. 9

Page 199

1. 12
2. 8
3. 13
4. 11
5. 8
6. 12

Page 200

1. 16
2. 13
3. 11
4. 15
5. 12
6. 12
7. 10
8. 15
9. 9

Page 201

1. 8
2. 9
3. 10
4. 11
5. 12
6. 13
7. 17
8. 14
9. 12
10. 16

Page 203

red: 3, 5, 7
yellow: 2, 8
blue: 1, 9
green: 4, 6

Page 204

1. 33
2. 29
3. 43
4. 29
5. 34
6. 53
7. 64

Page 205

1. 39
2. 47
3. 52
4. 72
5. 24
6. 27

Secret number: 27

Page 206

1. 97	5. 99
2. 76	6. 86
3. 68	7. 45
4. 78	

Page 207

1. 18
2. 65
3. 83
4. 20
5. 56
6. 59
7. 74
8. 92
9. 60
10. 47

Page 208

13 + 14 = 27 (a)
14 + 12 = 26 (c)
11 + 18 = 29 (l)
16 + 12 = 28 (o)
13 + 13 = 26 (c)
12 + 13 = 25 (k)

a clock

Page 209

a. 42
b. 35
c. 61
d. 29
e. 20
g. 37
i. 51
l. 53
m. 92
n. 84
o. 67
r. 31
s. 66
t. 25
u. 39
w. 48
y. 72

Message: Congratulations! You are adding two-digit numbers.

Answer Key *(cont.)*

Page 211

Sunday: 32
Monday: 30
Tuesday: 36
Wednesday: 34
Thursday: 31
Friday: 33
Saturday: 38

Page 212

1. 88
2. 75
3. 36
4. 96
5. 52
6. 63
7. 54
8. 45

Page 213

i = 31
r = 72
e = 100
t = 61
g = 73
o = 60
m = 91
p = 54
u = 81
Message: TIME TO REGROUP

Page 214

1. 119
2. 81
3. 41
4. 101
5. 90
6. 31
7. 71
8. 102
9. 93
10. 72
11. 81
12. 83
smallest sum: 31

Page 215

1. 71
2. 43
3. 86
4. 60
5. 67
6. 81
7. 62

Page 216

1. 48
2. 30
3. 61
4. 72
5. 27
6. 41
7. 101

Page 217

44 + 37 = 81
68 + 12 = 80
55 + 33 = 88
47 + 35 = 82
19 + 70 = 89
65 + 24 = 89

Page 218

a. 70
b. 102
c. 54
d. 83
e. 126
f. 82
g. 158
h. 151
i. 111
j. 135

Page 219

45 + 37 = 82 (a)
17 + 67 = 84 (c)
38 + 47 = 85 (r)
58 + 25 = 83 (o)
58 + 26 = 84 (c)
36 + 47 = 83 (o)
49 + 31 = 80 (d)
69 + 18 = 87 (i)
79 + 7 = 86 (l)
48 + 33 = 81 (e)
a crocodile

Page 220

yellow: 28 + 17 = 45, 29 + 16 = 45, 26 + 19 = 45
green: 27 + 33 = 60
red: 31 + 19 = 50, 36 + 14 = 50
orange: 27 + 28 = 55
brown: 47 + 18 = 65

Page 221

a. 16 + 14 + 22 = 52
b. 28 + 32 + 46 = 106
c. 27 + 23 + 52 = 102
d. 19 + 33 + 21 = 73

Page 222

The rainbow colors from outside to inside are red, orange, yellow, green, blue, purple, and violet.

Page 223

antennae

Page 224

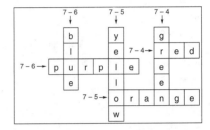

Page 225

9 – 8 = 1
8 – 6 = 2
9 – 6 = 3
9 – 5 = 4
8 – 3 = 5
9 – 3 = 6
9 – 2 = 7
9 – 1 = 8
9 – 0 = 9

Page 226

1. 0 (pink)
2. 3 (orange)
3. 7 (brown)
4. 1 (blue)
5. 4 (yellow)
6. 8 (white)
7. 2 (red)
8. 5 (green)
9. 9 (gray)
10. 6 (purple)

Page 228

a. 5 – 0 = 5
b. 7 – 1 = 6
c. 4 – 2 = 2
d. 8 – 3 = 5
e. 4 – 1 = 3
f. 10 – 5 = 5
g. 7 – 6 = 1
h. 7 – 3 = 4
i. 8 – 8 = 0
j. 9 – 6 = 3
k. 10 – 4 = 6

Answer Key *(cont.)*

Page 229

a. $1 - 0 = 1$
b. $8 - 1 = 7$
c. $5 - 2 = 3$
d. $4 - 3 = 1$
e. $8 - 4 = 4$
f. $5 - 4 = 1$
g. $9 - 6 = 3$
h. $7 - 7 = 0$
i. $8 - 7 = 1$
j. $10 - 5 = 5$
k. $9 - 3 = 6$

Page 230

a. $9 - 2 = 7$
b. $7 - 4 = 3$
c. $10 - 9 = 1$
d. $6 - 6 = 0$
e. $3 - 1 = 2$
f. $8 - 4 = 4$

Page 231

$7 - 5 = 2$ (a)
$8 - 7 = 1$ (f)
$9 - 6 = 3$ (o)
$3 - 0 = 3$ (o)
$6 - 1 = 5$ (t)
$9 - 5 = 4$ (b)
$9 - 7 = 2$ (a)
$1 - 1 = 0$ (l)
$5 - 5 = 0$ (l)
a football

Page 232

$5 - 4 = 1$ (pink)
$6 - 3 = 3$ (green)
$4 - 3 = 1$ (pink)
$6 - 6 = 0$ (yellow)
$7 - 5 = 2$ (brown)
$7 - 3 = 4$ (white)
$8 - 4 = 4$ (white)
$9 - 8 = 1$ (pink)
$5 - 3 = 2$ (brown)
$10 - 6 = 4$ (white)

Page 233

$11 - 11 = 0$
$11 - 10 = 1$
$11 - 8 = 3$
$11 - 7 = 4$
$11 - 2 = 9$
$11 - 9 = 2$
$11 - 3 = 8$
$11 - 6 = 5$
$11 - 5 = 6$
$11 - 4 = 7$
$11 - 1 = 10$
$11 - 0 = 11$

Page 234

1. $12 - 7 = 5$
2. $12 - 9 = 3$
3. $12 - 6 = 6$
4. $12 - 10 = 2$
5. $12 - 5 = 7$
6. $12 - 11 = 1$
7. $12 - 0 = 12$

Page 235

blue: $13 - 12 = 1$, $13 - 11 = 2$
green: $13 - 4 = 9$, $13 - 3 = 10$
yellow: $13 - 7 = 6$, $13 - 8 = 5$,
$13 - 9 = 4$, $13 - 10 = 3$
red: $13 - 6 = 7$, $13 - 5 = 8$
white: $13 - 1 = 12$, $13 - 2 = 11$

Page 236

1. 13
2. 6
3. 1
4. 2
5. 9
6. 12
7. 8
8. 3
9. 7
10. 11
11. 4
12. 10
13. 5

House # 7 matches the mailbox.

Page 237

1. $15 - 5 = 10$
2. $10 - 4 = 6$
3. $8 - 1 = 7$
4. $9 - 2 = 7$

Page 238

gray: $18 - 12 = 6$, $18 - 15 = 3$,
$18 - 7$, $18 - 13 = 5$, $17 - 12 = 5$,
$17 - 10 = 7$, $17 - 11 = 6$
blue: $18 - 3 = 15$, $17 - 2 = 15$,
$18 - 4 = 14$, $17 - 3 = 14$, $18 - 5 = 13$, $17 - 4 = 13$, $18 - 2 = 16$, $17 - 6 = 11$, $17 - 1 = 16$, $17 - 5 = 12$, $18 - 7 = 11$, $18 - 6 = 12$

Page 239

G = 5
A = 1
S = 12
B = 2
N = 9
E = 4
R = 11
K = 7
C = 3
L = 8
H = 6
O = 10
nose, nose, roll, hang, back, hognose

Page 240

a. $9 - 4 = 5$
b. $8 - 2 = 6$
c. $7 - 3 = 4$
d. $8 - 4 = 4$
e. $8 - 1 = 7$

Page 241

a. $7 - 6 = 1$
b. $9 - 3 - 6 - 0 = 0$
c. $10 - 1 - 6 = 3$
d. $5 - 3 - 1 = 1$

Page 243

$49 - 26 = 23$
$47 - 35 = 12$
$68 - 47 = 21$
$70 - 50 = 20$
$55 - 33 = 22$
$65 - 24 = 41$

Page 244

e = 17, i = 29, o = 26, r = 38, s = 43, t = 22
mystery animal: tortoise

Page 245

a. 32
b. 71
c. 25
d. 10
e. 15
f. 1

Page 246

1. $76 - 22 = 54$, $76 - 31 = 45$, $76 - 44 = 32$, $76 - 53 = 23$
2. $86 - 21 = 65$, $86 - 44 = 42$, $86 - 55 = 31$, $86 - 73 = 13$
3. $58 - 31 = 27$, $58 - 47 = 11$, $58 - 12 = 46$, $58 - 23 = 35$
4. $45 - 14 = 31$, $45 - 23 = 22$, $45 - 13 = 32$, $45 - 42 = 3$

Page 247

black: $42 - 21 = 21$, $49 - 28 = 21$, $21 - 0 = 21$
blue: $27 - 15 = 12$, $47 - 35 = 12$
green: $35 - 12 = 23$, $48 - 25 = 23$
yellow: $47 - 16 = 31$
red: $97 - 34 = 63$
gray: $58 - 32 = 26$, $36 - 10 = 26$, $26 - 0 = 26$

Answer Key *(cont.)*

Page 248

42 − 30 = 12 (a)
33 − 22 = 11 (b)
46 − 34 = 12 (a)
54 − 41 = 13 (n)
77 − 67 = 10 (j)
28 − 14 = 14 (o)
a banjo

Page 250

1. 81 − 3 = 78
2. 80 − 6 = 74
3. 80 − 3 = 77
4. 30 − 8 = 22
5. 35 − 7 = 28
6. 60 − 9 = 51
7. 37 − 8 = 29
8. 97 − 8 = 89
9. 31 − 6 = 25
elephant—orange
ostrich—green
cheetah—blue
bee—brown
dog—red
horse—pink
snail—purple
giraffe—yellow
turtle—black

Page 251

27, 69, 18
39, 17, 55
53, 21, 77

Page 252

1. 13
2. 4
3. 18
4. 57
5. 16
6. 37
Number 5 took the cookies.

Page 253

a. 60 − 48 = 12
b. 72 − 13 = 59
c. 32 − 23 = 9
d. 40 − 32 = 8
e. 61 − 15 = 46
f. 58 − 29 = 29
g. 83 − 38 = 45
h. 74 − 46 = 28
i. 22 − 18 = 4
j. 94 − 28 = 66

Page 254

73 − 48 = 25 (orange)
84 − 49 = 35 (yellow)
90 − 48 = 42 (purple)
61 − 16 = 45 (blue)
62 − 29 = 33 (green)
80 − 38 = 42 (purple)
93 − 48 = 45 (blue)
82 − 47 = 35 (yellow)
70 − 45 = 25 (orange)

Page 255

1. 78 − 16 = 62, 62 − 27 = 35,
   35 − 18 = 17
2. 85 − 7 = 78, 78 − 9 = 69,
   69 − 13 = 56
3. 56 − 9 = 47, 47 − 23 = 24,
   24 − 17 = 7
4. 91 − 18 = 73, 73 − 25 = 48,
   48 − 14 = 34

Page 256

Correct: 20 − 9 = 11, 20 − 8 = 12,
19 − 9 = 10, 32 − 6 = 26,
27 − 9 = 18, 25 − 8 = 17
Incorrect: 18 − 9 = 11,
24 − 8 = 17, 17 − 9 = 11,
21 − 9 = 18,
17 − 8 = 12, 42 − 6 = 44

Page 257

80 − 45 = 35 (a)
75 − 38 = 37 (j)
92 − 57 = 35 (a)
52 − 16 = 36 (c)
72 − 33 = 39 (k)
92 − 54 = 38 (e)
107 − 67 = 40 (t)
a jacket

Page 258

a. 93 − 68 = 25
b. 43 − 27 = 16
c. 53 − 28 = 25
d. 83 − 65 = 18

Page 260

1. 12, 12
2. 10, 10
3. 24, 24
4. 15, 15

Page 261

1. 3, 2, 6
2. 2, 4, 8
   4 + 4 = 8
   2 x 4 = 8

Page 262

1. 8, 8
2. 5, 5
3. 3, 3
4. 0, 0

Page 263

1. 0
2. 0
3. 0
4. 0
5. 0

Page 264

1. 1
2. 4
3. 8
4. 11
5. 7

Page 265

1. 2, 2
2. 4, 4
3. 6, 6
4. 8, 8
5. 10, 10
6. 12, 12
7. 14, 14
8. 16, 16
9. 18, 18
10. 20, 20
11. 22, 22
12. 24, 24

Page 266

1. 2
2. 12
3. 9
4. 0
5. 1
6. 10
7. 11
8. 10
9. 0
10. 6
11. 8
12. 4
13. 0
14. 0
15. 18
16. 7
17. 16
18. 3
19. 4
20. 0

Answer Key *(cont.)*

Page 267

1. 5
2. 6
3. 1
4. 22
5. 4
6. 0
7. 0
8. 10
9. 18
10. 0
11. 16
12. 4

Page 268

1. 12
2. 18
3. 27

Page 269

1. 3
2. 6
3. 9
4. 12
5. 15
6. 18
7. 21
8. 24
9. 27
10. 30
11. 33
12. 36

Page 270

1. 4
2. 28
3. 8
4. 32
5. 12
6. 36
7. 16
8. 40
9. 20
10. 44
11. 24
12. 48

Page 271

1. 5
2. 35
3. 10
4. 40
5. 15
6. 45
7. 20
8. 50
9. 25
10. 55
11. 30
12. 60

Page 272

1. 30
2. 10
3. 25
4. 60
5. 45
6. 35
7. 5
8. 45
9. 15
10. 40
11. 50
12. 20
13. 55
14. 25
15. 40

Page 273

1. 2/3
2. 1/4
3. 1/2
4. 1/3
5. 3/5
6. 2/5

Page 274

Sample Solutions:

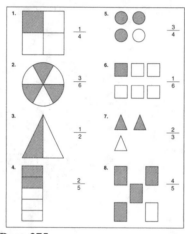

Page 275

Answers will vary.

Page 276

6 squares
3 circles
4 triangles
3 rectangles

Page 278

globe—sphere
pyramid—triangular prism
pencil—cylinder
ice cream cone—cone
alphabet blocks—cube

Page 280

1. 3 + 4 = 7
2. 5 + 2 = 7
3. 1 + 6 = 7

Page 281

1. reading
2. 6
3. science and physical education
4. mathematics
5. 2

Page 282

1. Sunday
2. 70 fish
3. Friday
4. Tuesday
5. yes—20 fish
6. 130 fish

Page 284

1. K A.M.: 20
   K p.m.: 5
   1st: 60
   2nd: 75
   3rd: 55
   4th: 50
   5th: 35
   6th: 20
2. 2nd grade
3. K A.M. and 6th grade
4. sixth graders
5. Answers will vary

Page 285

1. yes 10:15 to 11:45
2. calendar, music, lunch
3. sharing, reading, writing, math, science, art, recess

Page 286

1. Tuesday
2. August 12
3. Wednesday
4. 2
5. Monday and Friday

Page 287

1. □
2. △
3. ○
4. ♡
5. ○
6. □
7. D
8. △
9. ♡
10. □

Page 288

a. 9
b. 18
c. 35
d. 12
e. 6
f. 7
g. 1
h. 15
i. 29
j. 90
k. 6
l. 0
m. 3
n. 9

Practice
and
Learn

Part 2

Table of Contents
Part 2

What Kind of Noun?

Nouns are words that name a person, place, or thing.

Write each of the following words under the correct heading.

Adam	farmer	museum	state
attic	football	rainbow	zoo keeper
comb	hoe	room	artist
Dr. Roberts	London	Russia	playground
door	mother	scientist	
clock	motor		

Person

Place

Thing

_____ _____ _____

_____ _____ _____

_____ _____ _____

_____ _____ _____

_____ _____ _____

_____ _____ _____

#6455 Practice and Learn—Ages Seven to Nine

Find the Noun

A noun names

a person,   place,   or thing.

Underline each noun.

1. The dancer jumped in the air.

2. The boy watched television.

3. Mr. Smith teaches our class.

4. The baby cried for her mother.

5. The sisters walked to the store.

6. My school has two stories.

7. The teenagers rode their skateboards through the park.

8. The dentist treated a new patient.

9. A little dog picked a fight with a big cat.

10. There were presents, cake, and candles at my birthday party.

What Kind of Noun?

A noun names

a person,

place,

or thing.

Complete each sentence with the kind of noun written before the sentence.

person   1.   The _____ delivered the mail.

thing   2.   I can not find my _____.

thing   3.   The dog played with the _____.

person   4.   Jeff and _____ played

           ball in the park.

place   5.   I read my book at the _____.

person   6.   _____ played the piano.

place   7.   Can we go to the _____?

thing   8.   At the store, I bought _____.

Common and Proper Nouns

Proper nouns begin with capital letters, and **common nouns** are just regular nouns. The word **cat** is a common noun, but **Boots**, the cat's name, is a proper noun.

I have a **cat**.

His name is **Boots**.

Circle each word used as a common noun in the sentences below. Underline the words used as proper nouns.

1. I live in the green house on Elm Street.

2. My dog, Max, and I went for a walk.

3. There are three Ryans in my class.

4. My family is planning a trip to the Grand Canyon.

5. "Mom, where is my yellow shirt?" Jenny asked her mother.

6. Where is Primrose Park?

7. The only vegetable I like is broccoli.

8. Our neighbor's cat is named Sylvester.

9. My teacher is Mrs. Simms.

10. Ricky, Sam, and Tim are going to play football in the park.

How Proper Are You?

Fill in the blanks to name the proper nouns in your life.

Your name _____

Name of a family member _____

Pet's name (or the name of a pet you would
like to have) _____

Friend's name _____

Your street _____

Your city_____

Your country _____

Specific places you would like to visit _____

_____

Teacher's Name _____

Parents' Names_____

_____

Plural Nouns

In most cases, an *s* is added to a noun to name more than one.

If the noun ends in **s**, **x**, **ch**, or **sh**, *es* is added.

fox

foxes

Write the plural form of each noun.

1. cat _____

2. dog _____

3. house _____

4. gate _____

5. church _____

6. monkey_____

7. tree_____

8. class_____

9. door _____

10. chair_____

11. lunch_____

12. box _____

13. bush _____

14. glass_____

15. truck _____

16. brush _____

Plural Nouns Ending in Y

When a noun ends in **y**, change the **y** to **i** and add *es*.

bunny

bunnies

Write the plural forms of the nouns below.

1. penny _____

2. pony _____

3. berry _____

4. family _____

5. factory _____

6. candy _____

7. party _____

8. cherry _____

9. baby _____

10. filly _____

11. jelly _____

12. lily _____

13. lady _____

14. patty _____

15. fly _____

16. story _____

Unusual Plural Nouns

Some nouns do not follow the normal rules when they become plurals.

leaf   leaves

In the blanks, write the plural form of each underlined word.

1. The <u>woman</u> next door invited several _____ to tea.

2. Although one baby <u>tooth</u> fell out, many more must fall out before I have all my adult _____.

3. One <u>man</u> on my father's bowling team is much taller than the other _____.

4. I saw only one <u>child</u>, but I could hear many more _____ playing.

5. It is much more difficult to hop on one <u>foot</u> than it is to hop on both _____.

6. We caught one <u>mouse</u> in the trap, but we suspected there were other _____ in the attic as well.

7. The pioneer knew that one <u>ox</u> could not pull his wagon so he would need a team of _____.

8. One <u>wife</u> suggested that all of the _____ should meet for a morning walk.

9. The large <u>goose</u> bossed all the other _____ in the barnyard.

10. I added the hot <u>loaf</u> of bread to the other _____ I had baked in the morning.

Possessives

The **boy's kite** flew high in the sky.

Possessives show who or what owns something. Singular nouns are made possessive by adding an apostrophe and then an *s*. Plural possessives are formed by adding an apostrophe after the *s*. However, when a plural noun does not end with an *s*, an apostrophe and then an *s* are added.

Rewrite the underlined nouns in the sentences below to make them possessive.

1. The <u>baby</u> rattle fell to the ground. _____

2. <u>Mary</u> doll has brown hair. _____

3. Those <u>boys</u> skates are in the locker. _____

4. The <u>tree</u> leaves have turned red and gold. _____

5. <u>Ken</u> mother brought his lunch to school. _____

6. The lost <u>dogs</u> owner was very glad to see them again. _____

7. The <u>children</u> balloons flew away. _____

8. The <u>kitten</u> ball rolled under the couch. _____

9. Some <u>woman</u> hair was blowing in the wind. _____

10. The <u>pan</u> handle was very hot. _____

Action Verbs

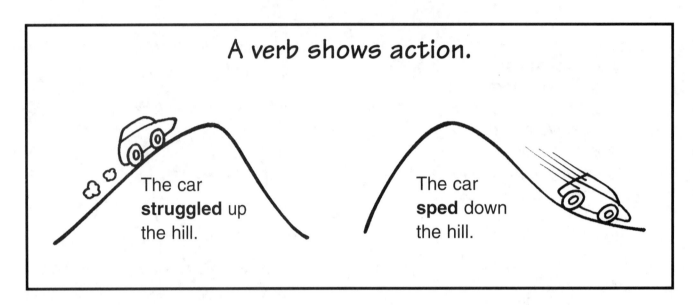

A verb shows action.

The car **struggled** up the hill.

The car **sped** down the hill.

Write the verb for each sentence on the line provided.

1. Barbara plays basketball well. _____

2. The bird flies over my head. _____

3. The bicycle makes Frank happy. _____

4. The children ran to the playground. _____

5. The balloon popped in front of me. _____

6. The pen ran out of ink. _____

7. I fell on the sidewalk. _____

8. I eat a piece of fruit each day. _____

9. The old horse stood quietly in the field. _____

10. Our teacher reads a story to us each day. _____

Take Action!

An **action verb** tells what the subject does or did. It shows action.

Examples

run/ran	laugh/laughed
swing/swung	see/saw
hear/heard	leap/leaped
jump/jumped	stop/stopped

There are 54 words used as action verbs in the following paragraph. Try to find at least 40 of them. When you find one, underline the action verb and then write it on a separate sheet of paper.

In the morning, Benjamin woke up and jumped out of bed. He landed on his brother, Timothy, who slept on the bottom bunk. Timothy sat up and rubbed his eyes. He grumbled at Benjamin and then fell back on his bed. Benjamin looked at Timothy for a long time. He wondered whether Timothy slept. Then Benjamin ran to the corner and grabbed his horn. Benjamin blew into his horn and played some musical notes. He liked the sound of his horn, but he heard another sound. He stopped and listened. A moan came from Timothy. Benjamin disliked that sound. He grabbed his horn and ran out the door. He sat on the front lawn and played some more music. The notes floated in the air. He played until he heard another sound. He stopped and listened. A groan came from his next-door neighbor. Benjamin ran into the backyard. He played his horn some more. He liked the notes. Then he heard another sound. He heard his mother. She called his name again. He went inside. His mother took his horn and put it away. Then she put Benjamin back in his bed. She told him he left his bed too early. Benjamin's mother went back to bed, too. Benjamin imagined the sounds of his horn. Suddenly, he heard another sound. He stopped and listened. Timothy snored again and again. Benjamin moaned. He stuck his fingers in his ears, but he still heard Timothy. So he covered his ears with his pillow. Soon he slept again.

Linking Verbs

You have learned that all sentences have verbs. A verb can be a word that tells what a subject does. When a verb tells what a subject does, it is called an **action verb**. However, a verb can also be a word that tells us what the subject is. When a verb describes what a subject is, it is called a **linking verb**.

Examples:

My friend **is** the owner of a dog. The linking verb is *is*.

The dog **is** nice. The linking verb is *is*.

We **were** on the boat with the dog. The linking verb is *were*.

Find the linking verbs in the following sentences. Underline them in the sentences. Then write them on the lines. The first one is done for you.

1. The turtle <u>seems</u> hungry.

2. The turtle is very small.

3. My cat Fluffy is furry.

4. My cat looks very sleepy.

5. My brothers are tall.

6. They are always busy.

7. The turtle and the cat were in the wagon.

8. My brothers are in trouble.

9. My cousins are taller than my brothers.

10. My sister is older than my brother.

1. _____ *seems* _____

2. _____

3. _____

4. _____

5. _____

6. _____

7. _____

8. _____

9. _____

10. _____

The Verb Is Superb

A **verb** can tell what the subject does. This is called an **action verb**.

> **Example:** Jacob runs home. (What does Jacob do? **runs** The action verb is runs.)

A verb can also describe the subject by telling what the subject was or is. This is called a **linking verb**.

> **Example:** Ruth is cold. (The linking verb is **is**.)

Circle the verbs in the following sentences. Then, on the line before each number, write an **A** if you circled an action verb or **L** if you circled a linking verb.

_____ 1. Marci sings in the choir.

_____ 2. Yoshi kicks the soccer ball.

_____ 3. Matt has the flu.

_____ 4. Leeann is really smart.

_____ 5. Mrs. Ross was my teacher.

_____ 6. The dog tipped over the trash can.

_____ 7. Next, the dog jumped on Leticia.

_____ 8. Mr. Carter's shirt is dirty.

_____ 9. They walked to the store.

_____10. Toby washes his shirt.

Past and Present

Verbs in the **present tense** show action that is happening now. In the **past tense**, verbs show action that already happened.

Today the bird **chirps.**

Yesterday the bird **chirped.**

Change each of these present-tense verbs to the past tense by adding *d* or *ed*.

1. walk _____

2. climb _____

3. jump _____

4. play _____

5. comb _____

6. roar _____

7. smile _____

8. fold _____

9. close _____

10. paint _____

Change each of the past-tense verbs to the present tense by removing the *d* or *ed*.

11. colored _____

12. scribbled _____

13. turned _____

14. cooked_____

15. washed _____

16. shared_____

17. stacked _____

18. typed _____

19. laughed _____

20. delivered _____

Irregular Verbs

Irregular verbs do not change from present to past tense by adding *d* or *ed*.
Other letters of the verb change to make the past tense. Draw lines to connect
the present-tense and past-tense of each irregular verb.

run	gave
see	brought
eat	saw
come	ate
make	built
build	ran
sleep	made
give	slept
take	took
bring	came
sing	sang

Changing Irregular Verbs

Change the following irregular verbs from present to past tense.

1. blow

   _____

2. come

   _____

3. sing

   _____

4. wear

   _____

5. take

   _____

6. cry

   _____

7. make

   _____

8. give

   _____

9. fall

   _____

10. fly

   _____

Change the irregular verbs from past to present tense.

11. caught

   _____

12. read

   _____

13. rode

   _____

14. drank

   _____

15. swung

   _____

16. shone

   _____

17. paid

   _____

18. wrote

   _____

19. swept

   _____

20. tore

   _____

Singular and Plural Verbs

When subjects and verbs are together in a sentence, they must agree in number.

The sandal (feel, feels) like it fits.

A **singular subject** (only one) takes a singular verb.

A **plural subject** (more than one) takes a plural verb.

Circle the correct singular or plural verb. Write the word **singular** or **plural** after each sentence.

1. The rabbit (hops, hop). _____

2. The sun (shines, shine). _____

3. The cakes (was, were) delicious. _____

4. Angry tigers (roars, roar) loudly. _____

5. The man (rides, ride) his bike to work. _____

6. Winter vacation (is, are) coming soon. _____

7. The boys (has, have) red shirts. _____

8. The flowers (is, are) blooming. _____

9. Karen (dances, dance) very well. _____

10. The tomatoes (is, are) ripe._____

Which Verb?

Circle the correct verb for each sentence.

The runners **race** to the finish line.

1. We _____ the book.	**read**	**reads**
2. They _____ the kite.	**fly**	**flies**
3. Mr. Kim _____ across the pool.	**swim**	**swims**
4. Lucky _____ the ball.	**chase**	**chases**
5. The panda _____ the tree.	**climb**	**climbs**
6. I _____ a mile.	**run**	**runs**
7. You _____ up the mountain.	hike	hikes
8. They _____ to 100.	count	counts
9. She _____ the violin.	play	plays
10. We _____ the circus.	watch	watches

Was/Were and Does/Do

was? were? does? do?

He **was** playing.

They **were** playing.

She **does** her chores.

They **do** their chores.

Write **was** or **were** in each sentence.

1. Where_____we supposed to meet?

2. Who_____with you?

3. I_____at school when the siren sounded.

4. We_____watching a play.

5. She_____confused about the homework.

6. They_____wondering where to go.

Write **do** or **does** in each sentence.

7. Where_____you keep the sugar?

8. I will_____the dishes.

9. They will_____the laundry after we leave.

10. She_____her best on all her work.

11. Kevin_____a good job when he hoes the garden.

12. Who_____the paperwork in the office?

Adjectives

Adjectives are words that describe. Write an adjective for each word.

1. _____stairs

2. _____windows

3. _____stories

4. _____chimney

5. _____hallway

6. _____apartment

7. _____families

8. _____neighbor

9. _____room

10. _____street

11. _____door

12. _____friend

(tall) building

326

Choose the Adjectives

Adjectives describe
people, places, and
things.

a
diamond
ring

many   **loose**   **funny**   **large**   **striped**

Use the words in boldface to add an adjective to each sentence.

1. The_____zebra is a beautiful animal.

2. My clothes are baggy and_____.

3. _____people watch television each day.

4. We laughed at the_____movie.

5. The giant was so_____he blocked the sun when
    he stood.

Add an adjective to each sentence below. Write the new sentences.

6. The monkeys swing from the trees.

    _____

7. The owl hooted in the night.

    _____

8. The farmer plants his crops.

    _____

9. Have you seen my shoes?

    _____

10. A hummingbird flew past the window.

    _____

How Would You Describe It?

Write a describing word (adjective) in each blank.

1. The _____ man came to my house.

2. A _____ puppy ran through the yard.

3. I like the _____ bike.

4. We can play with this _____ toy.

5. I am wearing a _____ pair of shoes.

6. My mother is _____.

7. The nurse is _____.

8. I saw a _____ show on television.

9. The _____ pig rolled in the mud.

10. There was a _____ spider hanging from its web.

Articles: A and An

Articles are a kind of adjective. The three most common articles are *the, a,* and *an.* *A* is used before words that begin with a consonant sound, *an* is used before words that begin with a vowel sound, and *the* may be used before words that begin with either a vowel or a consonant.

a house **an apple**

Write **a** or **an** in the blanks below.

1. _____ crayon

2. _____ ape

3. _____ saucer

4. _____ egg

5. _____ monkey

6. _____ pill

7. _____ itch

8. _____ orange

9. _____ blouse

10. _____ log

11. _____ ant crawled across the leaf.

12. Have you seen _____ purple butterfly?

13. I would like to eat _____ sandwich for lunch.

14. _____ apple a day keeps the doctor away.

15. _____ goat chewed on my pant leg!

When? Where? How?

Adverbs tell *when, where,* and *how.* Before each sentence write *when* if the underlined words tells about a time, *where* if it tells about a place, or *how* if it shows how something is done. The underlined words are adverbs in the sentences below.

When ? Where ? How ?

_____ 1. I walked <u>quietly</u> down the hall.

_____ 2. We will go <u>tomorrow</u>.

_____ 3. We can play <u>in the park</u>.

_____ 4. My cousins will come over <u>in the morning</u>.

_____ 5. The cheetah growled <u>fiercely</u>.

_____ 6. The waves rolled <u>gently</u> on the shore.

_____ 7. A new family of monkeys is moving <u>to the zoo</u>.

_____ 8. <u>After dinner</u> I will shoot some baskets.

_____ 9. The team played <u>well</u>.

_____ 10. He wrote his letter <u>quickly</u>.

Adverbs

Underline the words in each sentence that show when, where, or how. These are the adverbs or adverb phrases. After each sentence, write **when** if the underlined words tell about a time, **where** if it tells about a place, or **how** if it shows how something is done.

We enjoyed
the clown act
at the circus.

1. Joey ate an ice-cream cone after lunch. _____

2. She whispered softly. _____

3. The kitten jumped into the basket. _____

4. The cowboy rode his horse skillfully. _____

5. I can read this book tomorrow. _____

6. Linda reads well. _____

7. We will bake the cookies tonight. _____

8. The team made a basket after time ran out. _____

9. The flowers grew quickly. _____

10. The baby slept through the afternoon. _____

Finding the Adverbs

Adverbs are describing words that tell **when** (a time), **where** (a place), or **how** (how something is done).

The monkey chatters **noisily.**
(**how**)

Underline the adverbs. On the lines, write **how**, **where**, or **when** to show the way in which the adverb is used.

_____ 1. I walked quietly.

_____ 2. We will go tomorrow.

_____ 3. We can play later.

_____ 4. My cousins will come here.

_____ 5. The cheetah growled fiercely.

_____ 6. The mother sang softly.

_____ 7. The ballerina dances gracefully.

_____ 8. Yesterday I played baseball.

_____ 9. The orchestra played well.

_____ 10. He completed his homework quickly.

Pronouns

> **Pronouns** are words that are used in the place of nouns. Some pronouns are *I, we, you, it, he, she,* and *they.* There are other pronouns as well.

Read the sentences below. In each blank, write a pronoun to replace the bold noun.

1. The **boy** played baseball.   _____

2. The **girl** swam across the pool.   _____

3. The **children** climbed the trees.   _____

4. **Mary and Frank** rode their bikes to school.   _____

5. The team surprised **Lily** with a trophy.   _____

6. Kim saw the **dog** run across the street.   _____

7. **Mom** read the new bestseller.   _____

8. **Gary** saw a strange shadow.   _____

9. The girls walked to **Mary**'s house.   _____

10. The family found **kittens** in a basket on their porch.   _____

11. Where should I put the **presents**?   _____

12. My **dad** put gas in the car.   _____

13. The **players** won the championship!   _____

14. Where is the **key**?   _____

15. Please, give that to **Rick**.   _____

He, She, or They

Maria whispered, "We don't want to wake the sleeping babies."

She whispered, "We don't want to wake the sleeping babies."

Read the sentences below. Decide who is the speaker. Write **he**, **she**, or **they** on the line after each statement.

1. "Wow, ice cream for dessert!" yelled the students in 2-B. _____

2. "Who wants to play soccer today?" asked Diana. _____

3. "That is my favorite song!" shouted Grandfather. _____

4. "We're lost in the woods!" cried Hansel and Gretel. _____

5. "I wish I had a fairy godmother," sighed Cinderella. _____

6. "Line up for recess," said Mrs. Johnson with a smile. _____

7. "You need to do your homework after supper," said Father. _____

8. "Let's order pizza for dinner," suggested Mother. _____

I and We, Me and Us

I and *we* are used when the person or people are doing the action. *Me* and *us* are used when something is happening to the person or people.

Examples

I am going to have a party.

We are going to have a party.

Mom is having a party for *me*.

Mom is having a party for *us*.

Circle the correct pronoun in each sentence.

1. (We, Us) are going to the store.

2. Would you like to come with (with, us)?

3. (I, Me) played baseball after school.

4. Karen threw the ball to (I, me).

5. Our parents are taking (we, us) out to dinner tonight.

6. Did you hear that (I, me) won first prize?

7. Jim and (I, me) are neighbors.

8. When do you think (we, us) will go?

9. That secret is between Jose and (I, me).

10. Jill told (we, us) about the party.

Synonyms

When comparing and contrasting objects and ideas, it is helpful to use special words called synonyms. **Synonyms** are words that mean nearly the same thing. Look at the list of synonyms below.

good, helpful   big, large
fast, quick   gentle, mild
little, small   bad, evil
strong, powerful   tired, sleepy
sour, tart   bright, shiny

Circle the synonyms in each row.

1. busy	tired	active	bad
2. nibble	chew	hit	play
3. cook	flavorful	tasty	show
4. joyful	happy	sad	angry
5. fall	walk	stand	trip
6. huge	pretty	anxious	enormous
7. worried	anxious	smart	angry
8. mad	angry	funny	disappointed
9. talk	kick	chat	sing
10. rush	slow	hurry	mild

The Same Thing

Read each sentence. Write the word from the word box that means the same thing as the underlined word.

Let's **gather** some leaves for our art project.

Let's **collect** some leaves for our art project.

asked	bucket	eat	shore	small
big	decorate	quiet	slept	watched

_____ 1. The Martians <u>observed</u> the people of Earth.

_____ 2. The waves roll upon the <u>beach</u>.

_____ 3. We will <u>dine</u> at a nearby restaurant.

_____ 4. The children filled the <u>pail</u> with sand.

_____ 5. After playing, we all <u>napped</u> for awhile.

_____ 6. The teacher <u>questioned</u> the students about their homework.

_____ 7. In December some people <u>trim</u> a tree.

_____ 8. The insects were <u>tiny</u>.

_____ 9. A <u>large</u> storm is coming our way.

_____ 10. Everyone was <u>silent</u>.

More Synonyms

Draw a line to connect synonym pairs.

1.	neat	see
2.	sad	calm
3.	thin	chilly
4.	look	skinny
5.	plain	powerful
6.	strong	stingy
7.	cold	large
8.	big	small
9.	cheap	wealthy
10.	quiet	pointed

Nursery Rhyme Time

Rewrite the nursery rhyme by replacing synonyms for each circled word in the poem.

Hey, diddle, diddle,

The (cat) and the fiddle,

The cow (jumped) over the moon;

The (little) dog (laughed)

To (see) such (sport,)

And the (dish) (ran) (away) with the spoon.

_____

_____

_____

_____

_____

_____

_____

_____

_____

Antonym Match-Up

Antonyms are words with opposite meanings.

large   small

Draw a line to connect the antonyms.

1. happy   young

2. brave   far

3. right   afraid

4. fast   weak

5. big   little

6. rude   tame

7. old   sad

8. strong   answer

9. crowded   ugly

10. smile   frown

11. close   slow

12. loud   wrong

13. ask   easy

14. wild   quiet

15. beautiful   empty

16. hard   polite

Antonyms

Read each sentence. Write the word from the word box that means the opposite of the underlined word.

The lady **laughed** as she watched the movie.

The lady **cried** as she watched the movie.

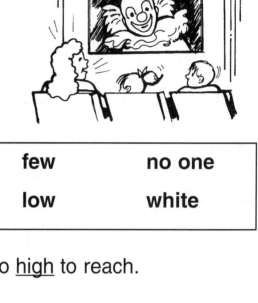

bad	**difficult**	**empty**	**few**	**no one**
calm	**down**	**everybody**	**low**	**white**

_____ 1. The leaf was too <u>high</u> to reach.

_____ 2. The bag was <u>full</u>.

_____ 3. The sun was <u>up</u> when we left.

_____ 4. <u>Many</u> people listen to the radio.

_____ 5. The drill team was dressed all in <u>black</u>.

_____ 6. The students thought the test was <u>easy</u>.

_____ 7. <u>Nobody</u> came to the play.

_____ 8. <u>Someone</u> is coming to the party.

_____ 9. The sea was <u>wild</u>.

_____ 10. Everyone had a <u>good</u> time at the show.

Opposites

Write an antonym for each word on the blank lines.

` 1. top _____

2. earth _____

3. true _____

4. fast _____

5. friend _____

6. fancy _____

7. loose _____

8. over _____

9. odd _____

10. part _____

11. positive _____

12. sunrise _____

13. sell _____

14. thick _____

15. dry _____

happy

sad

Homophones

> **Homophones** are words that sound the same but are spelled differently and have different meanings.

Jim **ate eight** slices of pizza today!

Choose the correct homophone to use in each sentence.

pail   pale   1. They collected sea shells in the_____.

Two   To   2. _____friends went to the concert.

here   hear   3. Do you_____that noise?

wear   where   4. I am going to_____my new sweater.

so   sew   5. He will have to_____his button onto his shirt.

hi   high   6. The snow fell_____in the mountains.

wood   would   7. Collect some_____for the fire.

be   bee   8. A honey_____flew to the hive.

blew   blue   9. The wind_____across the water.

knew   new   10. I_____you would come!

Which Word Shall I Use?

Circle the correct word on the right that matches the word or phrase on the left.
An example has been done for you.

listen = (hear)/here

1. relative   ant/aunt

2. cry   tear/tier

3. moisture   dew/do/due

4. jewel   purl/pearl

5. evening   night/knight

6. forbidden   band/banned

7. transparent   shear/sheer

8. character   roll/role

9. company   guest/guessed

10. small   we/wee

11. female deer   doe/dough

12. cold   chilly/chili

13. smash   brake/break

14. tree   fir/fur

Wally the Word Worm

Look carefully at the paragraph below. It has some incorrectly used homophones. How many incorrectly used homophones can you find in the paragraph below? Circle each one. Over each of the words that you circle, write the correct homophone. The first one has been done for you.

Wally Worm woke up early (won) knight. He *(one)* stretched and started down the rode in search of food. Just then too of his friends met hymn. They new wear sum red apples had fallen from the trees knot two far away. They offered too show hymn where he could find them. So together they inched there weigh two the orchard and dove inn. They eight until they could eat know more.

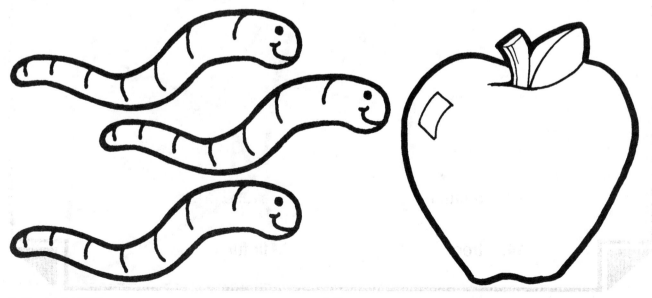

Synonym or Antonym?

Look at the word pairs. If they are synonyms, color the space red. If they are antonyms, color the space yellow.

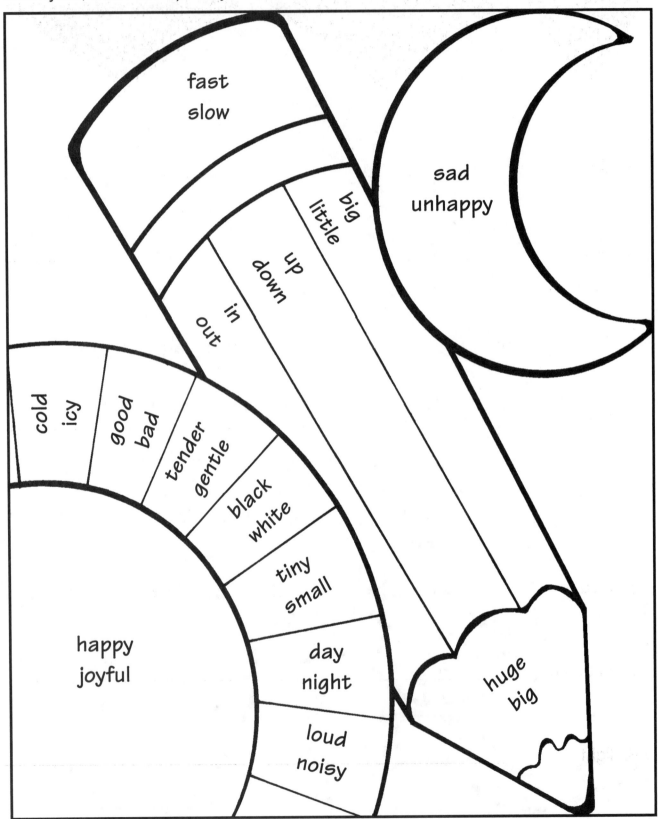

You Decide

Write a synonym and an antonym for each word listed below.

word	synonym	antonym

1. day   _____   _____

2. dirty   _____   _____

3. sad   _____   _____

4. thin   _____   _____

5. healthy   _____   _____

6. cloudy   _____   _____

7. beautiful   _____   _____

8. light   _____   _____

Synonyms, Antonyms, and Homophones

Synonyms	Antonyms	Homophones
big	happy	dear
large	sad	deer

Identify each pair of words as synonyms (**S**), antonyms (**A**), or homophones (**H**).

1. _____ near—far

2. _____ desire—want

3. _____ foe—friend

4. _____ close—near

5. _____ led—lead

6. _____ genuine—real

7. _____ healthy—sick

8. _____ maid—made

9. _____ hurry—rush

10. _____ meat—meet

11. _____ wide—narrow

12. _____ limp—slack

13. _____ clear—plain

14. _____ strong—weak

15. _____ none—nun

16. _____ mix—blend

17. _____ pale—pail

18. _____ often—seldom

More Synonyms, Antonyms, and Homophones

Identify each pair of words as synonyms (**S**), antonyms (**A**), or homophones (**H**).

1. _____ build—construct

2. _____ break—repair

3. _____ full—empty

4. _____ chord—cord

5. _____ dear—deer

6. _____ start—begin

7. _____ find—fined

8. _____ noise—quiet

9. _____ thanks—gratitude

10. _____ hard—soft

11. _____ guessed—guest

12. _____ vacant—empty

13. _____ flower—flour

14. _____ timid—fearful

15. _____ hoarse—horse

16. _____ tiny—small

17. _____ private—public

18. _____ remember—forget

That's Capital!

Some words need to be capitalized. This means they start with capital letters. You should always capitalize . . .

- the first word in a sentence.
- the word *I*.
- titles of people (such as *Dr.* Martin and *Mrs.* Garcia).
- the special names of people and places (such as *France* and the *Grand Canyon*).
- titles or family names when they are used in place of a person's name (such as "Good morning, *General*" and "Give the list to *Mom*.").
- the days of the week and months of the year.
- titles of books, movies, songs, plays, magazines, newspapers, and television shows.
- holidays.
- school subjects when they are the names of languages or subject titles (such as *English* or *Modern Art in America*).

The following sentences have some words that need to be capitalized. Cross out each letter that needs to be changed to a capital. Write the capital above the crossed out letter. The first letter is done for you.

       W

1. ̶When i went to the store, i saw my teacher, mrs. roe, buying strawberries.

2. my family will go to disneyland in july.

3. i am reading *old yeller* this week.

4. my sister, sarah, says her favorite subject is spanish.

5. on wednesday, we will celebrate groundhog day.

6. my brother said that mom was a cheerleader at roosevelt high school.

7. in august, we're going to visit aunt margaret in san francisco, california.

8. benjie, my little brother, had a birthday, and we sang, "happy birthday to you."

9. my friend, rosa, speaks spanish, and i speak english.

10. my neighbor, julia, is going to be an exchange student in paris, france, next august.

Capitalization

Proper nouns are the specific names of people, places, and things (including days, months, and holidays). All proper nouns must be capitalized. Put the proper nouns from the word box in their correct columns below. Be sure to add the capital letters!

rocky mountains	november	alexander	christmas	monday
mr. peterson	plum street	thursday	south america	sandy
saturday	august	thanksgiving	russia	february
mardi gras	spot	fluffy	colorado river	march

Names *(people and pets)*　　　　　　　　**Places**

_____　　_____

_____　　_____

_____　　_____

_____　　_____

_____　　_____

Days　　　　　　　**Months**　　　　　　　**Holidays**

_____　　_____　　_____

_____　　_____　　_____

_____　　_____　　_____

_____　　_____　　_____

Capital Review

It is time to see how much you have learned about capitalization. Circle all the letters below that should be capitals. *(Hint:* There are 64 of them.)

1. the first day of school is exciting.

2. freddy wilson's frog, peepers, hopped into mrs. woolsey's purse.

3. as i walked outside, i smelled smoke.

4. in the play, robin hood was played by lieutenant bronksy.

5. the fourth thursday in november is thanksgiving.

6. i like halloween best when it is on a saturday.

7. aunt susan went to yellowstone national park.

8. connie lives on maple street in bismarck, north dakota.

9. brazil, argentina, and peru are in south america.

10. the mediterranean sea and the atlantic ocean touch spain.

11. the letter was signed, "love always, esther."

12. davis medical center opened in january last year.

13. one of the religions practiced by many african people is islam.

14. italians and germans belong to the caucasian race.

15. last tuesday ruben walked his dog, spotty, down tulip street to central park.

Matching

Contractions are made by bringing two words together into one. Draw a line to match the contractions to the words.

she'll	they will
it's	you are
won't	I am
you'll	it is
you're	is not
isn't	she will
we're	he is
I'll	we are
they'll	can not
weren't	will not
I'm	you will
he's	they are
can't	are not
aren't	I will
they're	were not

Making Contractions

Write a contraction for each set of words.

> **Example:** would not = wouldn't

1. can not _____

2. he is _____

3. will not _____

4. does not _____

5. they are _____

6. we are _____

7. should not_____

8. it will _____

Write the words that make the contraction.

> **Example:** we'll = we will

9. she'll_____

10. it's_____

11. mustn't _____

12. you're _____

13. they'll _____

14. haven't _____

15. I'll _____

16. I'm _____

Write two sentences. Use at least one contraction in each.

_____

_____

_____

_____

_____

Correct Contractions

The turtle **is not** moving quickly.

The turtle **isn't** moving quickly.

Read each sentence and circle the correct contraction that fills in the blank.

1. We _____ be late for the party.

   aren't   won't   isn't

2. _____ feed his pet at dinner time.

   He'll   He's   I'm

3. _____ fun to build a snowman.

   Isn't   Wouldn't   It's

4. _____ the library?

   Where's   We're   Weren't

5. She _____ know the answer.

   don't   didn't   isn't

6. _____ go to the movies.

   He's   She's   Let's

7. I _____ come to soccer practice.

   can't   aren't   isn't

8. _____ be happy to help you.

   I'd   I'm   I've

End Marks

Every sentence must end with a punctuation mark. A sentence may end with a period, a question mark, or an exclamation point.

- A period comes at the end of a sentence that tells something.

    Examples: I have a purple bicycle.
    Turn left at the corner.

- A question mark comes at the end of a sentence that asks a question.

    Examples: What color is your bicycle?
    Is that your house?

- An exclamation point comes at the end of a sentence that contains a strong feeling.

    Examples: Watch out for that car!
    What a wonderful surprise!

The following sentences need punctuation marks at the end. Think about which kind of punctuation each sentence needs at the end. Then write the correct punctuation mark at the end of each sentence.

1. I love my purple bicycle ☐

2. I saved enough money to buy it last year ☐

3. Would you like to try it ☐

4. My brother has a blue bicycle ☐

5. One time he crashed into me, and I fell off my bike ☐

6. Have you ever fallen off your bike ☐

7. Did you skin your knee ☐

8. I was so mad at my brother ☐

9. He told me he was sorry ☐

10. I'm so glad that my bike did not break ☐

11. Watch out for the glass in the road ☐

12. Don't ride your bike in the street ☐

13. Can you park a bike right here ☐

14. I have to go inside now ☐

15. Will I see you tomorrow ☐

More End Marks

How many blocks do you see $\boxed{?}$

I see 18 blocks $\boxed{.}$

Add a period (.), a question mark (?), or an exclamation point (!) to the end of each sentence.

1. I will go with you $\square$

2. Where is it $\square$

3. Help me $\square$

4. Who ate the cookies $\square$

5. Go to the third house $\square$

6. I like to play basketball $\square$

7. What a great day $\square$

8. The children are in the yard $\square$

9. How many are there $\square$

10. What is happening here $\square$

11. When are we going to the game $\square$

12. I would like the sugar cookie, please $\square$

13. Is it time for bed $\square$

14. I'm so happy to see you $\square$

15. It's over there $\square$

Rules for Commas

Here are three rules for using commas in sentences.

A. Commas should be used to separate words in a series.

   Example: Joe and his sister love marshmallows, graham crackers, and chocolate.

B. A comma should be used after the words *yes*, *no*, and *well*.

   Example: Yes, I love s'mores.

C. When a person is spoken to, a comma should be used to set off that person's name.

   Example: Pedro, do you want a graham cracker?

Use the three comma rules to place commas in the sentences below.

1. No Mary does not like marshmallows.

2. Well maybe Bernard will try the s'mores.

3. Bobby would you like to try a s'more?

4. Alice wants a hot dog potato chips and a pickle.

5. We played baseball basketball and volleyball.

6. Harry would you like to dance?

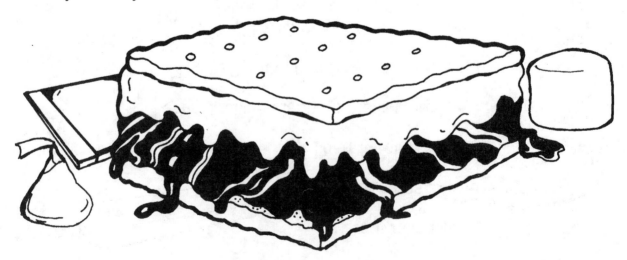

More Rules for Commas

Here are three more rules for using commas in sentences.

A. An appositive is a group of words that tells more about another word. Use commas to set off an appositive from the rest of the sentence.
> **Example:** Dr. Lee, David's father, is my dentist.

B. The day and the year in dates should be separated by commas.
> **Example:** My dental appointment is for January 16, 2000, the day after my birthday.

C. The names of cities and states should be separated by commas.
> **Example:** Dr. Lee will move his office from San Diego, California, to Oceanside next month.

Use the comma rules to place commas in the sentences that follow.

1. Jack my brother does not like to go to the dentist.

2. I like my dentist Dr. Lee.

3. Dr. Payce the dentist in the next office is also a good dentist.

4. On March 2 1999 Dr. Lee took David and me camping.

5. My first visit to Dr. Lee was on February 27 1994.

6. By June 30 2012 I will have become a dentist myself.

7. I was born in Brooklyn New York and so was Dr. Lee.

8. He visits Chicago Illinois every summer.

9. David wishes they would go to Orlando Florida each year instead.

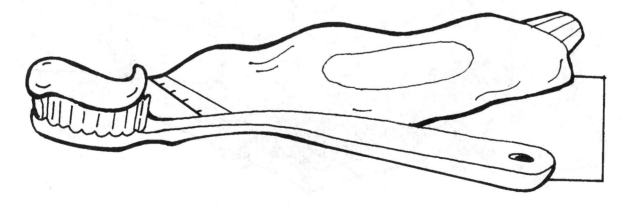

Compound Sentences

A **comma** should be placed before *and*, *but*, and *or* when they join two complete sentences to make a compound sentence.

Read the sentences and place the commas where they belong.

1. You wear your blue jeans and I'll wear my black jeans.

2. Your white T-shirt fits better but your red T-shirt is more colorful.

3. Do you want yellow patches on your jeans or do you want pink patches?

4. Jill's T-shirt looks great and Amy's jeans are terrific.

5. I have three pairs of blue jeans but I want another pair of green jeans.

6. You need to wash your old jeans and you should iron your new jeans.

7. This white T-shirt is mine but that white T-shirt is yours.

8. Let's all wear our blue jeans today and let's wear our red jeans tomorrow.

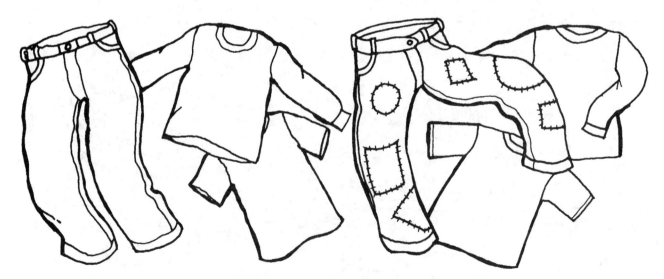

Commas Review

Add the commas where they belong.

1. Yes I would love to go to the movie.

2. We have potato chips cheese and chili.

3. Grandma could we please spend the night?

4. This red car belongs to my mom and this blue car belongs to my dad.

5. John may I borrow your football?

6. We saw swans ducks and an ostrich.

7. Invite Casey Jackie and Toby to go with us.

8. No we can't go to the zoo today.

9. My sister likes hot dogs and I like pizza.

10. Aunt Irene my mom's sister liked the book but I liked the movie.

More Commas Review

Add commas where they belong.

1. Tasha's birthday is March 4 1981.

2. Dennis my best friend lives in San Francisco California but he is moving to Oakland.

3. Our teacher Mr. Hill took us on a field trip to Boston Massachusetts.

4. July 16 1973 is my parents' anniversary.

5. The Davis family is moving to Orlando Florida on July 13 2001.

6. My friend Mrs. Allen is a nurse.

7. The airplane will land in Paris France after taking off from London England.

8. He visits Chicago Illinois every summer but this year he will go to Montreal Canada.

Apostrophes

An **apostrophe** is used to show ownership (possession) in writing. For example, another way to write **toy belonging to baby** is **baby's toy**.

boy's sneakers

Rewrite the phrases below using an **'s**. (**Note:** If the word ends in **s**, only add an apostrophe.)

1. food belonging to a dog _____

2. cage belonging to a bird _____

3. bike belonging to Kenny _____

4. store belonging to Mr. Stout _____

5. radio belonging to Janie _____

6. book belonging to Don _____

7. baseball belonging to the coach _____

8. desk belonging to the student _____

9. closet belonging to the class _____

10. pencil belonging to Mrs. Davis _____

Quotation in Conversation

When two or more people speak to each other in conversation, use quotation marks to show exactly what they are saying.

A direct quotation is the exact words spoken. Quotation marks are used before and after a direct quotation.

Example: "Thank you for the delicious slice of pizza," said Jim.

Notice that quotation marks are never used around the words that tell who is speaking and the comma always goes before the quotation mark.

Sometimes we write what a person says without showing exact words. When this happens, we do not use quotation marks. Never use quotation marks unless you are showing a speaker's exact words.

Example:
Janet thought that her tent was too small.

Place quotation marks around only what is said.

1. Yes, Ryan, Mom answered, Matt can come over after lunch.

2. Thanks, Mom, Ryan answered.

3. Ryan said that he and Matt would play basketball after school.

4. Mom said, While you play basketball, I'll bake cookies.

5. Ryan asked when Matt could come over to play.

6. Mom answered that Matt could come over after lunch.

Quotation Marks Review

Add the correct punctuation to complete the quotations.

1. Bobby yelled Mom where are my blue jeans?

2. A plane is flying overhead said Jim's dad.

3. Mindy said Look at the turtles.

4. Watch out yelled Sara The dog will get out!

5. Dad said that the boys could play all afternoon.

6. Grandma Joey cried will you tie my shoe?

7. The boys yelled Come out and play!

8. Mother said Change the channel, boys.

9. Amanda asked if her friend could come with her.

10. Can you ride a bicycle? asked Joseph.

Punctuation Review

Read the story below. Add the missing punctuation.

Have you ever been on a farm

Mrs Young took her third grade class to Mr Frank s

farm on Tuesday morning They saw cows chickens

and horses Mr Frank wanted to know if any students

would like to ride a horse Leslie screamed I do Also

John and Carl wanted to ride Mrs Young s class will

never forget the special day on the farm

Punctuation Challenge

Read the letter. There are 21 punctuation errors. Circle the punctuation that is wrong and correct it. Add any missing punctuation.

Dear Pen Pal

I love to go to the circus! On May 6 1999, the circus came to my hometown of Jackson Wyoming. A parade marched through our streets and soon the big top could be seen. Ken my best friend, and I went to watch the performers prepare for opening night. We saw clowns, acrobats, and even the ringmaster. What a sight? Have you ever seen anything like it. You should go if you ever get the chance.

I also really enjoy playing baseball. My favorite team is the New York Yankees but I also like the St. Louis Cardinals. When I grow up, I want to be a baseball pitcher, first baseman, or shortstop. Do you like baseball? What do you want to do when you grow up. I wish you could see my cool baseball card collection, but Kens collection is even better.

Oh, I almost forgot to tell you about my family! There are four people in my family. They are my mom my dad my brother and me. Scruffy my cat is also a family member. In August 2000 my grandpa will probably move in with us. I cant wait for that! Didn't you say your grandma lives with you. Ill bet you really like that.

Well thats all for now. Please, write back to me soon. See you!

Your pal,

Brent

Who and What

Who

(Circle) the subject in each sentence.

What

Underline the word or verb that shows what the subject of each sentence does.

The (leopard) ran toward the bushes.

1. The doctor checked the patient.

2. My sister ate a bag of chips.

3. The actor read his part in the play.

4. The neighbors mowed their lawn.

5. The hiker climbed the hill.

6. The child brushed his teeth.

7. The family swam in the ocean.

8. The singer stepped on stage.

9. The poet wrote a poem.

10. The grandmother visited her grandchildren.

What Is a Subject?

All sentences have subjects. A **subject** tells who or what a sentence is about.

Example: Blake loves to paint.
          Who loves to paint? **Blake** loves to paint.
          Blake is the subject of the sentence.

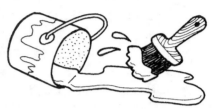

First, ask yourself who or what the sentence is about. Then, underline the subject of the sentence. Finally, write the subject of the sentence on the line. The first one is done for you.

1. Blake has a paintbox.
   Who has a paintbox? _____ Blake _____

2. The paintbox has three colors.
   What has three colors? _____

3. The colors are red, yellow, and blue.
   What are red, yellow, and blue?_____

4. Blake can make more colors.
   Who can make more colors? _____

5. Green is made by mixing together blue and yellow paints.
   What is made by mixing together blue and yellow paints? _____

6. Orange is made by mixing together yellow and red paints.
   What is made by mixing together yellow and red paints? _____

7. Blake loves to paint.
   Who loves to paint? _____

8. Blake's favorite color is blue.
   What is blue? _____

9. Mom hung Blake's painting.
   Who hung Blake's painting?_____

10. The painting is of a sailboat on the ocean.
    What is of a sailboat on the ocean?_____

What Is a Predicate?

Just as each sentence has a subject, it also will have a predicate. The predicate tells us important things about the subject. It tells us what the subject does, has, or is.

Examples

- Tommy had a cold.
  What did Tommy have? Tommy **had a cold.**
  The predicate of the sentence is *had a cold.*

- Felicia jumps into the lake.
  What does Felicia do? Felicia **jumps into the lake.**
  The predicate of the sentence is *jumps into the lake.*

- The inner tube is leaking air.
  What is the inner tube doing? The inner tube **is leaking air.**
  The predicate of the sentence is *is leaking air.*

First, ask yourself what the subject does, has, or is. Then, circle the predicate of the sentence. The first one is done for you.

1. The water is very cold.

2. We jump into the water.

3. Luke splashes us.

4. Tonia is cold.

5. She gets out of the water.

6. Nick does a handstand underwater.

7. Everyone claps for him.

8. The inner tube has a leak in it.

9. Luke throws the inner tube onto the shore.

10. Tonia sits on the inner tube.

11. The inner tube deflates with Tonia on it.

12. Everyone laughs with Tonia.

13. Tonia jumps into the water.

14. Luke swims as fast as he can.

What Is Missing?

Here are some sentences that are missing subjects or predicates. Choose a subject or predicate from the box to complete each sentence. Then, on the line before each number, write a **P** if you added a predicate or an **S** if you added a subject to the sentence. The first one is done for you.

The following subjects and predicates may be used more than once.

My teacher	An ugly grasshopper	fell on my toe
The mail carrier	The tree	is growling
My kitten	has an attitude	is singing in an opera
has a cute little hat	is crying	is really an alien
A ladybug	climbs on the furniture	is covered in stripes
Uncle Gerald	is lost in space	was under the house
My sister	Dinner	is as big as Australia
A cute little baby	My bed	is a spy
A suitcase	drove over the hills	The doctor
is very gross	ran on the playground	floats away
is drooling	snores	is purple with polka dots

__S__ 1. _____ My kitten _____ sat on the birthday cake.

_____ 2. _____ ate worms for breakfast.

_____ 3. Laurie _____ .

_____ 4. _____ slipped on a banana peel.

_____ 5. Mrs. Crabapple _____ .

_____ 6. _____ is a big, hairy beast.

_____ 7. A giant elephant _____ .

_____ 8. My little brother _____ .

_____ 9. The grizzly bear _____ .

_____ 10. _____ is very heavy.

_____ 11. _____ has the measles.

_____ 12. A jet plane _____ .

_____ 13. _____ is green.

_____ 14. My science book _____ .

_____ 15. _____ is growing blue fur.

Complete the Sentence

The **subject** of a sentence is **who** or **what** the sentence is about.

The **predicate** is what the subject **does, has,** or **is.**

The soccer player **(subject)**   kicked the ball toward the goal. **(predicate)**

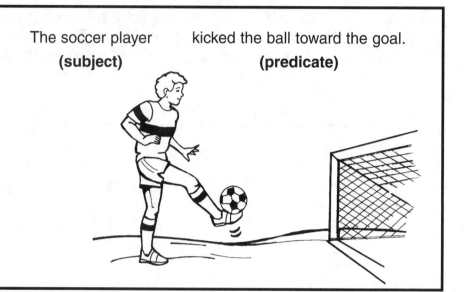

Fill in a subject for each sentence below.

1. _____ exploded.

2. _____ is beautiful.

3. _____ tripped over my foot.

4. _____ laughed loudly.

5. _____ should have gone to class.

Fill in a predicate for each sentence below.

1. Our teacher _____.

2. This movie _____.

3. The gray cat _____.

4. My grandmother _____.

5. The table _____.

More Sentences to Complete

Complete each sentence with either the missing subject or the missing predicate.

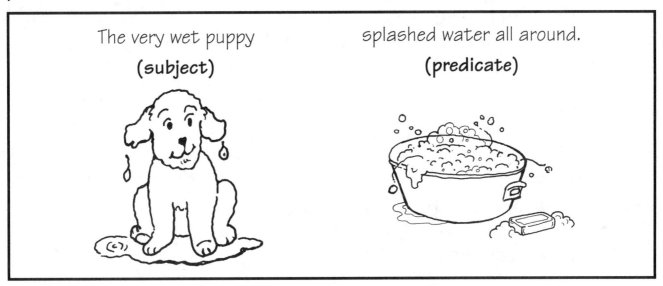

The very wet puppy
(subject)

splashed water all around.
(predicate)

1. The rabbit _____.

2. _____wore an old shoe.

3. A friendly mouse _____.

4. _____caught fire.

5. _____played by the river.

6. My best friend _____.

7. _____sang a song.

8. _____climbed over the fence.

9. The girl across the street _____.

10. _____ate the box of cereal.

Complements

Every predicate must contain a verb. Usually the predicate contains more than a verb. These additional words are called a complement. A **complement** is a word or group of words that complete the sense of the predicate.

The rabbit blinked.
The rabbit blinked at me through the bushes.

Add a complement to the sentence parts below.

1. The crowd screamed

   _____

   _____

2. Joe enjoys

   _____

   _____

3. My brother borrowed

   _____

   _____

4. Terry ate

   _____

   _____

5. A winter morning is

   _____

   _____

6. The pilot flew

   _____

   _____

My Complements!

Sentence complements complete the predicate of a sentence. The complement can drastically change the meaning of the sentence.

The car sped.

The car sped around the racetrack.

The car sped down the hill.

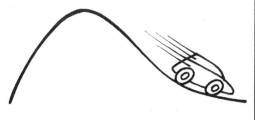

For each sentence beginning below, write two different complements. Follow the examples above.

1. The rabbit hopped _____

_____

2. I slept _____

_____

3. The movie was_____

_____

4. A gorilla climbed _____

_____

5. We wanted_____

_____

6. The train chugged _____

_____

7. The apple was _____

_____

8. The lightning flashed _____

_____

What Is a Sentence?

A sentence begins with a capital letter and ends with a period (.), a question mark (?), or an exclamation point (!).

A sentence can be a group of words that tells us something.

Examples: Jacob went to the beach.

I won first prize!

A sentence can also be a group of words that asks us a question.

Example: When did Nancy leave?

A sentence is always a complete thought.

Circle the sentences below. Remember that each sentence must start with a capital letter; end with a period, question mark, or exclamation point; and be a complete thought.

1. over the rainbow!
2. Becky writes a letter.
3. What does Jaime want?
4. strawberries and bananas
5. Watch out for the ball!
6. when school over?
7. I am in the pool.
8. When Derek

9. Do you like dogs?
10. I can see you!
11. If I stop
12. a house on the hill
13. why don't you
14. I painted my brother green.
15. It made my mom laugh.

Now write three sentences of your own. End one with a period, one with a question mark, and one with an exclamation point.

1. _____

_____

_____

2. _____

_____

_____

3. _____

_____

Practice Sentences

There are four different kinds of sentences—declarative, interrogative, declarative, and exclamatory. After you read the definition of each one, write a sentence that demonstrates that kind of sentence.

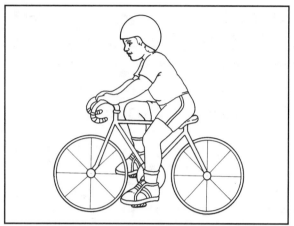

A **declarative** sentence makes a statement and ends in a period.

> **Example:** My mom gave me a new bicycle.

_____

_____

An **interrogative** sentence asks a question and ends in a question mark.

> **Example:** Would you like to ride my bicycle?

_____

_____

An **imperative** sentence gives a command and ends in a period.

> **Example:** Don't ride my bicycle in the street.

_____

_____

An **exclamatory** sentence shows great expression and ends in an exclamation point.

> **Example:** What a great bicycle ride that was!

_____

_____

Sentence Types and Their End Marks

Put a period, a question mark, or an exclamation mark at the end of each sentence below, and on the line after the sentence, write *declarative*, *interrogative*, *imperative*, or *exclamatory*.

1. Oh, boy, it's time for recess _____

2. I'm not sure where to go because I'm new here _____

3. Where do I go for recess _____

4. Do you mean way over there where it's all sandy _____

5. Oh, well, at least there are some swings over here _____

6. Hey, watch where you're going _____

7. Don't throw sand _____

8. Now that's an interesting looking ball _____

9. Where did you get it _____

10. Be careful where you throw that thing _____

11. Can I play, too _____

12. I'm not kidding; I really like to play _____

13. Oh, no, there goes the bell _____

14. Okay, class, let's line up _____

15. Did everyone have fun during recess _____

Sentence Scramble

Unscramble the words to make sentences. Be sure to add a capital letter at the beginning and punctuation at the end of each sentence.

1. bird cat the chased the

   _____

   _____

2. letter friend I a wrote my to

   _____

   _____

3. puzzle the made a family

   _____

   _____

4. a baker cake baked the

   _____

   _____

5. sea jumped into penguin a the

   _____

   _____

6. song to a puppets audience the sang the

   _____

   _____

Are You a Good Sentence Detective?

A **sentence** is a group of words that tells us something or asks us a question. It is always a complete thought.

Example: John cooks dinner.

What does the sentence tell us?

It tells us who it is about. *John*

It tells us what John does. *cooks dinner*

There are only 10 complete sentences shown in the magnifying glass. Write these 10 sentences on a separate paper.

I'm going swimming after school!
Tuesday.
Chris opens the door.
April
Will we go to the store tomorrow?
paper bag
My iguana ate my homework.
Juanita helps me.
Can you come with me?
the lights!
My best friend
Maria dances every day.
I have a cat.
That bicycle looks brand new!
Do you like candy?

Sentence Fragments

A **sentence fragment** is an incomplete sentence. It is missing either the subject or the predicate, and it does not make sense by itself.

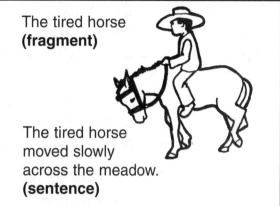

The tired horse
(fragment)

The tired horse moved slowly across the meadow. **(sentence)**

Make the fragments below into complete sentences.

1. the hungry bear

   _____

   _____

2. chews gum loudly

   _____

   _____

3. the mountains

   _____

   _____

4. my first birthday party

   _____

   _____

5. danced all night

   _____

   _____

6. the gigantic elephant

   _____

   _____

7. is my favorite present

   _____

   _____

Fragment or Sentence?

In the box there are four complete sentences and three sentences fragments. Rewrite the sentences, adding capitals and ending punctuations. Rewrite the fragments, adding either subjects or predicates.

1. i have many things in my room
2. there is a box of clothes under the bed
3. a rug is in front of the closet
4. two stuffed rabbits
5. i can see trees from my window
6. the bedspread and curtains
7. a large poster of

1. _____

_____

2. _____

_____

3. _____

_____

4. _____

_____

5. _____

_____

6. _____

_____

7. _____

_____

Sentence Run-Ons

You have learned that each sentence is a complete thought. What about sentences that do not stop when they should? A sentence that runs on to the next thought is called a run-on sentence.

Run-on: My birthday is tomorrow I hope I get a bike.

Correct: My birthday is tomorrow. I hope I get a bike.

Each of the following is a run-on sentence. Write each run-on as two complete sentences.

1. It is windy today I should fly my kite.

   _____

2. I like to read *James and the Giant Peach* is my favorite book.

   _____

3. Where are you going when will you be home?

   _____

4. The boy ran home after school then he did his homework.

   _____

5. The clown danced in the parade he gave balloons to all the children.

   _____

6. My sister really enjoys camping I do, too.

   _____

7. The puppies cried for their mother they were hungry.

   _____

8. I don't feel like going to bed I want to stay up to watch my show!

   _____

9. Who is there what do you want?

   _____

10. They wanted to climb the tree the branches were too high to reach.

    _____

Run-On or Sentence?

In the box there are four complete sentences and three run-ons. Rewrite the sentences, adding capitals and ending punctuations. Rewrite the run-ons to make them complete sentences.

---

1. the monkeys danced to the peddler's music
2. my sister cried for my mother she wouldn't stop
3. my favorite game to play is Chinese checkers
4. the students wondered what the teacher had planned for the day
5. they were late to the party everyone was worried about them
6. the birds were singing in the trees the flowers looked colorful in the sun
7. he knew that it would be an exciting day the moment he saw the pony

---

1. _____

   _____

2. _____

   _____

3. _____

   _____

4. _____

   _____

5. _____

   _____

6. _____

   _____

7. _____

   _____

Grammar Practice

Every sentence ends with a period, a question mark, or an exclamation point. Rewrite the sentences below. Be sure to begin each one with a capital letter. End each one with the correct punctuation mark.

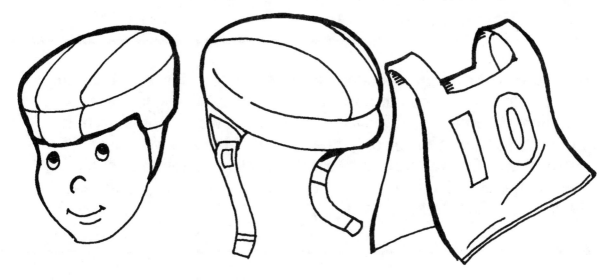

1. my cousin spent the night at my house

   _____

2. john said that I could look at his snake

   _____

3. jim entered the bicycle race

   _____

4. what a race it was

   _____

5. did he wear a helmet

   _____

6. who won the race

   _____

More Grammar Practice

Correct all the errors in the story below. Include your corrections as you rewrite the sentences on the lines below.

Making Butter

Today, Mrs. Banks announced, we are going to make your own butter she asked, c j and juan to passout the spoons. Napkins knives and empty margarine tubs. Sonya erin and Scott were chosen to help pour the Cream. You will only need two tablespoons of cream, warned Mrs. Banks. Next she told us to attach the lid and shake it hard. In a few minutes each us had a lump of Butter. We spread it on crackers. It was tasty treat.

_____

_____

_____

_____

_____

_____

_____

_____

_____

_____

_____

_____

_____

Grammar Review

Here is a story that has no punctuation and no capitalization whatsoever. Your mission: capitalize and punctuate. Using a colored pen, write a capital letter over any letter that needs one. Be careful. Don't capitalize anything that shouldn't be. Insert punctuation marks wherever you think they need to go. Good luck!

our class went on a very special field trip we saved up money from newspapers and recycling aluminum cans until we had enough for a group rate to disneyland isnt that exciting

we also had to save up enough for the bus which wasnt too expensive when the day finally came we were so excited we sang songs like bingo and the ants go marching in all the way there the bus driver said he was going to go crazy but he was just kidding he was also going to disneyland and he was happy about that

when we got there marisa said i see space mountain then luke said I see the matterhorn then hector said i see splash mountain and of course then olivia said i see big thunder mountain

the bus driver said maybe they should call it mountainland instead nobody said anything because just then we all saw the monorail go by I want to go on the monorail cassie said but mrs martinez said that we had to go through the entrance first

after we went through the entrance everybody forgot about the monorail we were divided into groups so we could go wherever our group wanted to go we could join with other groups too whenever we wanted to we all wore bright orange shirts so it wouldnt be too hard to find each other mrs martinez took a group and so did mr rawlings miss white mrs hojito and bill the bus driver guess what i was in bills group ill never forget this day our group had more fun than any other group because bill went on all the rides with us and he didnt complain at all in fact he said im having too much fun isnt that great bill even rode the bobsleds with us and he went on the autopia too he didnt get sick on dumbo or the merry go round and he even went on splash mountain thunder mountain and space mountain on indiana jones he covered his eyes when a snake hissed at him and on the jungle cruise he shrieked when a hippopotamus blew water on him he made us all laugh all the time at the very end bill got motion sickness on the teacups someone was coming to pick him up and to bring a new bus driver that meant we got to go back into disneyland for one more hour we felt sorry for bill but we were so glad to have another hour

Beginning Sounds

There is a sound at the beginning of every word. Often that sound is a consonant.
Consonants are all the letters of the alphabet except the vowels *a*, *e*, *i*, *o*, and *u*.

Look at these pictures. Say their names. What beginning consonant sound do you hear?

 _____at    _____ug   _____oor

 _____ouse    _____an    _____adder

When the beginning consonant changes, the word changes. Read the words. Then change the beginning consonant to make a new word. The first one has been done for you.

1. jump b_ump
2. car   _____ar
3. beat   _____eat
4. horn   _____orn
5. book   _____ook
6. pad   _____ad
7. mist   _____ist
8. can   _____an
9. fall   _____all
10. top   _____op

More Beginning Sounds

How many different words can you make with each group of letters? Write the beginning consonants on the lines below each letter group.

___an

_____

_____

_____

_____

_____

___ark

_____

_____

_____

_____

_____

___eat

_____

_____

_____

_____

_____

___ame

_____

_____

_____

_____

_____

___ear

_____

_____

_____

_____

_____

___our

_____

_____

_____

_____

_____

___ine

_____

_____

_____

_____

_____

___ice

_____

_____

_____

_____

_____

___up

_____

_____

_____

_____

_____

Blends

Consonant blends are formed when two or more consonants are side by side in a word, and you can hear both consonant sounds when you say them. For example, say the word *play*. If you listen closely, you will hear the *p* sound and the *l* sound. Write a consonant blend to complete the name of each picture.

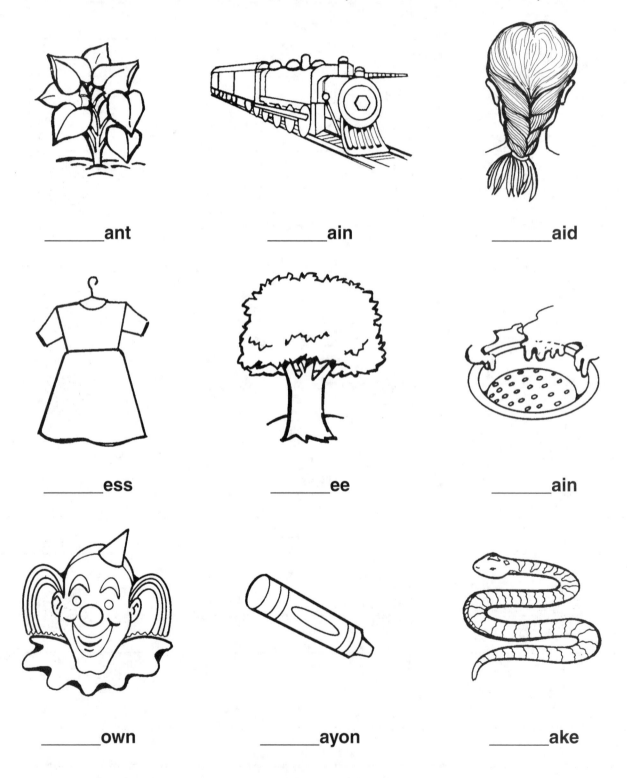

_____ant　　　　　　_____ain　　　　　　_____aid

_____ess　　　　　　_____ee　　　　　　_____ain

_____own　　　　　　_____ayon　　　　　　_____ake

More Blends

List all the words you can think of that begin with the following consonant blends.

bl   **br**   **cl**   **cr**

_____   _____   _____   _____

_____   _____   _____   _____

_____   _____   _____   _____

_____   _____   _____   _____

dr   **fl**   **fr**   **gl**

_____   _____   _____   _____

_____   _____   _____   _____

_____   _____   _____   _____

gr   **pl**   **pr**   **sl**

_____   _____   _____   _____

_____   _____   _____   _____

_____   _____   _____   _____

sp   **st**   **str**   **tr**

_____   _____   _____   _____

_____   _____   _____   _____

_____   _____   _____   _____

Digraphs

When two consonants are placed together and form one consonant sound, they are called a **digraph**. *Ch, sh, th,* and *wh* are the most common digraphs. When you say them together, you only hear one sound. Digraphs can come at the beginning, middle, or end of a word.

ship   **wh**eel   **ch**ur**ch**   fi**sh**

Add one of the four digraphs—**ch**, **sh**, **th**, **wh**—to each letter group. Say the words you have formed.

1. _____ick

2. _____oose

3. _____op

4. _____ape

5. ma_____

6. _____ank

7. _____eese

8. _____eck

9. _____irst

10. _____istle

11. ba_____

12. wi_____

13. _____ip

14. ben_____

15. wa_____ing

16. tra_____

Long Vowel Quilt Square

Listen for the long vowel sound in each word. Color the spaces this way:

long a = red   long e = purple   long i = yellow

long o = green   long u = blue

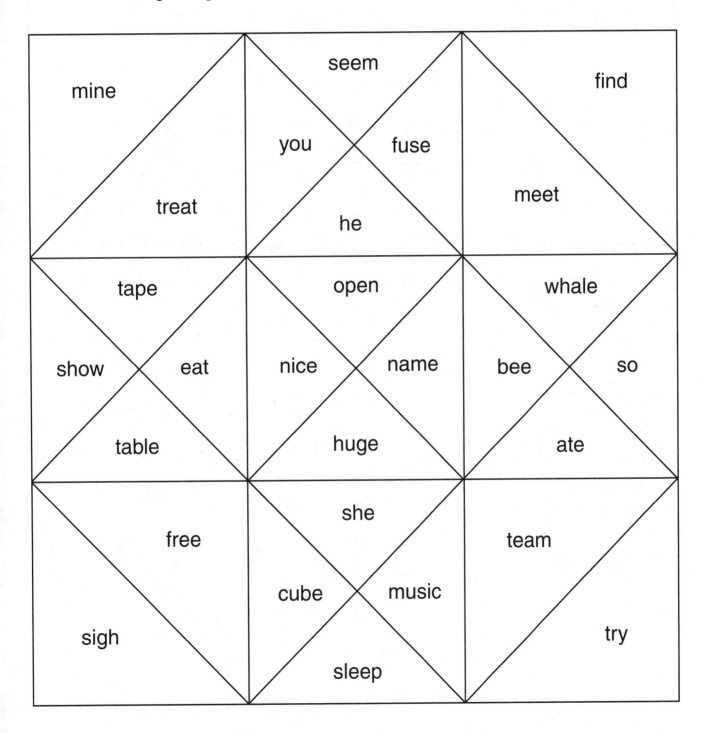

Short Vowel Quilt Square

Listen for the short vowel sound in each word. Color the spaces this way:

short a = purple   short e = blue

short i = red   short o = yellow

short u = green

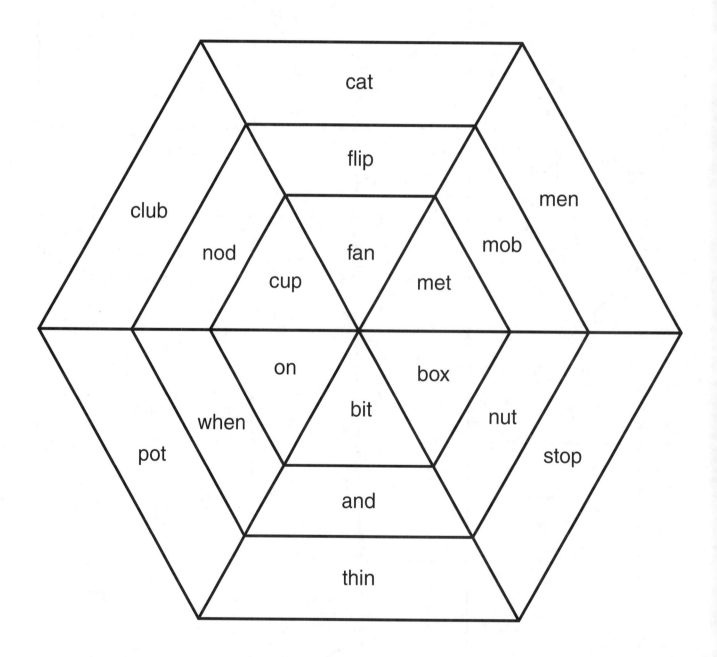

Long and Short

Read the words in the word box. If the vowel sound is long, write the word in the top hat. If the vowel sound is short, write the word under the cap.

mule	chick	jump	fish
flown	track	pond	bike
dime	bay	side	coat
six	meat	cake	frog
nest	hat	tree	use
	sun	net	

Ai or Ay

Say the picture names. Write **ai** or **ay** to complete the words.

1.

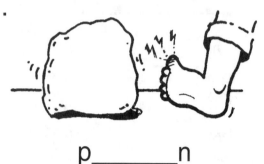

p_____n

2.

h_____

3.

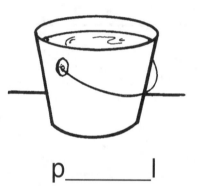

p_____l

4.

tr_____n

5.

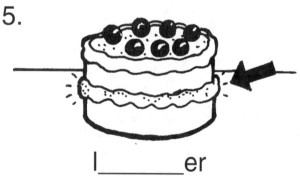

l_____er

6.

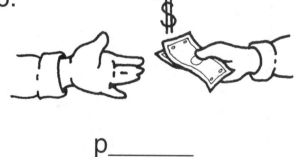

p_____

7.

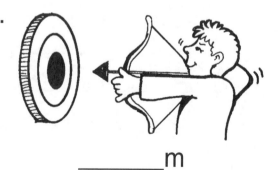

_____m

8.

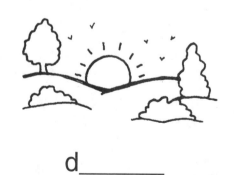

d_____

Oi and Oy

Say the picture names. Write **oi** or **oy** to complete the words.

1. b_____	2. t_____
3. j_____nt	4. j_____
5. s_____l	6. c_____n
7. r_____al	8. b_____l

Ie, Y, and Ey

Say the picture names. Write **ie**, **y**, or **ey** to complete the words.

1.  monk_____	2.  cook_____
3.  mon_____	4.  donk_____
5.  cand_____	6.  pupp_____s
7.  bab_____	8.  happ_____

Ar, Er, Ir, Or, and Ur

Say the picture names. Write **ar, er, ir, or,** or **ur** to complete the words.

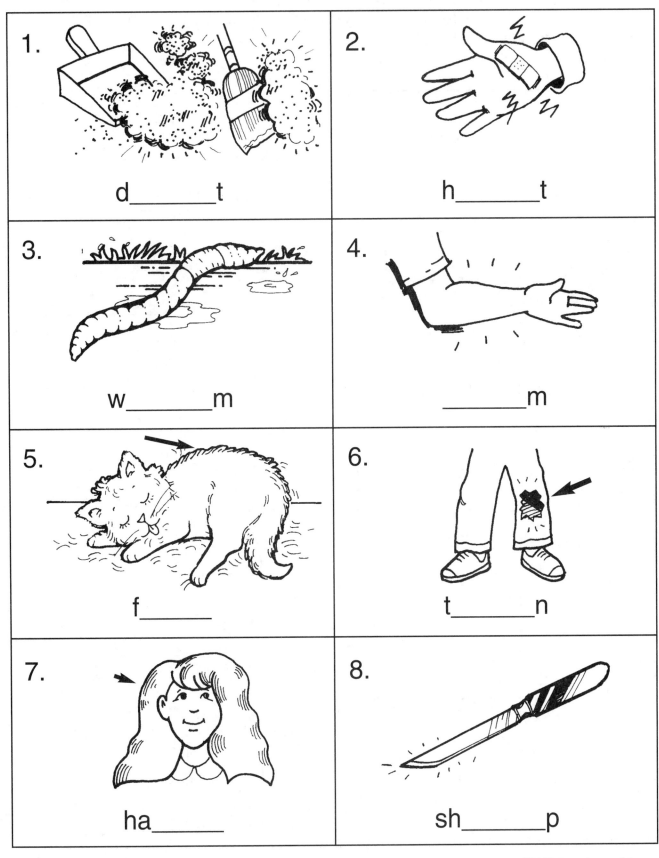

1. d_____t

2. h_____t

3. w_____m

4. _____m

5. f_____

6. t_____n

7. ha_____

8. sh_____p

Silent E

Sometimes the letter *e* in a word has no sound, but its job is still important. It changes a short vowel sound to a long one. Read the words below. Then write the word on the blank, adding an *e*. Read the new words.

1. can	2. sit	3. cap
4. tub		
5. dot		
6. not		
7. rat		
8. lob	9. bit	
10. cub		
11. grim		
12. fin		
13. bath	14. van	15. plan

1. _____

2. _____

3. _____

4. _____

5. _____

6. _____

7. _____

8. _____

9. _____

10. _____

11. _____

12. _____

13. _____

14. _____

15. _____

Silent Letters

Letters other than *e* in a word may be silent. Sometimes they change the sounds of the other letters and sometimes they do not. There are no easy rules for these silent letters. You must practice them to learn them.

Each word below is missing a silent letter. Choose a letter from the letter bank to complete the word. (Be sure to use a letter that is silent in the word.) Then say the words aloud.

b	h	k	t	w

1. _____rite

2. wi_____ch

3. _____hole

4. dum_____

5. _____not

6. no_____ch

7. _____new

8. com_____

9. _____onest

10. lam_____

11. g_____ost

12. w_____ale

13. _____rench

14. ba_____ch

15. w_____ip

16. _____our

17. ca_____ch

18. _____rong

19. _____rinkle

20. ma_____ch

21. _____night

22. _____nee

23. crum_____

24. _____nife

25. thum_____

26. _____nit

The Phunny Elefant?

The *f* sound is created in different ways. Sometimes the sound is made by the letter *f*. Other times it is made by *ff*, a *ph*, or a *gh*. Choose an **f**, **ph**, **ff**, or **gh** to complete each of the words below.

al_____abet

aw_____ul

cou_____

dol_____in

ele_____ant

el_____

enou_____

_____antastic

_____ish

_____un

gira_____e

lau_____

mu_____

_____onics

rou_____

ta_____y

tele_____one

tou_____

Gh

The letters *gh* are pronounced two ways. Sometimes they make the *f* sound as in *cough*. Other times, they are silent as in *sigh*.

Read the words. Write each word in the correct column.

cough	naughty	slough
daughter	night	taught
dough	right	though
enough	rough	tough
knight	sigh	trough
light	sight	high

F Sound	**Silent**

The K Sound

The *k* sound can be made in four different ways: *c*, *k*, *ck*, and *ch*. Fill in the blanks with the correct letters to make the *k* sound. Read the words.

c	k	ck	ch

1. a_____e
2. ba_____
3. ban_____
4. bea_____
5. _____ane
6. _____ut
7. _____rumb
8. do_____
9. ja_____
10. _____eep
11. _____ey
12. _____ind
13. loo_____

14. ma_____e
15. ne_____
16. ni_____el
17. pa_____
18. po_____et
19. s_____are
20. s_____ool
21. s_____in
22. so_____
23. spo_____e
24. stoma_____
25. wal_____
26. ra_____e

Identifying Final Sounds

Circle the word in each box that has the same ending sound as the picture.

look far spoon	the run cap	not dog doll	pass hat can
will what bus	this then book	door dirt girl	jam coat lion
pen room big	hair hand hang	foot ring light	sun bar hug

Rhymes

Rhyming words have the same end sounds, but those end sounds are not always spelled in the same way. Match the rhyming pairs by coloring each matching pair the same color.

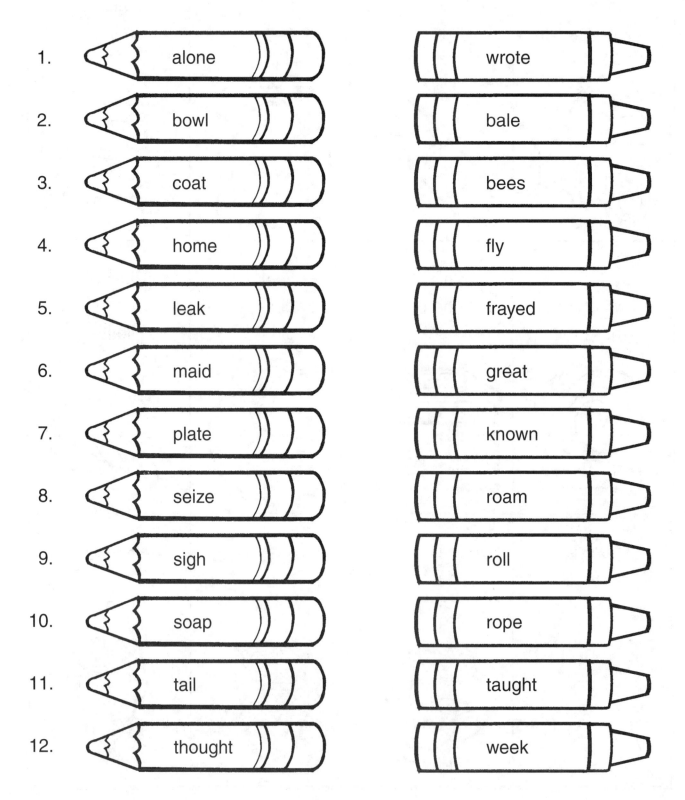

1. alone	wrote
2. bowl	bale
3. coat	bees
4. home	fly
5. leak	frayed
6. maid	great
7. plate	known
8. seize	roam
9. sigh	roll
10. soap	rope
11. tail	taught
12. thought	week

Animal Antics

When words rhyme, they end with the same sound.

Example: *wig* and *jig* rhyme with *pig.*

Fill each animal with words that rhyme with its name.

Puzzling Rhymes

To discover the hidden picture, follow the directions carefully. Color red the sections with words that rhyme with *gate*, *line*, and *bend*. Color blue the sections with words that rhyme with *seat*, *bird*, and *car*.

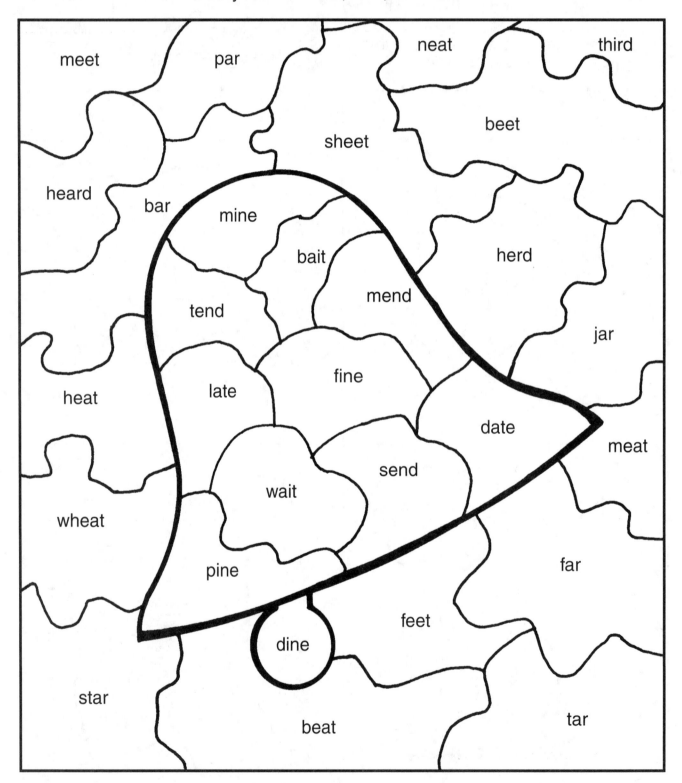

Compound Words

A compound word is made up of two smaller words. For example, **honeymoon** consists of two words, **honey** and **moon.** See how many compound words you can make from the single words below.

honey	road	rail	sail	person
play	boat	wood	snake	over
head	rattle	ply	sales	light
moon	rain	take	ground	bow

1. _____

2. _____

3. _____

4. _____

5. _____

6. _____

7. _____

8. _____

9. _____

10. _____

11. _____

12. _____

More Compound Words

Write a word in the blank between each set of words. The trick is that the new word must complete a compound word both to the left and to the right of it. The first one has been done for you.

1. dug   __out__   side

2. foot   _____   ladder

3. arrow   _____   line

4. country   _____   walk

5. tea   _____   belly

6. camp   _____   place

7. basket   _____   room

8. touch   _____   stairs

9. drug   _____   keeper

10. base   _____   park

11. flash   _____   house

12. hill   _____   ways

13. look   _____   doors

14. quarter   _____   bone

15. some   _____   ever

Compound Bubble Gum

Color the compound words red. Color all other words blue.

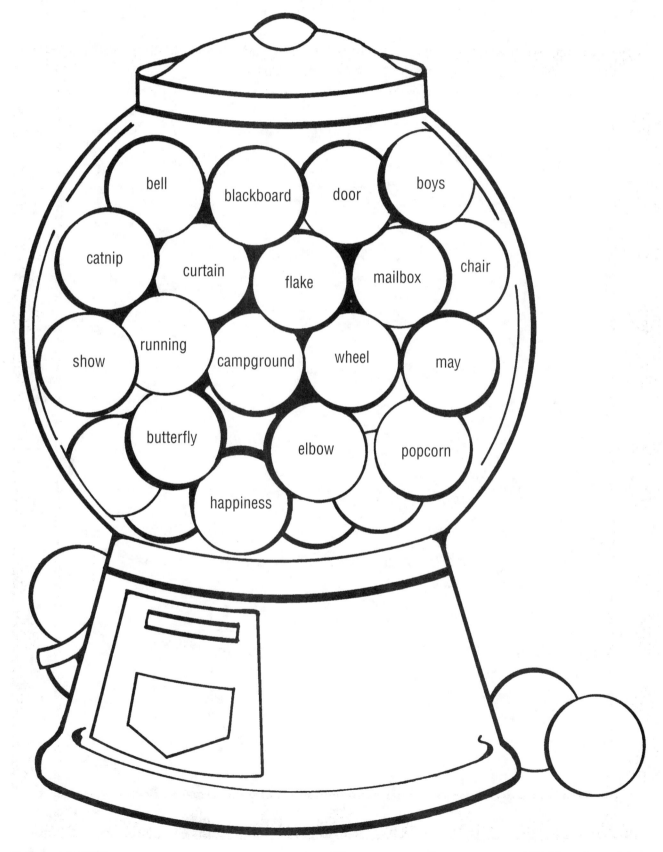

Syllable Solo

A one-syllable word is never divided. Keep in mind that a word with one syllable may have one or more vowels.

Find the one-syllable words in the following song and circle them. Then choose any five of these words and write them in the starts.

"Twinkle, twinkle, little star

How I wonder what you are.

Up above the world so high

Like a diamond in the sky.

Twinkle, twinkle, little star

How I wonder what you are."

Double Trouble

When two consonants come between two vowels in a word, the word is usually divided between the two consonants.

Examples:　bat-ter　　　mar-ket　　　roc-ket

Write the word that names each picture. Use a hyphen to divide it into syllables.

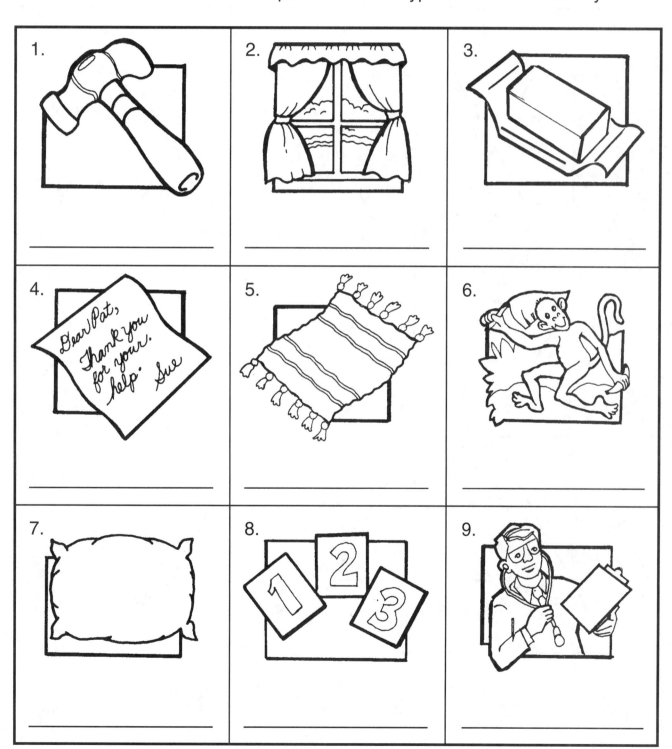

Syllable Quilt

Listen for the syllables in each word. Color the spaces in the following way:

1 syllable = red	2 syllables = blue	3 syllables = green

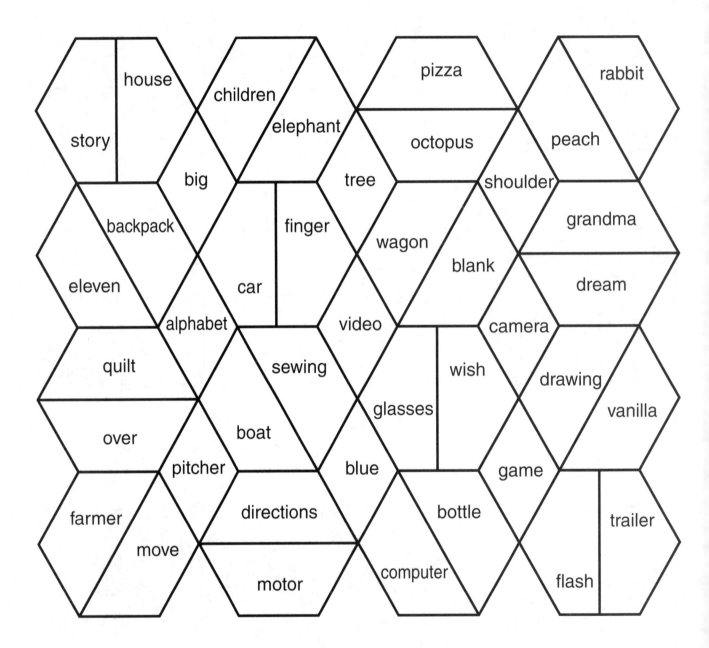

Juggling Vowels

When a vowel is sounded alone in a word, it is a syllable by itself. Divide each word into syllables. Write one syllable in each of the balls that the clowns are juggling.

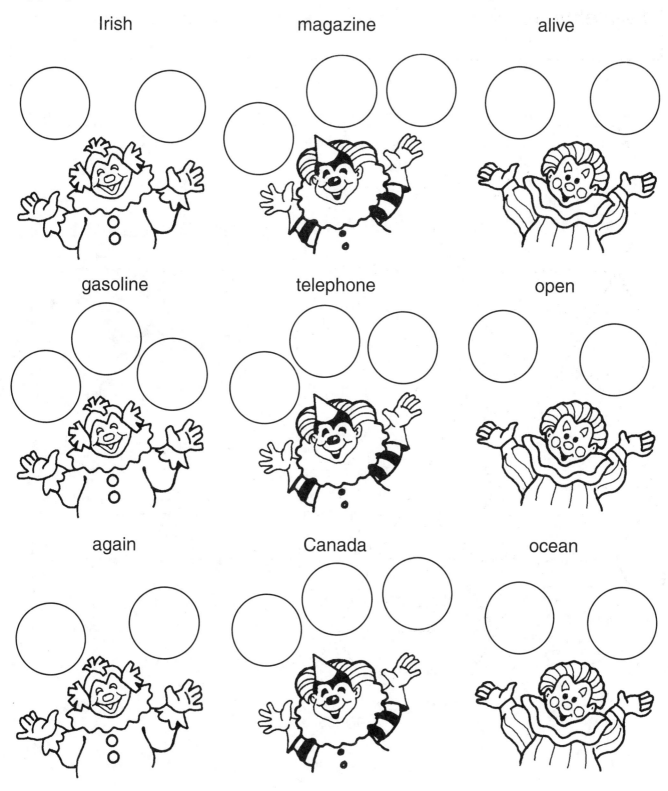

Irish

magazine

alive

gasoline

telephone

open

again

Canada

ocean

Getting to the Root of It

Sometimes a word has letters added to the beginning or end of it that change the meaning of the word. The main word is called the **root word**, and the added letters are **prefixes** or **suffixes**. For example, in the word **soundless**, the root word is **sound**, and in the word **unusual** the root word is **usual**. Notice how the meanings of these two words change with the added letters.

Read the words below. Circle the root words.

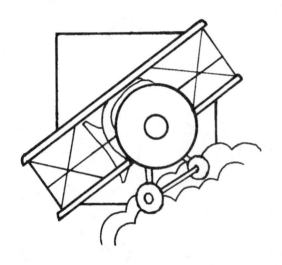

1. irregular

2. misspell

3. prideful

4. useless

5. impossible

6. disloyal

7. unknown

8. prearrange

9. mermaid

10. biplane

11. joyous

12. uniform

13. tricycle

14. nonstop

15. royalty

Brush Up on Root Words

On each brush is the name of a person who does an action. Find the root word in each and write it on the tooth.

Example: farmer, farm

1.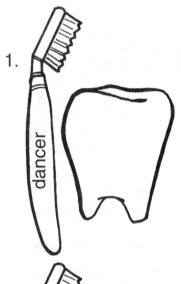

2.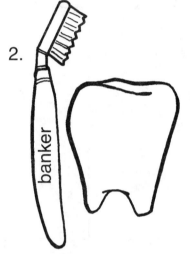

3.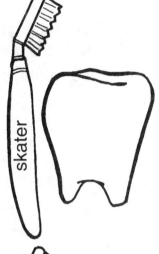

4.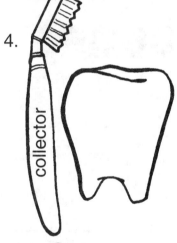

5.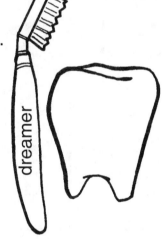

6.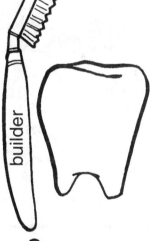

7.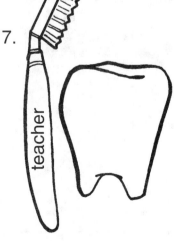

8.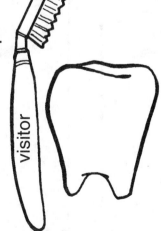

9.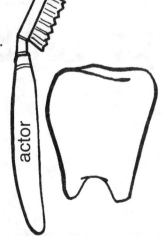

Prefix Parade

A **prefix** is one or more syllables at the beginning of a root word. When a word has a prefix, the syllable division is between the prefix and the root word. Circle the prefixes in the following cards. Write the word on the cards using hyphens to divide it into syllables.

unwrap	**refill**
discover	**nonsense**
preschool	**misspell**

Prepare for Prefixes

Here are six common prefixes. How many words can you find that begin with these prefixes? Write them in the columns. One word in each column has been done for you.

un	dis	pre
unusual	discover	preorder

under	re	mis
understand	remake	mistake

Prefix Practice

Find the words with prefixes in the following sentences and underline them.
Write the prefix, root word, and definition in the correct column. Use a dictionary
to help you if you need it.

Sentence	Prefix	Root	Definition
1. John reread the book because it was good.			
2. Ann came to class unprepared.			
3. Did you go to preschool?			
4. Bob misspelled California.			
5. The plant was underwatered.			
6. Joe felt overjoyed when he won.			
7. The students misjudged her.			
8. In health class, we learned not to overeat.			

Surfing with Suffixes

A **suffix** is one or more syllables at the end of a root word. When a word has a suffix, the syllable division is between the suffix and the root word. Circle the suffixes in the waves and then write the word on the wave with a hyphen to divide it into syllables.

1. kindness

2. careful

3. helpful

4. seedless

5. clearly

6. healthful

Bubbling Over with Suffixes

The suffix **less** can mean *without*. The suffix **ous** can mean *full of.* Circle the suffix in each bubble. Read the clues in the bubble box. Find the word in the bubbles that goes with the meaning. Color each bubble when you use the word.

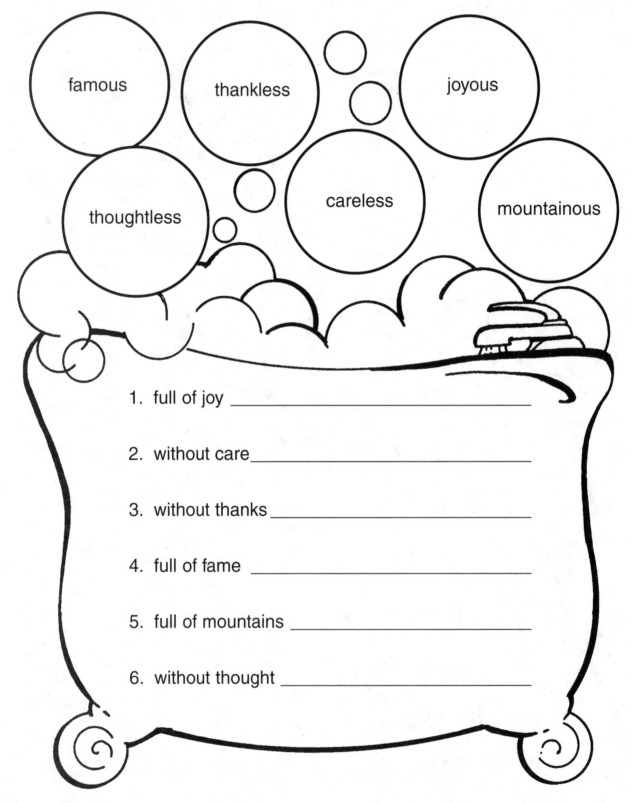

famous

thankless

joyous

thoughtless

careless

mountainous

1. full of joy _____

2. without care_____

3. without thanks _____

4. full of fame _____

5. full of mountains _____

6. without thought _____

Spotting Suffixes

Read the words in the bones. Color the bones yellow that have a word with a prefix. Color the bones blue that have a suffix.

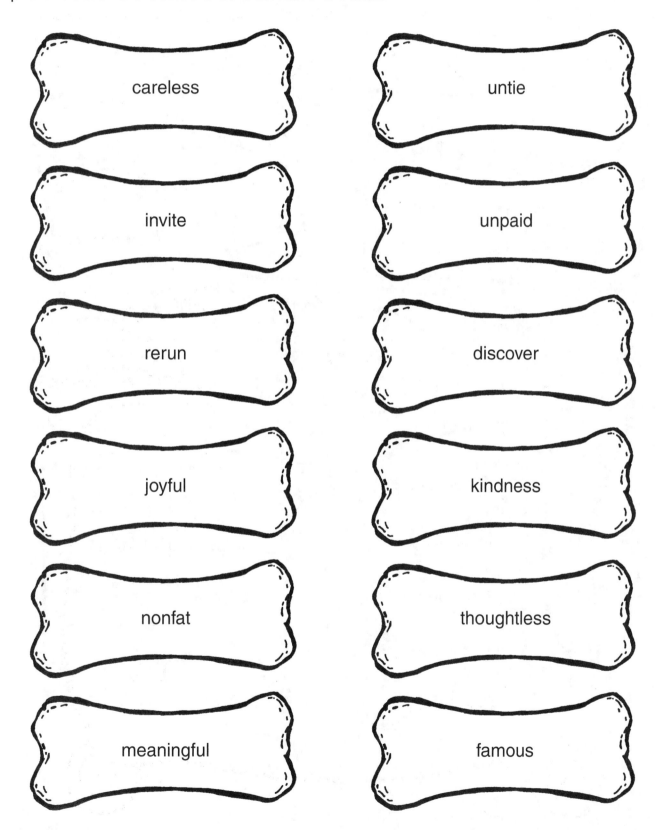

careless

untie

invite

unpaid

rerun

discover

joyful

kindness

nonfat

thoughtless

meaningful

famous

Sine Maker?

Help! The sign maker has lost his glasses! A word on every sign is misspelled. Find the misspelled word on each sign and circle it. Write the word correctly in each sign.

Janie's Homework

Janie did her homework, but she had some trouble spelling. Help her correct her paper before she gives it to her teacher. First, read her homework. Then correct the misspelled words on the lines below.

One day a boy woke up for skool. He washed his fase and coombed his hare. Then he put on the read shirt and blew jeens that his mother had lade out for him. It took some time to put on his shose becawse the laces were tied in double nots. Finaly, he did it. Afterwards, he went to the kitchin to eat some cereul and milk. It was verry good. Then he remembered that he didn't pak a lunch! He made a peanut butter and jelly sandwitch, and he put it in his lunchbox with an appel and some cookeys. Now he was reedy. But, wait! He forgot to bruch his teath. He brushed them quickly, just in time for the bus to get thare. Then he waz off too school.

_____

_____

_____

_____

_____

_____

_____

_____

_____

Correct or Not?

Some of the words below are spelled correctly and some are not. Correct the misspelled words. Write the word *correct* next to each word that is spelled correctly.

1. cloo _____   11. fich _____

2. shake _____   12. cookey _____

3. row _____   13. monkie _____

4. lin _____   14. donkey _____

5. freze _____   15. name _____

6. bote _____   16. eech _____

7. sayl _____   17. lowd _____

8. march _____   18. gurl _____

9. tea _____   19. boy _____

10. womin _____   20. loe _____

Double Letters

Each word or phrase below is a clue for a word that contains consecutive double letters. Write the word on the blank line. An example has been done for you.

The color of bananas = yellow

1. A place to learn _____

2. Very thin _____

3. Lovely _____

4. The day after today _____

5. Scrambled or sunnyside up _____

6. Not awake _____

7. The number after fourteen _____

8. Color of grass _____

9. Red fruit _____

10. Everything _____

11. You stand on this _____

12. Group of Girl Scouts _____

13. Porcupines have them _____

14. Found at the beach _____

15. Middle of the day _____

Anagrams

Rearrange the letters of each word below to make a new word. An example has been done for you.

mug = gum

1. arm _____

2. tea _____

3. mace _____

4. pal _____

5. pan _____

6. rats _____

7. peek _____

8. cape _____

9. dear _____

10. tame _____

11. hint _____

12. miles _____

13. pit _____

14. pot _____

15. scar _____

16. tar _____

17. team _____

18. its _____

19. ten _____

20. slip _____

Go, Team, Go!

Each phrase below is a clue for a word or phrase that contains the word *go*.
Be careful; some of these are challenging!

1. Animal _____

2. Sport _____

3. Water taxi _____

4. Valuable mineral _____

5. Past tense of go _____

6. Guiding principle _____

7. Type of dog _____

8. End or aim _____

9. Another name for a peanut _____

10. Intermediary _____

11. To eat hurriedly _____

12. Mischievous or scary elf _____

13. Beautiful _____

14. Ape _____

15. Drinking glass with a stem _____

16. Spectacles used to protect the eyes _____

17. Loose, flowing garment _____

18. Dance _____

19. Fruit of a trailing or climbing plant _____

20. Type of bird _____

What's to Eat?

List food items that begin with each letter of the alphabet.

A			
B			
C			
D			
E			
F			
G			
H			
I			
J			
K			
L			
M			
N			
O			
P			
Q			
R			
S			
T			
U			
V			
W			
X			
Y			
Z			

Animal Word Find

Try to find all of the 30 animals hidden in this word maze.

```
A  A  R  D  V  A  R  K  I  S  S  M  O  L  A  E  S
C  A  M  O  L  R  A  B  B  I  T  O  M  O  W  L  U
A  E  A  G  L  E  A  R  L  Y  C  H  E  E  T  A  H
T  O  G  L  U  E  B  A  B  O  O  N  O  L  O  H  U
O  G  O  T  J  A  G  U  A  R  U  N  A  E  X  W  R
H  I  P  P  O  P  O  T  A  M  U  S  L  P  O  T  T
C  R  H  O  X  L  A  H  N  U  T  L  E  H  T  X  U
I  A  E  P  L  A  T  E  A  L  L  I  G  A  T  O  R
R  F  R  Z  E  B  R  A  C  A  N  O  N  N  H  F  T
T  F  E  R  R  E  T  X  O  W  N  N  I  T  E  O  L
S  E  R  F  I  C  K  A  N  G  A  R  O  O  N  O  E
O  A  L  A  O  K  A  N  D  Y  M  U  S  K  R  A  T
T  O  E  I  G  U  A  N  A  T  S  U  R  L  A  W  E
W  A  N  A  R  O  U  M  I  P  P  O  C  U  E  L  R
```

Making New Words

Can you turn a word into a new word by repeating one of the letters in the word?
Example: If you add *e* to *red* you get *reed*. Remember, you have to add one of
the letters that is already in the word. You cannot add *a* to *red* to make *read*
because there isn't already an *a* in the word.

1. go_____

2. lose _____

3. diner_____

4. chose_____

5. met_____

6. coma _____

7. super _____

8. desert _____

9. lot_____

10. be_____

11. fed _____

12. god_____

13. son_____

14. in _____

15. lop _____

16. coral_____

Abbreviations

An abbreviation is a shortened form of a word that is usually followed by a period. An abbreviation is never used by itself as a word. It is always used with other words or names.

- You **wouldn't** write . . .

  I live on the St. next to the park.

- You **would** write . . .

  I live at 4342 Pumpkin St. next to the park.

- And you **wouldn't** write . . .

  That's a Mt. I would like to climb.

- But you **would** write . . .

  Someday I want to climb Mt. Whitney.

Common Abbreviations

apt.	apartment	cont.	continued	Jr.	Junior
Aug.	August	Corp.	Corporation	kg	kilogram
Ave.	Avenue	Dec.	December	lb.	pound
Bldg.	Building	Dept.	Department	Oct.	October
Blvd.	Boulevard	ft.	feet	oz.	ounces
Capt.	Captain	in.	inches	Rd.	Road
cm	centimeters	Jan.	January		

Match the abbreviations with the words they stand for. Then copy the abbreviation correctly. Don't forget periods!

Letter

_____ 1. Wed.

_____ 2. Mr.

_____ 3. St.

_____ 4. Dec.

_____ 5. U.S.

_____ 6. Capt.

_____ 7. Tbs.

_____ 8. Blvd.

_____ 9. Aug.

_____ 10. Gov.

_____ 11. Jr.

_____ 12. gal.

_____ 13. Dr.

_____ 14. Tues.

_____ 15. yr.

Abbreviation

a. Boulevard _____

b. Mister _____

c. year _____

d. Governor_____

e. December _____

f. tablespoon _____

g. Tuesday_____

h. Street _____

i. gallon _____

j. Captain _____

k. Doctor _____

l. United States _____

m. Junior _____

n. Wednesday_____

o. August_____

More Abbreviations

Write the meaning of each abbreviation.

1. N _____

2. St. _____

3. RR_____

4. S.A. _____

5. M.C._____

6. C.O.D. _____

7. Wed. _____

8. A.M._____

9. chap. _____

10. doz. _____

11. qt. _____

12. pkg. _____

13. max. _____

14. Ave. _____

15. Sept. _____

16. yr. _____

17. bldg. _____

18. no. _____

19. temp. _____

20. P.O. _____

Alike Yet Different

Some words are spelled the same but are pronounced differently and have different meanings.

re´cord	record´	desert´	de´sert
con´test	contest´	con´tent	content´
re´fuse	refuse´	read (rēd)	read (red)
close (clos)	close (cloz)	sub´ject	subject´
con´duct	conduct´	ad´dress	address´

Choose the correct way of pronouncing the underlined word in each sentence below. Write the word at the end of the sentence and put the accent mark or vowel marks where they belong.

1. Our teacher will <u>record</u> us as we sing the national anthem.

   _____

2. We are studying about <u>desert</u> plants and animals. _____

3. Our little kitten was very <u>content</u> after we fed her._____

4. Kim and I entered the art <u>contest</u>. _____

5. How can anyone <u>refuse</u> to do an act of kindness? _____

6. My mother <u>read</u> the directions for the recipe. _____

7. Please <u>close</u> the door gently._____

8. Our <u>conduct</u> should be appropriate at all times. _____

9. What is your favorite <u>subject</u>? _____

10. My <u>address</u> is 221 Main Street. _____

Pronunciation Keys

When you use the dictionary, you will find guides to each word's pronunciation in parentheses. The dictionary will also give you a guide about how to read the pronunciation. However, if you know some basics, it will help. Use these tips.

A vowel written by itself makes the short vowel sound.

Examples: a, e, i, o, u

A vowel written with a straight line above it makes the long vowel sound.

Examples: ā, ē, ī, ō, ū

Using the two vowel tips above, write the words on the lines.

1. mat _____

2. māt_____

3. tīn_____

4. tin_____

5. fed _____

6. fēd _____

7. us_____

8. ūs _____

9. mēt _____

10. met _____

What's the Word?

Read the pronunciation guides. Write the words on the lines provided.

1. gōst _____

2. māl _____

3. pōst _____

4. lā´-zē _____

5. plās _____

6. rō _____

7. fū´-əl _____

8. tō´-təl _____

9. ōk _____

10. sprā _____

11. vāl _____

12. ri-pār´ _____

13. ri-plī´ _____

14. əb-zērv´ _____

15. whī _____

Alphabetical Order

List these words in alphabetical order.

river	friend	vest	jump
moon	house	silent	light
cart	ghost	tunnel	umbrella

_____   _____   _____

_____   _____   _____

_____   _____   _____

_____   _____   _____

List these words in alphabetical order. You will need to look at the second letters as well as the first.

dog	game	same	science
sort	lunch	grass	cell
loop	cane	lion	deer

_____   _____   _____

_____   _____   _____

_____   _____   _____

_____   _____   _____

Alphabetizing

When you are alphabetizing, what do you do if you have more than one word that starts with the same letter? Look at the alphabetizing steps below.

1. Begin putting the words in ABC order. When you find two or more words that start with the same letter, put them in a neat stack.

   dog
   dad
   doctor

2. Cross out or cover up the first letter of each of the words.

   d̶og
   d̶ad
   d̶octor

3. Put these in ABC order. You know *ad* will be first because *a* comes before *o*. Put the *d* back on the word and put *dad* first. That will leave these:

   dad
   og
   octo

4. Cross out or cover the *o* because both words start with the same letter. That leaves:

   o̶g
   o̶ctor

5. *C* comes before *g*, so *doctor* is before *dog* in alphabetical order.

Circle the lists that are in ABC order.

bear	cheetah	llama	manatee
billy goat	cat	parakeet	monkey
bobcat	leopard	parrot	lynx
cougar	lion	penguin	moose

Sight Words

Read the basic sight words out loud to someone. Put a check by the words that you do not know. Later, make word cards to practice the words you do not know. If you learn these basic sight words, your reading skills and speed will improve.

a	the	take	why
has	red	going	they
for	we	only	then
far	down	an	let
you	she	black	put
fast	good	eat	laugh
run	of	once	it
or	I	shall	cold
thank	his	these	him
done	blue	is	ask
went	at	made	when
and	found	hot	her
full	be	buy	ten
walk	drum	over	six
got	about	long	help
did	sit	where	please
if	read	he	have
saw	us	on	use
does	clean	around	funny
pick	go	wash	not

More Basic Sight Words

Read these basic sight words out loud to someone. Put a check by the words that you do not know. Make word cards to practice the words you do not know. Accept the challenge to learn all of these words.

came	show	every	wish
we're	pull	tell	into
own	find	may	by
been	green	five	my
soon	play	much	two
live	bear	water	box
garden	hand	time	cow
name	brother	sister	bed
chair	thing	watch	men
feet	home	nest	ate
very	light	pizza	could
new	because	cute	stop
say	your	knit	bring
ran	together	again	in
will	seven	round	all
under	white	first	yes
blue	orange	purple	tin
add	work	lucky	me
swam	mouse	knock	up
price	borrow	button	miss

More Basic Sight Words (cont.)

Read these basic sight words out loud to someone. Put a check by the words that you do not know. Make word cards to practice the words you do not know. If you stumble over the basic sight words, reading will be difficult for you. So learn them all.

yellow	stop	jump	eight
cut	see	their	today
call	as	out	grow
old	no	better	ride
open	that	four	kind
like	try	never	this
now	just	can	write
to	had	must	get
which	do	make	but
with	said	what	fall
there	from	hold	how
was	am	off	best
warm	its	fly	some
so	big	think	any
drink	three	brown	carry
one	who	myself	sing
well	shall	little	come
pretty	don't	work	give
many	sleep	are	

Sight Nouns

Read these basic sight words out loud to someone. Each of these words is a noun. A noun names a person or thing. Put a check by the ones that you do not know. Make word cards to practice the words you do not know. Reading will be a snap if you know the basic sight words!

window	lamb	birthday	carrot
baby	game	paper	girl
home	robin	wood	eye
men	nest	seed	father
picture	bread	fire	doll
name	sister	floor	toy
garden	corn	shoe	table
pig	thing	rain	street
boat	party	duck	coat
kitty	brother	feet	farmer
ball	time	watch	house
bell	fish	flower	cow
tree	sheep	grass	let
way	wind	house	night
rabbit	car	box	head
cat	dog	day	chair
cake	song	top	bear
ring	egg	money	picnic
chicken	milk	sun	hand
stock	mother	apple	farm
boy	bird	horse	leg
snowman	hill	back	kangaroo

Which Meaning?

Choose the meaning of the word as it is used in each sentence. Write the letter of the meaning used on the line before each sentence. Then, choose a meaning and write its letter in the box. Write a sentence using the meaning you choose.

part	A. a role in a play
	B. a piece of a whole
	C. divide

_____ 1. I will take a part of the pie.

_____ 2. Where do you part your hair?

_____ 3. The actress took the part of the mother.

_____ 4. What did this part come from?

_____ 5. My part in the skit is small.

Meaning ☐ _____

cross	A. intersect
	B. a problem or burden
	C. angry

_____ 6. The highways cross in the north.

_____ 7. The drought is a cross to the farmers.

_____ 8. The child missed his nap and is feeling cross.

_____ 9. What are you so cross about?

_____ 10. I will cross these lines here.

Meaning ☐ _____

444

What Do You Mean?

Choose the meaning of the word as it is used in the sentence. Write the letter of the meaning on the line before each sentence. Then, choose a meaning and write its letter in the box. Write a sentence using the meaning you choose.

record	A. write down B. all the known facts C. highest achievement in a competition D. sound recording

_____ 1. Alice earned the team record when she scored more baskets than anyone else had.

_____ 2. The police officer kept a record of what everyone saw.

_____ 3. Do you have a record of our agreement?

_____ 4. Will the secretary please record the minutes of our meeting?

_____ 5. My mother has an old record of Elvis Presley singing.

Meaning ☐ _____

_____

close	A. shut	C. near to
	B. finish	D. secretive

_____ 6. Tomorrow we will close the deal.

_____ 7. Will you close the cupboard, please?

_____ 8. He is so closed off, it is hard to figure him out.

_____ 9. Don't stand so close to the heater.

_____ 10. The store is close to the park.

Meaning ☐ _____

_____

Which Meaning Is It?

Choose the meaning of the word as it is used in the sentence. Write the letter of the meaning on the line before each sentence. Then, choose a meaning and write its letter in the box. Write a sentence using the meaning you choose.

conduct
A. act as a leader; guide
B. transmit
C. behavior

_____ 1. Their conduct was excellent during the field trip.

_____ 2. The scout master will conduct the hike.

_____ 3. Their parents expected better conduct from them.

_____ 4. Electricity will conduct the message through the telephone wire.

_____ 5. Can you conduct an orchestra?

Meaning [ ] _____

_____

form
A. document with blanks to be filled in
B. a shape or structure
C. to shape or develop

_____ 6. I will form this clay into a pot.

_____ 7. The form of the building is unusual.

_____ 8. The children liked to form the mud into pies in their backyard.

_____ 9. The employee had to complete an emergency form before he started work.

_____ 10. The form can be very long when you go to the doctor's office.

Meaning [ ] _____

Practice Following Directions

Use your imagination and writing skills to follow each direction found below.

1. Write the word *visit.* Add the suffix *or.* _____

   Use the new word in a sentence.

   _____

2. Write the number 22. Double the number. Add five more. Use the answer to complete the rhyme.

   Fifty elephants stood in a line

   One dropped out and there were _____.

3. Begin with the number 4. Triple the number. Subtract 2. Use your answer to complete the rhyme.

   Fifteen zebras grazed in a pen.

   Five escaped and that left _____.

4. Begin with the number 5. Multiply it by 10. Subtract 0. Use your answer to complete the rhyme.

   The monkeys eat peanuts.

   I think that's nifty.

   We fed them a bunch

   One hundred and _____.

5. Begin with the word *orangutan*. Change one vowel to another vowel. Put a space between some letters and spell two color words.

_____ and _____

Following Cookie Directions

On a trip to the zoo, you may see reindeer. These animals can be recognized by their antlers. In the recipe that follows, you can use pretzel sticks to make edible antlers. Read the directions carefully, and try to imagine how the antlers will look. Draw a picture of what you think the reindeer cookies will look like in the box below. Try the recipe to see whether you correctly followed the directions in your imagination.

1. Use a serrated plastic knife to slice a graham cracker in half diagonally. Then you will have two triangles.

2. Spread the cracker pieces with vanilla icing.

3. Put each cracker piece on a plate so that the point of the triangle faces down.

4. Use thin pretzel sticks to make antlers at the top corners of the reindeer's head.

5. Use red cinnamon candies to make the reindeer's eyes, nose, and mouth.

By the Number

Color this picture by using the numbers and colors in the chart.

Color by Number

number	color to use		number	color to use
1	green		3	gray
2	blue		4	brown

From Words to Pictures

Make a map from the words on this page. Don't forget to fill in the key to your map. After you have made your map, reread the words. Does your map match the words exactly?

1. There are mountains in the north.

2. A lake is in the southeast corner.

3. A river runs from the mountains to the lake.

4. There is a thick forest on the west side of the river.

5. There is a town on the east side of the river about halfway between the mountains and the lake.

Key N W E S

forest

mountains

lake

river

town

Picture Sequence

Number the pictures in order. Color the pictures.

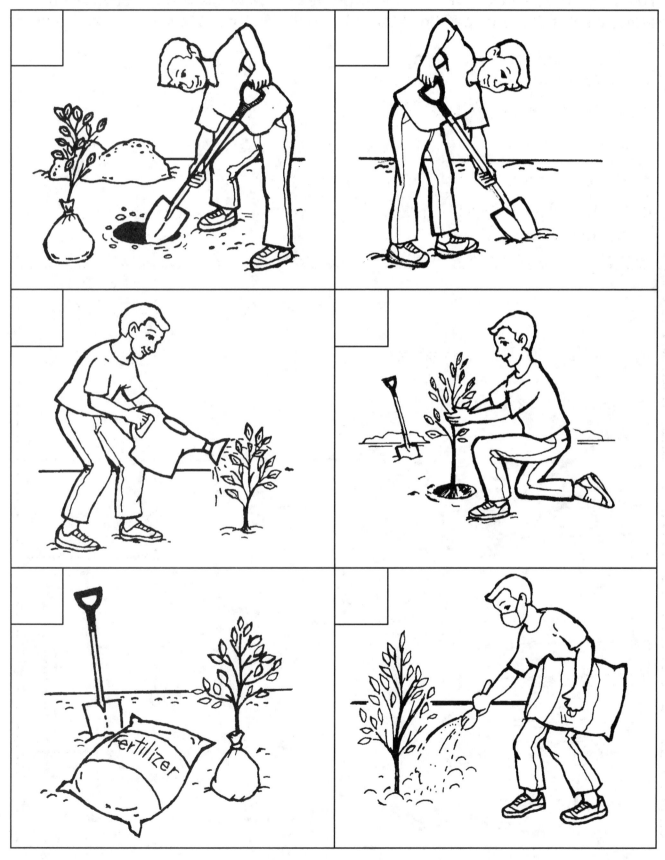

Making Brownies

Read over the directions for making brownies. Next, label the directions in sequence. The first step is done for you.

a. Add ½ cup water and 1 egg. _____

b. Preheat oven to 350° F. ____1____

c. Pour into prepared pan. _____

d. Empty brownie mix into bowl. _____

e. Cut, serve, and enjoy when cool. _____

f. Prepare pan with shortening or nonstick cooking spray. _____

g. Bake at 350° F for 25 minutes. _____

h. Stir 100 strokes by hand. _____

Sequencing the Story

Read the sentences below. Cut them out and glue them in order.

Finally, her wobbly legs pushed her up.

Next, she put her front hooves firmly on the grass.

At first, the new pony lay quietly on the ground.

The new pony was standing on her own!

Then, she lifted her nose into the air.

Reading Adventures

Read each story and then answer the questions.

Miles and Robin wanted to go to the zoo. Their mother said they could go after they finished their chores. First, they cleaned their rooms. Next, they mopped the kitchen floor. After that, they washed the family's car. Finally, they got ready to go to the zoo.

1. What did Miles and Robin do first? _____

_____

2. What did the boys do after they mopped the floor?_____

_____

3. What was the final thing the boys did? _____

_____

Miles and Robin were on an imaginary safari. First, their mother gave them a map of the zoo. Then, the boys went to the shark pool. Next, they found their way to the tiger cage. After that, they visited the wolf den. Finally, they met their mother at the alligator exhibit. Miles and Robin had a busy afternoon!

4. What animal did the boys visit first? _____

_____

5. Where did the boys go after they saw the tiger? _____

_____

6. What did the boys do last? _____

_____

Your Day

Think about some of the things you have done since you woke up this morning.

- Did you eat breakfast?

- Did you play?

- Did you go somewhere?

If you wanted to tell a friend about your day, it would be easy. Just tell about your day in the order in which things happened. This is called the **sequence of events**.

Write six things you did today in sequence (order).

1. _____

_____

2. _____

_____

3. _____

_____

4. _____

_____

5. _____

_____

6. _____

_____

Paragraph Maze

Find your way through the maze by making a paragraph. Some words in the paragraph are written right to left and bottom to top, so read carefully! Write the finished paragraph on another paper.

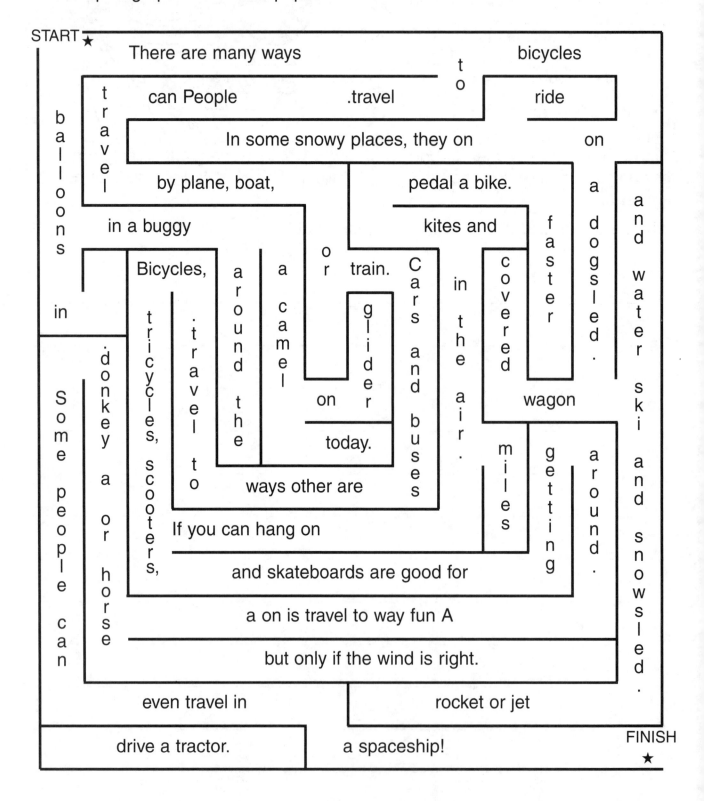

What's the Big Idea?

A paragraph should tell the reader about one idea. In the Ideas Bank below, you will find 10 ideas or topics. There are 10 lists on this page that need a main idea. Take the ideas from the box and write them at the top of the lists below.

Ideas Bank

favorite foods   summer
homework   pet peeves
favorite rides   ice cream
school   travel
sports   chores

---

1. _____

    cleaning your room

    taking out the trash

    setting the table

2. _____

    pizza

    candy

    burritos

3. _____

    recess

    study hall

    library

4. _____

    people who cut in line

    losing my lunch money

    alarm clocks

5. _____

    creamy, cold, and sweet

    banana splits

    hot fudge sundaes

6. _____

    books

    assignment schedule

    where to work at home

7. _____

    roller coasters

    loop rides

    spinning rides

8. _____

    packing

    tickets and reservations

    souvenirs

9. _____

    swimming

    ice cream

    vacations

10. _____

    basketball

    hockey

    baseball

Matching Pictures with Text

Underline the sentence that tells about each picture.

The lion roars.

Lions eat meat.

Lions sleep a lot.

The alligator swims.

Two alligators rest.

The alligator sleeps.

The bear dives into the water.

The bear eats a fish.

The bear rolls in the grass.

Ice cream is a nice treat.

Cupcakes are good.

I had spaghetti for lunch.

Titles Tell the Main Idea

If you read the title of a story, poem, or book, you will find a clue about the main idea. Read each title and description below. Draw a line to connect the pairs of mittens.

1. "The Snow Sunday"

A. Animals and plants are still alive, even though the pond is frozen.

2. "Ice Is Nice"

B. One very cold day, Sue learned that pets need special winter care.

3. "Winter at the Pond"

C. Every Sunday the aunts visited May Lie's house, except for the day that it snowed.

4. "The Coldest Day of the Year"

D. Ice has many important uses.

5. "Disaster at the Ice Skating Party"

E. Skating on the ice can be very dangerous.

Every Picture Tells a Story

Under each picture write a sentence that tells the main idea of what is happening. Color the pictures.

About Barn Owls

Read the paragraph below. Color the owl that has the main idea.

Barn owls learn to fly before they leave their nests.

Barn owls can hunt for food by 12 weeks of age.

Barn owls are fully grown by about 12 weeks of age.

Barn owls are fully grown by about 12 weeks of age. First, they hatch from eggs. At three weeks, their eyes are open, and they can jump and walk. Three weeks later, their feathers begin to grow. By eight weeks, they are practicing flight and are ready to leave their nests. Two weeks later, they begin to explore on their own. Finally, by 12 weeks they are grown and can hunt for food on their own.

First Sentence

The first sentence of each paragraph often tells the main idea of the whole paragraph. Always read the first sentence of a paragraph carefully. Read the paragraph below and underline the first sentence with a blue crayon. Circle the important details with a red crayon. Then answer the questions at the bottom of the page.

You can learn to make friends at school. First, be friendly. Smile at other people and say, "Hello." Share your crayons and snacks. Be kind. Don't wait for others to talk to you. Go up to them first, even if they look shy or do not act friendly at first. These are some of the ways you can make friends. If you do some of these things, you will have lots of friends in no time!

1. How many details did you circle? _____

2. Did the first sentence tell you the main idea of the paragraph?

   _____

3. List three ways that you can make friends.

   _____

   _____

   _____

Main Idea of a Paragraph

Sometimes you will want to tell about a paragraph you have read, but you do not have time to tell everything about it. You will need to decide what one idea the whole paragraph is about. The one idea that a whole paragraph is about is called the **main idea**. Finding the main idea of a paragraph is easy if you think about the details: **who**, **what**, and **why**. Read the paragraph below carefully.

A very young boy named Mark visited the American Zoo last Monday. While he was there, several penguin eggs hatched. Mark was one of the first people to see the baby penguins because he happened to be near the penguin exhibit when the babies were born. Mark was happy to be part of this very exciting event!!

Think about the three Ws. Answer each question.

1. Who is the paragraph about? _____

2. What did he do?_____

_____

3. Why did it happen? _____

_____

4. Write a main idea sentence from your answers.

_____

_____

George Washington

Read the story and then answer the questions.

One of the greatest leaders in United States history is George Washington. He was a general in the Revolutionary War against the British. The people of the new nation were proud of the work he did during the war, and many people thought he would be the best person to lead the country as its first president. General Washington became president for eight years, and he is still remembered as an excellent leader.

1. Who is the paragraph about?

   _____

2. What is this person remembered for?

   _____

   _____

3. Why is this person known in this way?

   _____

   _____

4. Use your answers to write a main idea sentence.

   _____

   _____

Main Idea Rephrasing

When we retell something we have read or heard, we usually cannot remember the exact words. So we tell the most important parts. This is called **rephrasing**. Read the example below.

> At the zoo, Antonio heard a worker tell about penguins.
>
> The worker said, "Penguins are flightless birds."

When Antonio told his friend Nicholas what he heard, Antonio could not remember the exact words the zoo worker had used. Antonio said instead, "Penguins are birds, but they cannot fly."

On the strips below, there are pairs of sentences that say basically the same thing. One sentence strip is a rephrasing of the other. Find the matching sentence strips and color each pair the same color.

Their tickets were lost!
The boys rode the bus to the game.
My favorite book is that one.
They lost their tickets.
My blue shirt has a rip.
That book is my favorite one.
The bus took the boys to the game.
My blue shirt is torn.

Lunchtime

Read the story. Answer the questions at the end.

"I am hungry! Let's stop for a few minutes to eat our lunch," said Anna. She, Mark, and Mark's father had been hiking through some nearby hills throughout the morning, and now it was lunchtime.

"Good idea," replied Mark. "I made these tuna salad sandwiches myself. You will love them, Anna."

Anna and Mark stopped at a large flat rock near a stream. They unwrapped the sandwiches. "Yuck! What smells so bad?" asked Anna, wrinkling her nose.

"I think it's the tuna salad," said Mark, "but I don't know what's wrong."

"It is spoiled, Mark. See how soggy and slimy it looks," said Anna.

"But I mixed all the ingredients and spread them on the bread last night, exactly as the recipe told me to do," complained Mark. "What could be wrong?"

"I know what's wrong," added Mr. Mitchell, Mark's father, as he joined them at the rock. "Did you read all the directions on the recipe, Mark? Did you chill the sandwiches overnight?"

Mark looked sheepish. "No, I stopped when I got to the part about spreading the tuna on the bread. I didn't think the rest was important."

"Maybe we can find some wild berries," sighed Anna. "I sure am hungry."

1. Which step of the recipe directions did Mark forget?

   _____

   _____

2. What happened to the sandwiches because Mark did not do that step?

   _____

   _____

   _____

My Dream

Read the story and then answer the questions.

I had a dream last night that I was five inches tall. In my dream, I climbed down my bedpost and onto the floor. I walked right under my bed and across the room. It was a good thing my mom wasn't in the dream because if she had seen everything stuffed under my bed, she would have made me clean my room! Instead, I walked over to my dollhouse and through the front door. Everything was just my size! I arranged all the furniture for a party, and I invited all my dolls to come over. We danced around the dollhouse, told jokes, and ate the cookies on my nightstand, left over from my bedtime snack. We had such a great time, I decided to live in the dollhouse forever. I went upstairs to the doll bedroom, and stretching out on the tiny bed, I fell asleep.

When I woke up from my dream, I smiled as I remembered it. Then I looked inside my dollhouse and wondered, "How did those cookie crumbs get in there?"

1. How did the girl get down from her bed?_____

_____

2. What was the girl glad her mother did not see? _____

_____

3. What did the girl do to get ready for the party?_____

_____

4. What did the partygoers eat? _____

_____

5. What surprised the girl when she woke from her dream?_____

_____

Inferences

When you use clues to draw conclusions about things, you are inferring. Read the paragraph below and make an inference.

"I could eat a horse! Lunch in the cafeteria wasn't very good today, so I didn't eat much," said Henry. "Do we have any cheese and crackers or some apples?" asked Henry as soon as he got home from school.

Henry was . . . happy to be home.   hungry.   hurried.

If you said hungry, you are right. List three clues in the story that tell you that Henry is hungry.

1. _____

_____

2. _____

_____

3. _____

_____

Making Inferences

Read the examples and answer the questions that follow each example.

"It sure is dark in here. Could we turn on some lights?" asked Wendy and Jack.

"The Fun House is too spooky!" said Jack as he walked through it.

"I'm ready to go on the Ferris wheel," said Wendy.

---

1. What can you infer? _____

_____

2. What clues did you find to prove you inferred correctly? _____

_____

_____

"I am not jealous of your new dress," said Mary. "I don't like that color on me anyway. My mother buys me more expensive things than that. I think the material looks like it would rip easily and not wash well. Where did you buy it? Was that the only one they had left?" asked Mary.

---

1. What can you infer? _____

_____

2. What clues did you find to prove you inferred correctly? _____

_____

_____

_____

Drawing Conclusions

Read the sentences below and then answer the questions.

	Answer
1. I live on a farm. I have feathers and wings. I wake up the farm in the morning. What am I?	
2. You watch me in a large building. There are a screen and a projector. People eat popcorn and drink soda while I am playing. What am I?	
3. Some people use me to write, other people use me to play games, and many people use me to find information and to send messages to each other. I can be found in many homes and most businesses. What am I?	
4. I grow from the ground. I smell sweet. My stem has thorns, but I am beautiful. What am I?	
5. I make beautiful sounds. I have a long neck and strings. Some people use a pick to play me. They strum my strings, and the sound vibrates. What am I?	

What Next?

Finish the story below by drawing a cartoon and writing a conclusion.

"It was sure hot today!" said one of the children. They were in their bathing suits and ready to jump in the pool. Just then a swarm of buzzing bees flew near.

Conclusion:

_____

_____

_____

_____

Predicting Outcomes

Read the words and look at the pictures. What do you think will happen?
Complete the last box with a picture and a sentence.

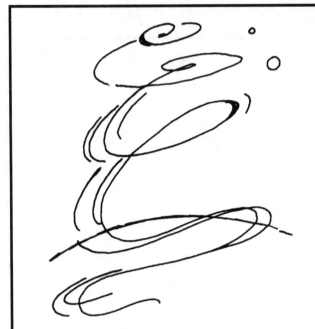

1. A big wind started to blow.

2. Leaves flew in whirlpools of air.

3. The old tree swayed and bent in the wind.

4.

Cause and Effect

Everything that happens (**effect**) is caused by something else (**cause**). Read the causes in the first column and the effects in the second column. Then match each cause with its effect.

Cause   **Effect**

_____ 1. rain   A. smiling

_____ 2. wind   B. success

_____ 3. sunshine   C. wet ground

_____ 4. darkness   D. scoring

_____ 5. hunger   E. hair blown

_____ 6. sadness   F. difficulty seeing

_____ 7. joy   G. late arrival

_____ 8. traffic   H. good health

_____ 9. hard work   I. warmth

_____ 10. home run   J. learning

_____ 11. going to school   K. crying

_____ 12. exercise   L. eating

More Cause and Effect

A **cause** is the reason why something happens.
The **effect** is what happens.

Cause   Effect

Read each cause. Write an effect.

1. The class had perfect attendance._____

   _____

2. The monkey ate all the bananas._____

   _____

3. The girl forgot her homework. _____

   _____

4. The clock stopped ticking. _____

   _____

Read each effect. Write a cause.

5. There was a traffic jam on the highway. _____

   _____

6. Ice cream spilled on the floor. _____

   _____

7. The baby started to cry. _____

   _____

8. Everyone shouted, "Hooray!" _____

   _____

Opinion

Facts are ideas that are true. They can be proven. People agree that the fact is true. **Example:**

Fact: Zebras are black and white.

You can prove that statement by looking at a zebra. Everyone who sees a zebra would agree it is black and white. An opinion is one person's thoughts about a subject. An opinion cannot be proven, and not everyone has to agree with it. **Example:**

Opinion: Zebras are pretty animals.

Not everyone believes that zebras are pretty. Some people may even think that zebras are ugly. People can have different opinions about the same thing. Below are words that can sometimes let the reader know that a sentence is an opinion and not a fact.

I believe   I think   my idea   my thought   I feel

Write **fact** or **opinion** next to each statement below.

1. Josephine is nine years old. _____

2. Kyle is a great painter. _____

3. The students spent all day at the zoo. _____

4. Reading is easy. _____

5. I'm going to win the award. _____

6. Everyone should read a book. _____

7. The math problems were difficult to do. _____

8. George Washington was the first American president. _____

Opinion

A fact is a statement that can be proven and that everyone accepts as true. An opinion is one person's idea. Everyone does not have to accept that it is correct. Read the story. Use red to underline the sentences that are facts. Use green to underline the sentences that are opinions.

A Visit to the Zoo

"I think panthers are beautiful!" exclaimed Haley.

"They are scary," said Ellen.

"Panthers belong to the cat family," said Courtney. "They weigh more than 100 pounds."

"A panther would be a great pet," Haley added.

"No, it wouldn't," announced Courtney. "It is against the law to keep a wild animal as a pet."

"This is the best trip we have ever taken," John told his sister.

Chelsea agreed, "I think it is fun, too. The zoo has many animals for us to see."

"There are six different types of monkeys at this zoo," John said. "I think they're the best animals here!"

"My favorites are the reindeer," said Chelsea. "They live where the weather is very cold."

"We learned a lot at the zoo today," said the teacher as everyone climbed on the bus to go back to school. "Tomorrow we will write stories about the things we have learned," added the teacher.

Tones Tell the Tale

Can words make you feel certain ways? Yes. Words can make you feel happy, sad, excited, silly, or even afraid. Words that add feeling to a story set the **tone**. Look at the flowers below. Read each word on the petals. Write a word in the center of the flower that tells you what the tone of each set of words might be.

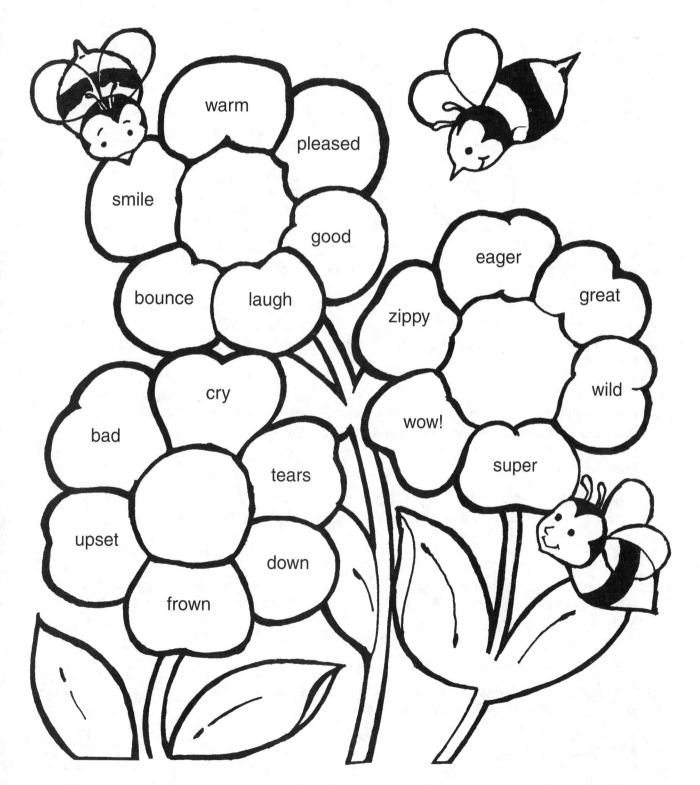

warm

pleased

smile

good

bounce

laugh

eager

great

zippy

wild

cry

wow!

bad

super

tears

upset

down

frown

What's the Tone?

The **tone** of a story is the feeling it has and the feeling it makes the reader have. A tone can be happy, sad, excited, fearful, or many others.

Word Bank

Read each paragraph below. Then write the tone each word sets. Choose from the words in the word bank above.

1. Wow! Today is my birthday. I know it will be a great day. We are having a chocolate cake and are playing lots of games. I can hardly wait until my friends arrive.

   Tone:_____

2. I can't believe my best friend is moving away. I want to cry. Even the sky looks gray and rainy today. Nothing will ever be the same without my friend.

   Tone:_____

3. Can a pig learn tricks? My pet pig, Sally, can roll over and shake hands. Or should I say shake snouts? She is a funny pig who really likes to "hog the show."

   Tone:_____

4. I can't believe our arithmetic test is today. I forgot to study, and I don't understand multiplication. I just know I will fail this test. This could ruin my math grade. Oh, why didn't I study last night?

   Tone:_____

5. It is a beautiful day today! The sun is shining, the birds are singing, and the air smells sweet and fresh. It feels good to be alive!

   Tone:_____

Identifying the Speaker

Read the story and answer the questions below.

Tracy had a big surprise when he took the trash out one night. He saw a small, furry animal hanging upside down in the trash can. "Get out of there!" yelled Tracy.

"What is going on?" called his father.

"Raccoons are hunting in our garbage," said the boy. He went back into the house and got a broom to chase the raccoons away. But when he came back, the furry raccoons were already gone. "I guess I'd better make sure that the lid is on tightly," he said.

1. How many speakers are in the story? _____

2. Who are the speakers? _____

3. Who said that he should make sure that the lid was on tightly?

_____

4. How do you know Tracy is a boy? _____

_____

First Person Voice

Read the entry in the diary below. The author, Ashley, recorded her thoughts and feelings. She used the words *I* and *me* often. When she reads her diary again, she will know that she means herself when she reads those pronouns. When you read something with the words *I* or *me*, meaning the author, that it is written in what is called the **voice of the first person**. The diary is written in the voice of the first person.

Dear Diary,

I wonder how the animals in the zoo feel when the weather is this cold? I worry that their fur and feathers will not keep them warm enough. It bothers me to think that the animals may be cold. Tomorrow, I will ask my teacher about how animals keep warm.

Ashley

Put a check after the sentences below that are written in the first person.

1. I am happy about our trip to the zoo. _____

2. The three girls watched the polar bear dance. _____

3. The zookeeper let me hold the owl. _____

4. I could feel the smooth skin of the snake. _____

5. The old monkey fussed at the younger ones. _____

Third Person Voice

Read the story below.

> Two kangaroos shared a cage at the zoo. Matilda kept her side of the cage as neat a pin. Elsie never picked up her belongings. Matilda often thought that Elsie was lazy about housekeeping, but she never fussed at Elsie about it. The two kangaroos lived peacefully together.

The author wrote about the kangaroos as if she were an invisible person in their cage. They did not know she was there, but she pretended to see and hear them all of the time. She could even pretend to know what they were thinking. When an author writes about someone else and pretends to know what he says, does, and thinks, the author is writing in the **voice of the third person**. Remember, when the author is the person speaking in the story, that is the **voice of the first person**. Write a 1 by the sentences written in the first person. Write a 3 by the sentences written in the third person.

1. _____ The boys were excited about the new movie.

2. _____ I am anxious to go to the zoo.

3. _____ Please walk with me to the hippopotamus exhibit.

4. _____ Seven seals swam happily back and forth in the pool.

Idiom Mania

Idioms are sayings or figures of speech which can be quite confusing if taken literally. Explain the meaning of each idiom below. Then choose one idiom and illustrate its literal meaning with a drawing on the back of this page. For instance, "She has a heart of gold" means that she is very kind. The literal picture would show a girl whose heart is actually made out of gold.

Idiom	Explanation
1. It's none of your bees-wax.	
2. I put my foot in my mouth.	
3. It's water under the bridge.	
4. Don't let the cat out of the bag.	
5. She's too big for her britches.	
6. She's hot under the collar.	
7. I'm in the doghouse.	
8. Don't pass the buck.	
9. Let's break the ice.	
10. Don't spill the beans.	

Idioms

An **idiom** is a phrase or expression that has a meaning different from what the words suggest in their usual meaning.

    Example: My little brother gets in my hair!

           This doesn't mean that the brother actually touches hair. It means he is a pest.

In each box below, there is an idiom. Draw a picture of the actual meaning of the words. Under the picture, write what the idiom really means.

1. I'm a chicken when it comes to climbing trees.	2. Doing math is a piece of cake.
3. Kathy is the teacher's pet.	4. Jimmy is in hot water with the coach.

What Does It Mean?

Explain the meaning of each phrase below.

1. Kit and caboodle _____

2. Get your goat _____

3. Cold feet _____

4. On the house _____

5. Drop me a line _____

6. Green thumb _____

7. Turn a deaf ear _____

8. Eat like a bird _____

9. Throw in the towel _____

10. Hit the books _____

11. Get the picture _____

12. Crack a book _____

13. Keep a straight face _____

14. Hit a bull's eye _____

15. Have a heart _____

Complete the Analogies

Words can relate to each other in different ways. Sometimes they are opposites.
Sometimes they are similar. Sometimes they have to do with the same thing.
There are many ways in which they can relate.

Analogies are a way to show the relationship between words. First,
two words are presented that compare in some way to each other.
Then a third word is provided. A fourth word must be found that will
relate to the third word in the same way the first two words relate.

Example: *hot* is to *cold* as *up* is to _____*down*_____

In this example, the word pairs are opposites.

Example: *up* is to *high* as *down* is to _____*low*_____

In this example, the word pairs are similar.

Can you complete these analogies?

1. pen is to paper as chalk is to_____

2. dog is to bark as a duck is to_____

3. bedroom is to sleep as kitchen is to _____

4. east is to west as north is to _____

5. ear is to hearing as eye is to _____

6. fur is to cat as scales are to_____

7. hockey is to arena as baseball is to_____

8. toe is to foot as finger is to_____

9. screw is to screwdriver as nail is to _____

10. in is to out as near is to _____

11. man is to woman as boy is to _____

12. bear is to forest as monkey is to _____

Practicing Analogies

Read the words that are being compared. Fill in each blank with the best word from the word box.

Cat is to **pet**   as   **car** is to **vehicle.**

bird	**goal**	**night**	**skin**	**winter**
coloring	**head**	**quack**	**swim**	**year**

1. Chicken is to cluck as duck is to _____.

2. Banana is to peel as apple is to _____.

3. Football is to touchdown as hockey is to _____.

4. Bird is to fly as fish is to _____.

5. Leaf is to tree as feather is to _____.

6. Pencil is to write as crayon is to _____.

7. Light is to day as dark is to _____.

8. Day is to week as month is to _____.

9. Hot is to summer as cold is to _____.

10. Roof is to house as hat is to _____.

Scattered Analogies

Analogies are comparisons.

Example: Nephew is to uncle as niece is to aunt.

Complete each analogy below.

1. _____ is to wings as fish is to fins.

2. Tennis is to _____ as baseball is to bat.

3. Jim is to James as Betsy is to _____.

4. Author is to story as poet is to _____.

5. Wide is to narrow as _____ is to short.

6. Lincoln is to _____ as Roosevelt is to Theodore.

7. _____ is to shell as pea is to pod.

8. Hard is to _____ as big is to small.

9. Dirt is to forest as _____ is to desert.

10. Frame is to picture as curtain is to _____.

11. Sing is to song as _____ is to book.

12. Braces are to _____ as contact lenses are to eyes.

13. _____ is to flake as rain is to drop.

14. Scissors is to _____ as pen is to write.

15. Hat is to head as _____ is to foot.

16. Hammer is to nail as screwdriver is to _____.

17. Necklace is to neck as _____ is to finger.

18. Fingers are to _____ as toes are to feet.

19. _____ is to pig as neigh is to horse.

20. Second is to _____ as day is to week.

All Together Now

Each set of words belongs to a different group. Classify the group by writing its name on the line.

1. Oak, maple, and pine are _____.

2. Kenneth, Brent, and Ryan are _____.

3. Main, Elm, and First are _____.

4. London, Paris, and Los Angeles are_____.

5. Ladybug, fly, and grasshopper are _____.

6. *The Cat in the Hat, Charlotte's Web,* and *Goodnight Moon* are _____.

7. Happy, sad, and angry are _____.

8. Norway, China, and Peru are _____.

9. Doll, top, and blocks are _____.

10. Jeans, sweatshirt, and pajamas are _____.

11. Pacific, Atlantic, and Indian are_____.

12. Sandals, loafers, and slippers are_____.

13. Corn, broccoli, and asparagus are _____.

14. Turkey, pastrami, and peanut butter and jelly are_____.

15. Baseball, football, and hockey are _____.

Categorizing

In the word box below are 42 words, each of which belongs in one of the six categories—wood, metals, water, space, colors, or furniture. Place each of the words under the correct category. For example, **bay** would belong in the water category. Seven words belong under each category.

bay	lumber	dresser	chest	steel	iron	chartreuse
Mars	tin	tan	pond	blue	forest	aluminum
rocket	mirror	scarlet	orbit	green	nail	weightless
creek	oak	bronze	board	river	rocker	countdown
sea	lake	red	cabinet	beige	walnut	pencil
lamp	ocean	moon	couch	copper	astronaut	maple

wood

_____
_____
_____
_____
_____
_____
_____

metals

_____
_____
_____
_____
_____
_____
_____

water

_____
_____
_____
_____
_____
_____
_____

space

_____
_____
_____
_____
_____
_____
_____

colors

_____
_____
_____
_____
_____
_____
_____

furniture

_____
_____
_____
_____
_____
_____
_____

Summarizing

When you write a summary, you pick out the main idea and a few details. Leave out the extra words and facts that take up space and time. Practice summarizing by reading the list of facts and ideas about frogs and toads. Put a green **S** by the ones that should go in a summary. Put a red **E** by the extra words.

_____ green and slimy	_____ amphibians	_____ live near water
_____ eat insects	_____ are funny	_____ strong legs
_____ croak and sing	_____ swim	_____ baby tadpoles
_____ lay eggs	_____ bulging eyes	_____ webbed feet
_____ big heads	_____ short necks	_____ like lily pads

Write a short paragraph about frogs and toads, using the important details you marked green.

_____

_____

_____

_____

_____

Practice Summarizing

Write a paragraph about your favorite animal. You can use the facts from your science book or an encyclopedia. Be sure to begin each sentence with a capital letter and end each sentence with correct punctuation.

_____

_____

_____

_____

_____

_____

_____

Write two sentences that summarize your paragraph. Give the main idea and the most important details.

_____

_____

_____

_____

Baby Animals

Read the story. Cross out the extra details. Rewrite the remaining sentences to make a summary.

Every animal has babies. Sometimes the mother takes care of the baby until it can take care of itself. Baby animals are cute. Sometimes the whole group of animals cares for the babies. Baby bears are called cubs. Cubs like to eat honey. Baby animals must eat. Mothers and fathers protect their babies. The babies are small and cannot find food for themselves. Some baby animals, like kangaroos, live in pouches. Other baby animals travel on their mothers' backs.   Possums and monkeys carry babies on their backs. Baby animals are fun to watch.

Summary

_____

_____

_____

_____

_____

_____

_____

_____

_____

_____

Your Day

On the blank lines, write in order everything you can remember doing today (beginning with waking up).

_____   _____

_____   _____

_____   _____

_____   _____

_____   _____

_____   _____

Now take what you wrote above, and group the ideas together under three or four headings (such as *getting ready* or *being at school*). Write your group names here.

_____   _____

_____   _____

_____   _____

Finally, write a summary of your day, using your group names. Write the summary in no more than three sentences.

_____

_____

_____

_____

_____

_____

Read All About It

Find an article in a newspaper or magazine that you think is interesting.
Read the article and then answer these questions.

What is the topic of the article?

_____

_____

_____

_____

What new things did you learn about the topic?

_____

_____

_____

_____

What else would you like to learn about the topic?

_____

_____

_____

_____

Why is this article interesting?

_____

_____

_____

_____

Pick a Part

Read a book. Write about your favorite parts.

The part that was the funniest was _____

_____

_____

_____

The part that was the saddest was _____

_____

_____

_____

The part that was the most unbelievable was _____

_____

_____

_____

The part I liked best was _____

_____

because _____

_____

Character Web

You can see this is a special kind of web. It is a **character web.**

Read a book. Draw a picture of the main character in the center circle. In each of the spaces, answer the question about the character.

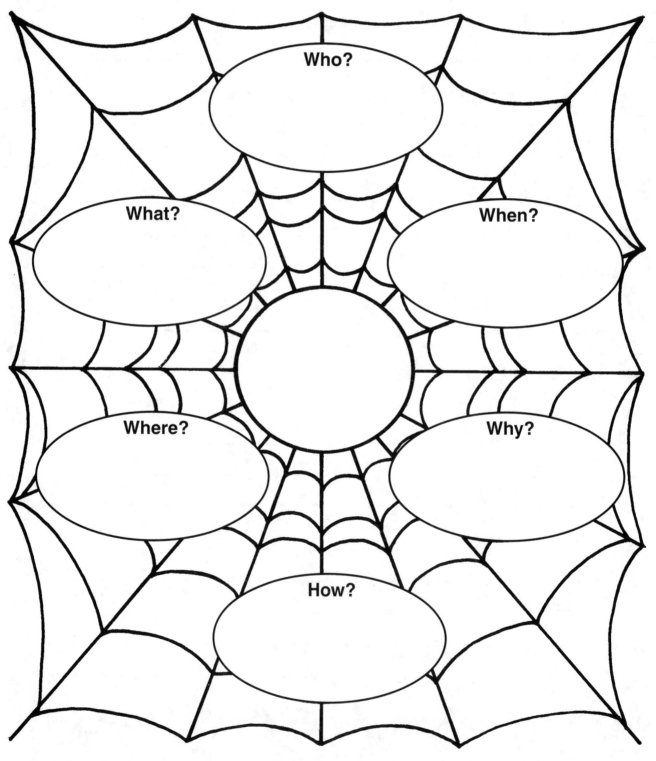

Complete the Sentences

Complete each sentence. Draw a picture of yourself in the box.

1. My name is _____

   _____.

2. I am_____years old.

3. I like to_____

   _____.

4. I am best at_____.

5. My friends think that I am _____.

6. My parents think that I am _____.

7. I wish I had a _____ .

8. I wish I could _____.

9. My favorite thing about myself is _____

   _____.

10. I am proud of_____.

Write a Sentence

Write a sentence for each picture.

 1. _____

_____

_____

 2. _____

_____

_____

 3. _____

_____

_____

 4. _____

_____

_____

 5. _____

_____

_____

 6. _____

_____

_____

 7. _____

_____

Start with a Noun and a Verb

Match each noun to a verb.

dog	**twinkles**
bird	**meows**
cat	**gallops**
horse	**learn**
star	**play**
sun	**sings**
students	**barks**
children	**shines**

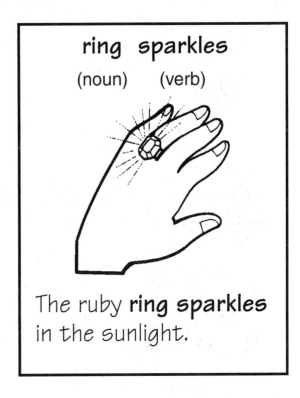

ring sparkles
(noun) (verb)

The ruby **ring sparkles** in the sunlight.

Write a sentence for each noun/verb pair above.

1. _____

2. _____

3. _____

4. _____

5. _____

6. _____

7. _____

8. _____

Sentence Expansions

The sentences below are complete because they each have a subject and a predicate. However, they are the simplest sentences possible. An example has been done for you.

> Boy walks.
>
> The small, tired boy walks slowly to his bed and climbs under the covers.

Add words to each sentence to make it more interesting.

1. Girl disappeared.

   _____

   _____

2. Horses galloped.

   _____

   _____

3. Dishes broke.

   _____

   _____

4. Radio plays.

   _____

   _____

5. Motorcycle roared.

   _____

   _____

6. Artist paints.

   _____

   _____

What Do You Think?

You have learned that every sentence must begin with a capital letter and end with a period, question mark, or exclamation point. You have also learned that a sentence must be a complete thought. A sentence needs to have enough information to make sense. It needs to ask you a complete question or tell you a complete idea. There are 10 incomplete sentences on this page. Rewrite the sentences to make them complete.

1. Jennifer wants to

   _____

2. Yesterday, while it was raining, I

   _____

3. Do you

   _____

4. all the way down the hill

   _____

5. is very annoying

   _____

6. I wish I had

   _____

7. Did they try

   _____

8. Watch out for the

   _____

9. is a big, scary monster

   _____

10. jumped into the spaghetti

   _____

Word Muncher

A word muncher is a kind of monster that only eats parts of sentences. You can tell that a word muncher has been here because these sentences are full of holes. See if you can save these sentences by filling in the missing subjects or predicates.

1. The word muncher _____

   _____

2. _____ (was, were) very hungry.

3. _____ jumped up and down on my bed.

4. Twelve gorillas _____

   _____

5. _____ fell into the trunk of my neighbor's car.

6. A tiny little dancer _____

   _____

7. _____ sat on a mushroom.

8. A large box of soap _____

   _____

9. My Aunt Gertrude _____

   _____

10. _____ (is, are) sloshing around in my pocket.

11. _____(is, are) tumbling down the front steps.

12. My friend, Tiffany, _____

    _____

13. _____ bit my ear!

14. _____escaped from (his, her, their, its) cage.

15. Your elbow _____

    _____

Combining Sentences

Combine these simple sentences into compound sentences. **Compound sentences** will combine two or more complete sentences with commas and conjunctions.

1. Camels have big, flat feet.

   Their feet do not sink into the soft sand.

   _____

   _____

2. Apples contain vitamin C.

   Apples have very little sodium.

   Apples contain vitamin A.

   _____

   _____

3. Rain forests receive four to eight meters of rain per year.

   Rain forests are located near the equator.

   _____

   _____

4. A crab is covered by a hard shell.

   A crab has 10 jointed legs.

   A crab's eyes rest on raised stalks.

   _____

   _____

5. The whale shark is very strong and powerful.

   It eats only plankton and small fish.

   _____

   _____

Let Me Tell You

The **topic sentence** may be the most important sentence in a paragraph because it tells the reader what the paragraph is about. Underline the topic sentence in the following paragraph.

> Trees give us many things. They give us shade on hot days. Their wood helps to build our homes. Their leaves give oxygen to the air to help us breathe. They are beautiful to look at, too. What would we do without trees?

Create a topic sentence for each main idea below.

1. Dancing

   Dancing is a great way to exercise.

2. Encyclopedias

   _____

3. Running shoes

   _____

4. Dogs

   _____

5. Bubble gum

   _____

6. Winter

   _____

7. Grandparents

   _____

8. Birthdays

   _____

9. Vegetables

   _____

10. Books

    _____

Let Me Tell You (cont.)

Write topic sentences for each paragraph below.

There are lions and tigers in outdoor pens. Wild birds are flying in large, tree-filled cages. Also a visitor at the zoo can see snakes and reptiles of many different sizes. My favorite thing to see at the zoo is the monkey that swings on a trapeze in a cage by the popcorn stands.

First, you must listen carefully in class. Next, you must study for your tests and quizzes. Finally, you must do all the homework the teacher assigns. If you follow these steps, good grades will be yours!

It starts slowly and then destroys everything in its way. It can ruin homes and land. It can kill people and animals. So before you strike a match, remember how dangerous fire can be.

Check your paragraphs. Do all of your topic sentences make sense in the paragraphs? Do all the sentences relate to each topic sentence?

We Need Some Body

The **body of a paragraph** consists of the sentences which tell about the subject. It is the main part of the paragraph. This is where one uses specific details such as who, what, when, where, why, and how. All the sentences of a paragraph make up the body, except for the first (topic sentence) and last (closing) sentences. The body paragraph sentences need to be related to the topic sentence, and they need to help explain the topic and make it more interesting. The sentences need to be arranged in an order that makes sense.

Here are three topic sentences along with their closing sentences. Put a letter in the blank to show which body sentences belong between the two sentences.

1. Students should be required to wear uniforms to school. _____ I think uniforms would be a good idea because students would be more focused on school.

2. Stormy days are great. _____ So, you see, every cloud has a silver lining.

3. My cat is an alien from Jupiter. _____ I just hope they don't come back for her, ever.

A. If you were to spend any time at all at my house, you would agree with me. First of all, you would probably see her slowly climbing up the wallpaper until she got to the ceiling. At the ceiling she might leap out into the room and land on someone, or she might jump onto the ceiling fan and go for a ride until she got too dizzy to hold on any longer. Then, she might play for about two hours with her imaginary enemies. This is the funniest thing to see. She attacks and retreats as if there were another creature there, but we can't see it. Another thing she does is to crawl into strange places. We might find her in the bottom of the laundry hamper or behind a chest of drawers. She walks around with dirty socks and dust balls hanging off her fur. Once, she proudly walked through the living room, covered in flour! We all looked at each other, wondering where she'd been. It's obvious to anyone who has seen her that she is from another planet.

B. First of all, the cost of a back-to-school wardrobe would be reduced, and there would be no need to dress to impress. Secondly, students would be able to get right to work instead of spending time looking around to see what everyone else is wearing. Students would spend less time thinking about and shopping for clothes and more time getting homework done. Finally, students would behave better while dressed in their school uniforms. The uniforms would not be "fun" or "play" clothes, so students would be more serious while in school. They could always change after school.

C. People complain about them, but I think they have some advantages. On a stormy day we can have a fire in the fireplace or a cup of hot chocolate and play games with our families. These things make us feel cozy. If the electricity goes out, we can play "sardines" by candlelight. If the storm is really bad, school will be closed!

We Need Some Body (cont.)

Here are some unfinished paragraphs for you to complete by writing the body sentences. Be sure that each sentence you write supports the topic sentence.

1. Last night, space invaders landed in my backyard.

   _____

   _____

   _____

   I was lucky to get out with my life!

   (*Writing hint:* What happened? Were you afraid?)

2. The pet you have is the most adorable pet I have ever seen.

   _____

   _____

   _____

   May I take her home?

   (*Writing hint:* What kind of pet is this? What makes the pet so adorable?)

3. I would like to go to Disneyland next weekend.

   _____

   _____

   _____

   So now it is clear why I really need to go to Disneyland.

   (*Writing hint:* What are your best, most convincing reasons?)

Finally!

The final sentence of your paragraph is the concluding or closing sentence. It comes after all the details and explanations have been included in the body sentences of your paragraph. The closing sentence needs to express the specific feeling, attitude, or point of the paragraph.

Here are some paragraph starts. Finish them with a few more details and a closing sentence.

✦   ✦   ✦

   I would make a fantastic president! First of all, I am used to bossing people around. I am always telling my little sister (brother) what to do. Also, I know how to say things so that they sound really good, no matter what. _____

_____

_____

_____

_____

✦   ✦   ✦

   Winter is not so bad at the beach. Sometimes it is still warm. People at the beach sometimes have their best weather in the winter. Another thing about the beach in the winter is that there are no tourists. The beach is nicer because there are no crowds and a lot less litter. _____

_____

_____

_____

_____

✦   ✦   ✦

   Vegetables were put on earth to torture little kids. First, they are green. Why would anyone want to eat something that is green? Next, they have strange textures. Take celery, for example. _____

_____

_____

_____

_____

Complete the Paragraph

A **paragraph** is a group of sentences that tells about one topic.
The sentences in a paragraph should be written in order.

On the lines below, write a paragraph, using the words provided for the beginning of each sentence.

Imagine you are the teacher for a day. What will you do in your classroom?

If I were teacher for a day, first _____

_____

_____

Next, _____

_____

_____

Then, _____

_____

_____

Finally, _____

_____

_____

_____

_____

What's Missing!

Your paragraph assignment is missing some sentences. You can read some of what you wrote. The rest has mysteriously vanished. Now you will have to write parts of your paragraph over again.

I like all the things in my room, but there are three things I especially like. One of my favorite things is _____

_____

because _____

_____.

Another thing I really like is _____

_____

because _____

_____.

Finally, I like _____

_____

because _____

_____

_____.

I'm so glad I have these three things in my room.

Favorite Holiday

What is your favorite holiday? _____

After deciding, write a paragraph about your favorite holiday.

Beginning: In a complete sentence, tell which holiday is your favorite.

_____

_____

Middle: In several complete sentences, tell why it is your favorite and how you and your family celebrate it.

_____

_____

_____

_____

_____

Ending: Tell the name of the holiday again and repeat why it is your favorite.

_____

_____

Favorite Holiday (cont.)

First, revise and edit the previous paragraph about your favorite holiday. Next, write your final paragraph by putting together all three parts: the beginning, the middle, and the end. Remember to indent, capitalize, and use the correct punctuation.

_____

_____

_____

_____

_____

_____

_____

_____

Illustrate your favorite holiday in the box below.

Spotlight on You

Think of one of your favorite parts of a story. Draw a picture of **yourself** in this part of the story. Write a paragraph describing what **you** would do if **you** were a character in this story.

_____

_____

_____

_____

_____

_____

Mind Mapping

When preparing to write, you can make a diagram of your ideas. A diagram of ideas is called a **mind map**.

Look at the mind map Nick made for his birthday party.

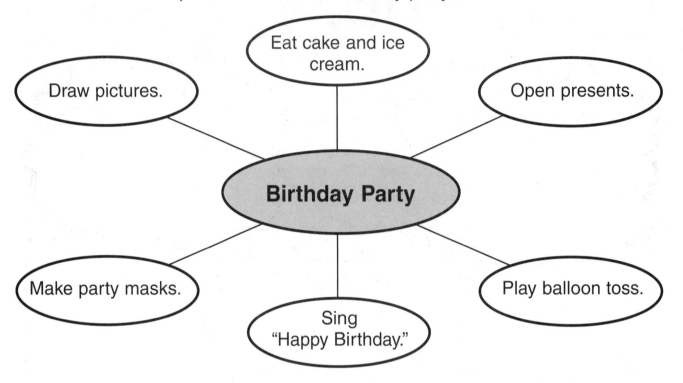

Make a mind map of six things you can do on a rainy day.

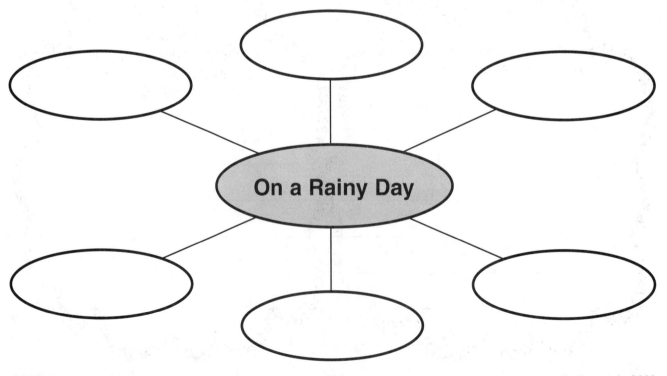

Dreams Make Stories Come True

It's time to write a story. Imagine you are preparing to write a story. Think of a character that would make a great hero. Then complete the story diagram on this page.

Author: _____
(your name)

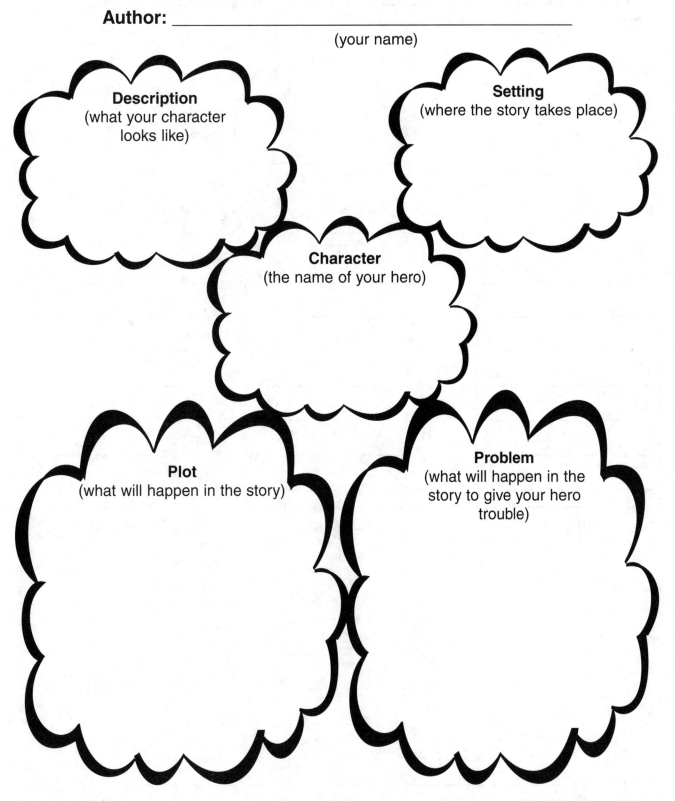

Description
(what your character looks like)

Setting
(where the story takes place)

Character
(the name of your hero)

Plot
(what will happen in the story)

Problem
(what will happen in the story to give your hero trouble)

Getting Your Paragraph Organized

Use this form to help you organize your paragraphs. Write a topic sentence in the circle at the top. Write three supporting ideas in the rectangles. Write your conclusion sentence in the triangle. Use these sentences to build your paragraph, adding any other words and details that you need to make it complete.

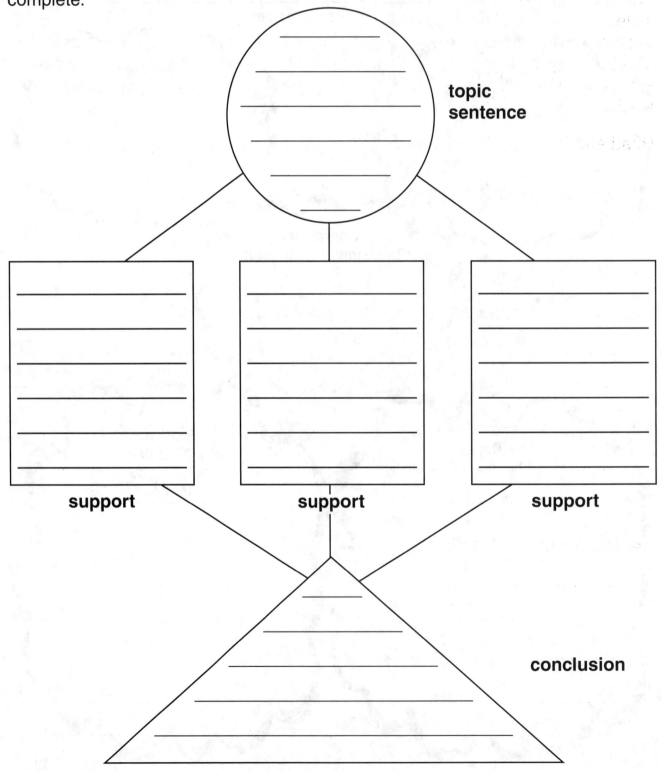

topic
sentence

support   support   support

conclusion

Writing by Sense

One of the best ways to write descriptively is to use your senses. Think about how something looks, smells, sounds, tastes, and feels, and then write about it, keeping those senses in mind. For example, instead of writing, "The flower smells nice," you can write, "The sweet nectar of the flowers tickles my nose." This gives an idea of exactly how the flower smells. For another example, instead of writing, "The puppies are cute," write, "The playful puppies roll over each other and tumble into a ball of fur and pink noses." This gives an idea of exactly how the puppies look. The sentences that use the senses to describe are much more interesting to read, and they make the images seem real for the reader.

Read and follow each direction below, using "sense" writing.

1. In a sentence, describe how a rainbow looks.

_____

_____

2. In a sentence, describe how a dirty dog smells.

_____

_____

3. In a sentence, describe how bacon sounds when it is frying.

_____

_____

4. In a sentence, describe how pizza tastes.

_____

_____

5. In a sentence, describe how a teddy bear feels.

_____

_____

Practicing Similes

Similes compare two different things, using *like* or *as*. "The cat was as still as a statue," is an example of a simile.

To write similes, complete each comparison found below.

1. An orange is as _____ as _____ .

2. A puppy is as _____ as _____ .

3. A star is as _____ as _____ .

4. Ice is as _____ as _____ .

5. The water is as _____ as _____ .

6. The rock is as _____ as _____ .

7. The color is as _____ as _____ .

8. The clouds are as _____ as _____ .

9. Snow is as _____ as _____ .

10. My kitten is as _____ as _____ .

Similes

> A **simile** is a figure of speech in which two things are compared with the words *like* or *as*.
>
> **Example:** He moved as quick as a wink.

Complete the following similes.

1. As blind as _____

2. As cool as _____

3. As mad as _____

4. As happy as _____

5. As busy as _____

6. As neat as _____

7. As flat as _____

8. As pale as _____

9. As easy as _____

10. As proud as _____

11. As fresh as _____

12. As hard as _____

13. As light as _____

14. As sharp as _____

15. As wise as _____

Creating Metaphors

Metaphors compare two different things without using *like* or *as*. Use comparison words to complete the metaphors below.

1. The cloud is a _____ .

2. The tree is a _____ .

3. The eagle is _____ .

4. The ice was _____ .

5. The moon was _____ .

6. The wolf was _____ .

7. The rain is _____ .

8. The rock is _____ .

9. The baby is _____ .

10. The ocean is _____ .

Simile and Metaphor Review

> A **simile** is a way of comparing two things by using the words *like* or *as*.
>
> A **metaphor** describes by comparing one thing to another without using the words *like* or *as*.

Read the sentences below. Put an **S** in the box if it is a simile. Put an **M** in the box if it is a metaphor.

☐   1. The wall was as hard as a rock.

☐   2. The ice was as slick as glass.

☐   3. The moon was a bright diamond in the sky.

☐   4. The cat is as soft as velvet.

☐   5. The flock of birds made a rainbow in the sky.

☐   6. The lake was as smooth as a fine piece of china.

☐   7. The puffy clouds are like cotton balls hanging in the sky.

☐   8. The star is a beacon lighting the way.

☐   9. The small child playing in the garden was as playful as a puppy.

☐   10. The earth is like a round marble.

Writing Stories in Parts

Use the next two pages to create a story about one of the following topics. Write the story in three parts: introduction, body, and conclusion.

- The Day I Got Lost
- My Pet Saved the Day
- When I Grow Up

- Best Friends Have an Adventure
- My Adventures in Space
- The Most Unforgettable Day of My Life

Part One: Introduction or beginning

_____

_____

_____

_____

_____

_____

Part Two: Body or middle of the story

_____

_____

_____

_____

_____

_____

_____

Writing Stories in Parts (cont.)

Part Two *(cont.):*

_____

_____

_____

_____

Part Three: Conclusion or ending of story

_____

_____

_____

_____

_____

_____

Check yourself.

1. Did you begin the story with an attention getter? ☐

2. Did you tell in the beginning who was in the story? ☐

3. Did you give lots of details in the middle? ☐

4. Did you bring the story to a close in the ending? ☐

5. Did you check your spelling? ☐

6. Did you write neatly? ☐

Practice What You've Learned

Write a descriptive paragraph about the place where you sleep. Remember all you have learned about writing descriptive paragraphs. When you go home today, look at the place and see how many of the details you included in your description.

_____

_____

_____

_____

_____

_____

_____

_____

_____

_____

_____

_____

Popcorn

Pretend you are a kernel of popcorn. Describe what it is like to be a kernel while all those around you are popping. Include how it feels to burst open as a large, white, fluffy piece of popcorn yourself!

_____

_____

_____

_____

_____

_____

_____

_____

_____

_____

_____

_____

Honeybee

Imagine you are a honeybee on a warm summer day. Describe what life is like for you. Make your story realistic, sweet, or funny. Be sure to add plenty of detail, keeping in mind all that you have learned about creative writing.

_____

_____

_____

_____

_____

_____

_____

_____

_____

_____

_____

_____

_____

_____

_____

_____

Writing an Invitation

An invitation has five parts. It is important to use all five. If not, your party guests might not get to your party on time, they might go to the wrong address, or they might arrive for the party on the wrong day. Pretend that you are having a birthday party. Use the example below as a guide to creating invitations to welcome friends to your party.

Heading: the date

Greeting: includes the word *Dear* and the name of the person to whom the invitation is sent

Body: includes the date, the time, and the location of the party (You might also want to include the type of clothes to wear.)

Closing: ends the invitation (examples: *Your friend*, *Yours truly*, or *Sincerely*,)

Signature: the sender's name

                                                             #6455 Practice and Learn

Writing a Thank-You Note

The object of this lesson is to write a thank-you note. A thank-you note has five parts. Follow these steps to write a thank-you note.

Heading: the date

Greeting: includes the word *Dear* and the name of the person to whom the thank you is sent

Body: says thank you by stating what the writer is thankful for, what he or she plans to do with the gift, and that the writer will think of the giver when using the gift

Closing: ends the thank you note (examples: *Love, Sincerely,* or *With thanks,*)

Signature: the sender's name

Writing a Friendly Letter

A friendly letter has five parts. Use the definitions below to write a friendly letter.

Heading: the date

Greeting: the word *Dear* followed by the name of the person you are writing

Body: the main part and the message you are writing

Closing: ends the letter with words like *Yours truly, Sincerely,* or *Your friend,*

Signature: your name

Writing Directions

Directions tell the reader exactly how to do something. Since you will be giving directions, it is very important for you to write down all the necessary steps in the correct order so that your reader will understand what to do.

Try your hand at writing directions. Pretend you are having friends over for lunch. You are going to serve your favorite sandwich. Write the directions for making your favorite sandwich.

1. _____

2. _____

3. _____

4. _____

5. _____

6. _____

7. _____

8. _____

Curves

Trace the shapes and then try the curves on your own.

Loops

Trace the shapes and then try the loops on your own.

Slants and Curves

Trace the shapes and then try the slants and curves on your own.

 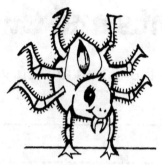

acrobatic

arachnid

Trace the letters and words and then practice them on your own.

a   a   a   a   a

a   a   a   a   a

apple ant

busy beaver

Trace the letters and words and then practice them on your own.

B B B B B

b b b b b

busy buy

clever

cow

Trace the letters and words and then practice them on your own.

C C C C C

x x x x x

cream cow

divine

dessert

Trace the letters and words and then practice them on your own.

𝒟 𝒟 𝒟 𝒟 𝒟

𝒹 𝒹 𝒹 𝒹 𝒹

daisy dear

elegant
elephant

Trace the letters and words and then practice them on your own.

egg eating

fabulous
fudge

Trace the letters and words and then practice them on your own.

$\mathcal{F}$ $\mathcal{F}$ $\mathcal{F}$ $\mathcal{F}$ $\mathcal{F}$

f f f f f

friend farm

graceful
gazelle

Trace the letters and words and then practice them on your own.

great goose

happy

hippo

Trace the letters and words and then practice them on your own.

$\mathcal{H}$ $\mathcal{H}$ $\mathcal{H}$ $\mathcal{H}$ $\mathcal{H}$ $\mathcal{H}$

h   *h*   *h*   *h*   *h*

hand heart

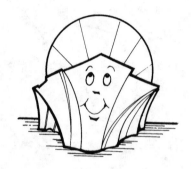

incredible

iceberg

Trace the letters and words and then practice them on your own.

l   l   l   l   l

i   i   i   i   i

inch icicle

jumping

jack rabbit

Trace the letters and words and then practice them on your own.

juice joy

kicking
kangaroo

Trace the letters and words and then practice them on your own.

K K K K K

l l l l l

kite knee

luscious
lollipop

Trace the letters and words and then practice them on your own.

L L L L L L

l l l l l l

lamp learn

marvelous

milkshake

Trace the letters and words and then practice them on your own.

m m m m m m

m m m m m m

main monkey

nifty
necktie

Trace the letters and words and then practice them on your own.

$\mathcal{N}$ $\mathcal{N}$ $\mathcal{N}$ $\mathcal{N}$ $\mathcal{N}$

$\mathcal{M}$ $\mathcal{M}$ $\mathcal{M}$ $\mathcal{M}$ $\mathcal{M}$

niece   north

odd

octopus

Trace the letters and words and then practice them on your own.

O O O O O

o o o o o

otter old

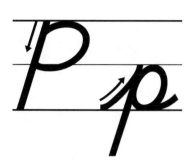

perky
pet

Trace the letters and words and then practice them on your own.

P   *P*   *P*   *P*   *P*

p   *p*   *p*   *p*   *p*

panda perch

quick

quail

Trace the letters and words and then practice them on your own.

2 2 2 2 2

q q q q q

queen quilt

refined

rat

Trace the letters and words and then practice them on your own.

R R R R R

r r r r r

royal race

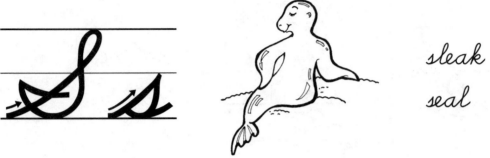

sleak

seal

Trace the letters and words and then practice them on your own.

sun sound

tasty

treat

Trace the letters and words and then practice them on your own.

T T T T T

t t t t t

tall trade

unique

umbrella

Trace the letters and words and then practice them on your own.

$\mathcal{U}$ $\mathcal{U}$ $\mathcal{U}$ $\mathcal{U}$ $\mathcal{U}$

u u u u u

uncle useful

venomous
viper

Trace the letters and words and then practice them on your own.

very voice

wiggly
worm

Trace the letters and words and then practice them on your own.

W W W W W

w w w w w

wand   wool

excellent

xylophone

Trace the letters and words and then practice them on your own.

$\mathcal{X}$ $\mathcal{X}$ $\mathcal{X}$ $\mathcal{X}$ $\mathcal{X}$

x x x x x

exact oxen

yummy

yam

Trace the letters and words and then practice them on your own.

Y Y Y Y Y Y

y y y y y y

yam yeast

zealous

zebra

Trace the letters and words and then practice them on your own.

zipper zoo

Understanding Place Value

 This block represents 100.

This block represents 10.

☐ This block represents 1.

These blocks together can represent other numbers. For example,

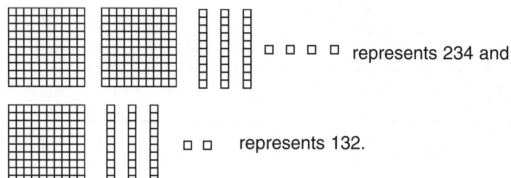 represents 234 and

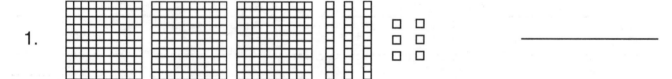 represents 132.

Write a number for each set of blocks.

1. 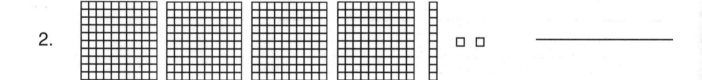 _____

2. _____

3. _____

4. 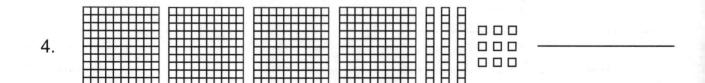 _____

Ones, Tens, and Hundreds

Look at the number blocks. Complete the place value charts.

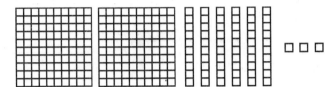

hundreds	tens	ones

1.

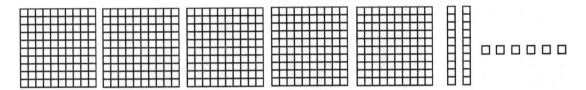

hundreds	tens	ones

2.

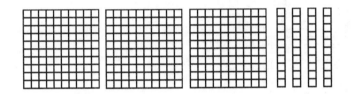

hundreds	tens	ones

3.

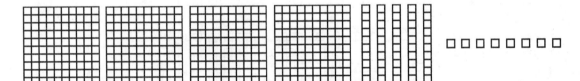

hundreds	tens	ones

4.

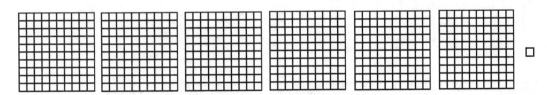

hundreds	tens	ones

5.

Which Is It?

Write the number that each set of blocks represents.

1.  _____

2.  _____

3.  _____

4. 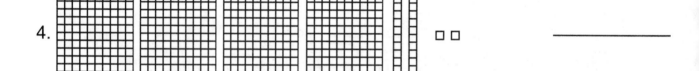 _____

5. 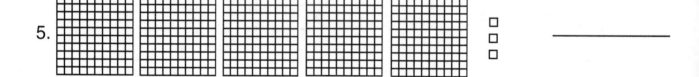 _____

6. 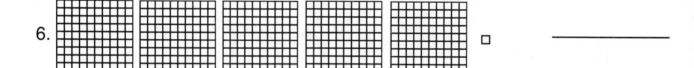 _____

7. 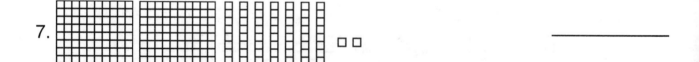 _____

8. 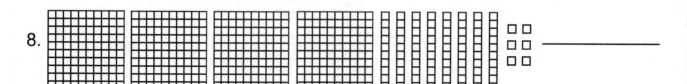 _____

Rounding

Sometimes you will just need the general value of a number. To get it, you will round. Rounding is not the exact number, but it is close.

There are some basic rules for rounding.

+ If the number is 5 or above, round up to the next tens place. For example, 26 is rounded to 30.
+ If the number is less than 5, round down to the last tens. For example, 13 is rounded to 10.
+ If the number is more than 100, round up to the nearest hundreds place for numbers bigger than 50. For example, 162 is rounded to 200.
+ If the number is more than 100, round down to the last hundreds place for numbers less than 50. For example, 123 is rounded to 100.

Now it is your turn. For each number given, circle the correct rounded number.

1. 48 → 40 or 50?

2. 62 → 60 or 70?

3. 93 → 90 or 100?

4. 15 → 10 or 20?

5. 67 → 60 or 70?

6. 11 → 10 or 20?

7. 19 → 10 or 20?

8. 408 → 400 or 500?

9. 559 → 500 or 600?

10. 232 → 200 or 300?

11. 875 → 800 or 900?

12. 845 → 800 or 900?

13. 341 → 300 or 400?

14. 633 → 600 or 700?

15. 196 → 100 or 200?

16. 255 → 250 or 260?

How Odd!

Odd numbers are all whole numbers that cannot be divided equally in half as whole numbers. Color the odd numbers.

1	2	3	5	4	7	9	6	11
8	13	10	12	15	14	16	17	18
19	20	21	23	22	25	27	24	29
26	31	28	30	33	32	34	35	36
37	38	39	41	40	43	45	42	47
44	49	46	48	51	50	52	53	54
55	56	57	59	58	61	63	60	65
62	67	64	66	69	68	70	71	72
73	74	75	77	76	79	81	78	83
80	85	82	84	87	86	88	89	90
91	92	93	95	94	97	99	96	0

Even Steven

Even numbers are all whole numbers that can be divided equally in half and remain whole numbers. Color the even numbers.

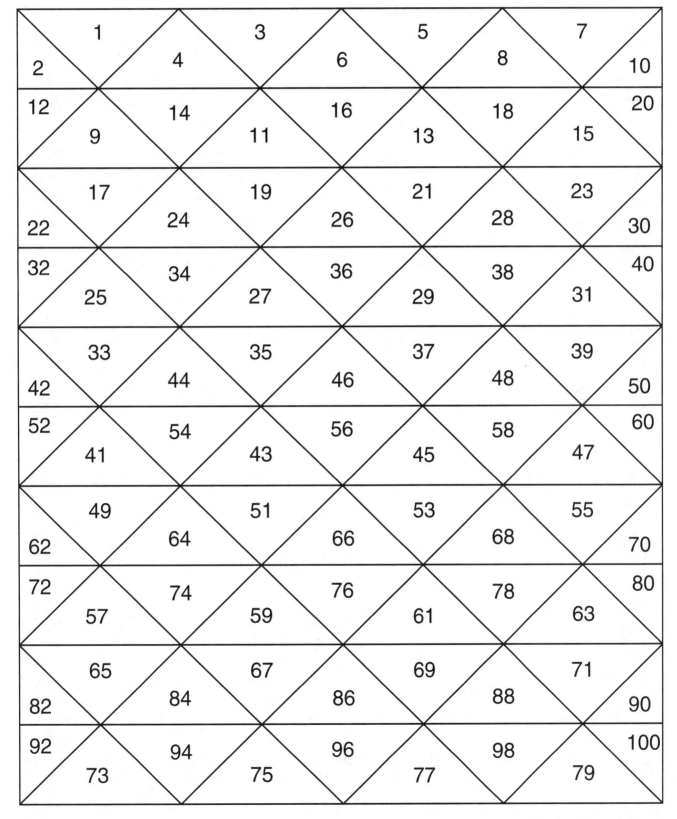

Add It Up

Find the sums to the addition problems below.

1. 1 + 3 = _____   11. 7 + 7 = _____

2. 5 + 8 = _____   12. 3 + 5 = _____

3. 3 + 7 = _____   13. 4 + 2 = _____

4. 9 + 3 = _____   14. 9 + 2 = _____

5. 6 + 1 = _____   15. 6 + 9 = _____

6. 2 + 4 = _____   16. 3 + 2 = _____

7. 1 + 2 = _____   17. 2 + 0 = _____

8. 8 + 0 = _____   18. 6 + 2 = _____

9. 0 + 3 = _____   19. 9 + 5 = _____

10. 4 + 6 = _____   20. 1 + 6 = _____

The Cat's Meow

Cross out each answer on the cat as you solve the problems.

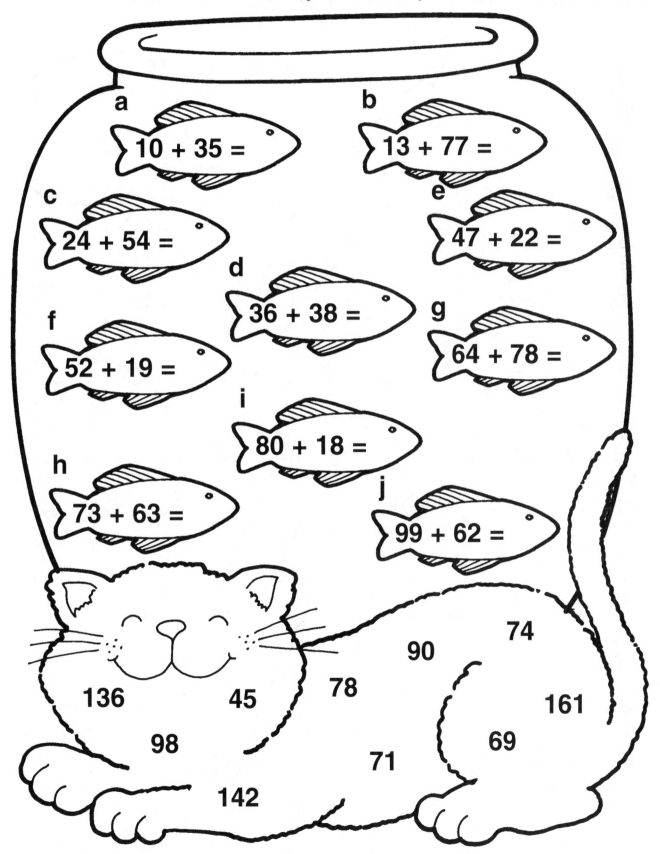

a   10 + 35 =

b   13 + 77 =

c   24 + 54 =

e   47 + 22 =

d   36 + 38 =

f   52 + 19 =

g   64 + 78 =

i   80 + 18 =

h   73 + 63 =

j   99 + 62 =

74

90

78

136   45

161

98

69

71

142

Lightning Quick

Solve the problems. Draw a line from the lightning to the cloud with the sum of 43. Color the lightning bolt.

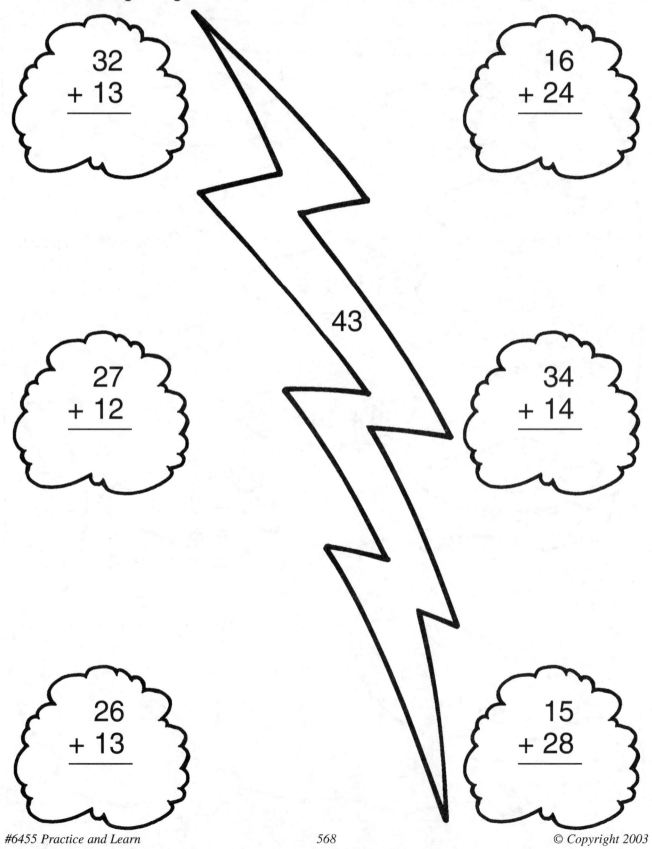

$$\begin{array}{r} 32 \\ + 13 \\ \hline \end{array}$$

$$\begin{array}{r} 16 \\ + 24 \\ \hline \end{array}$$

$$\begin{array}{r} 27 \\ + 12 \\ \hline \end{array}$$

43

$$\begin{array}{r} 34 \\ + 14 \\ \hline \end{array}$$

$$\begin{array}{r} 26 \\ + 13 \\ \hline \end{array}$$

$$\begin{array}{r} 15 \\ + 28 \\ \hline \end{array}$$

Addition Word Problems

Read each word problem. In the box, write the number sentence it shows. Find the sum.

a

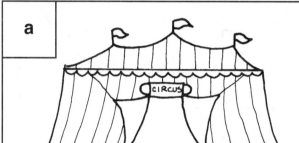

At the circus, Kenny saw 12 tigers, 14 horses, and 22 monkeys. How many animals did he see in all?

b

When Sandra went to the tidepools, she counted 28 starfish, 32 fish, and 46 shells. How many things did she see in all?

c

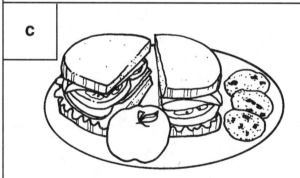

During one month, Jared ate 27 sandwiches, 23 apples, and 52 cookies. How many things did he eat in all?

d

Emily did 14 addition problems and 33 subtraction problems at school. At home, her mother gave her 21 more. How many problems did she solve in all?

Find the Sums

Find the sums.

a. 29 + 48	**g.** 14 + 75	**m.** 74 + 68	**s.** 97 + 50
b. 37 + 95	**h.** 20 + 52	**n.** 38 + 15	**t.** 45 + 29
c. 10 + 36	**i.** 41 + 52	**o.** 25 + 49	**u.** 34 + 17
d. 56 + 26	**j.** 27 + 30	**p.** 39 + 27	**v.** 74 + 19
e. 40 + 33	**k.** 52 + 73	**q.** 10 + 64	**w.** 27 + 28
f. 86 + 56	**l.** 67 + 70	**r.** 86 + 16	**x.** 55 + 54

Add Three

Find the sums.

a. 39 57 + 47	**g.** 39 12 + 72	**m.** 26 71 + 59	**s.** 17 79 + 54
b. 33 75 + 23	**h.** 51 24 + 88	**n.** 52 30 + 18	**t.** 39 95 + 48
c. 21 53 + 17	**i.** 42 84 + 19	**o.** 13 38 + 42	**u.** 27 77 + 70
d. 42 26 + 49	**j.** 23 14 + 92	**p.** 52 38 + 42	**v.** 59 44 + 16
e. 68 62 + 56	**k.** 84 36 + 65	**q.** 52 66 + 83	**w.** 51 36 + 24
f. 61 33 + 63	**l.** 34 42 + 30	**r.** 98 61 + 15	**x.** 67 73 + 30

Oh, Nuts!

Cross out each answer on the squirrel as you solve the problems.

a.
$$35 - 11$$

b.
$$77 - 13$$

c.
$$54 - 24$$

d.
$$38 - 36$$

e.
$$47 - 22$$

f.
$$52 - 19$$

g.
$$74 - 68$$

h.
$$73 - 63$$

i.
$$80 - 18$$

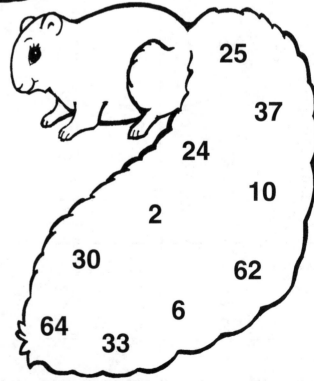

25
37
24
10
2
30
62
64
6
33

j.
$$99 - 62$$

Home Run!

Cross out each answer in the mitt as you solve the problems.

a.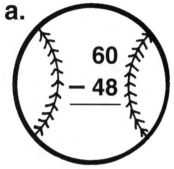
$$\begin{array}{r} 60 \\ -\ 48 \\ \hline \end{array}$$

b.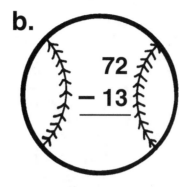
$$\begin{array}{r} 72 \\ -\ 13 \\ \hline \end{array}$$

c.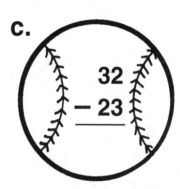
$$\begin{array}{r} 32 \\ -\ 23 \\ \hline \end{array}$$

d.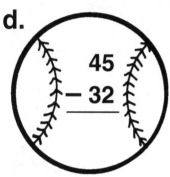
$$\begin{array}{r} 45 \\ -\ 32 \\ \hline \end{array}$$

e.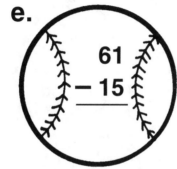
$$\begin{array}{r} 61 \\ -\ 15 \\ \hline \end{array}$$

f.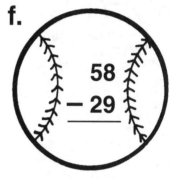
$$\begin{array}{r} 58 \\ -\ 29 \\ \hline \end{array}$$

g.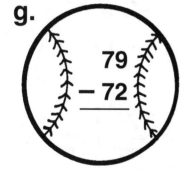
$$\begin{array}{r} 79 \\ -\ 72 \\ \hline \end{array}$$

h.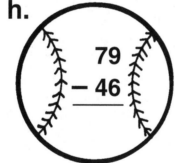
$$\begin{array}{r} 79 \\ -\ 46 \\ \hline \end{array}$$

i.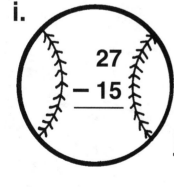
$$\begin{array}{r} 27 \\ -\ 15 \\ \hline \end{array}$$

j.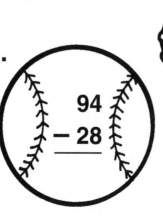
$$\begin{array}{r} 94 \\ -\ 28 \\ \hline \end{array}$$

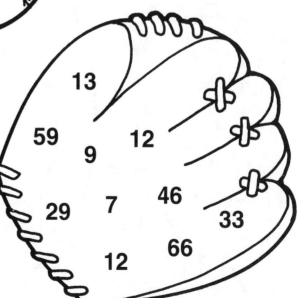

13
59
12
9
29
7
46
33
12
66

Hop to It

Help the mother kangaroo find her baby. Solve the problems below. Draw a line from the mother to the baby with the answer of 23. Color the mother kangaroo.

42
− 13
_____

34
− 11
_____

54
− 20
_____

26
− 13
_____

23

27
− 12
_____

48
− 29
_____

Subtraction Word Problems

Read each word problem. Write the number sentence it shows. Find the difference.

a

The snail and the rabbit had a race. If it took the rabbit 15 minutes to finish the race and it took the snail 25 minutes more, how long did it take the snail to finish the race?

b

Emily scored 41 points in her basketball game. Claire scored 32. What is the difference in points each earned?

c

Grace was reading a mystery book. She read 45 pages. If there are 96 pages in the book, how many more pages does Grace need to read to finish her book?

d

Benita counted 93 ants at the picnic. Sara counted 48. What is the difference in the ants counted?

Find the Differences

Find the differences.

a. $\begin{array}{r} 49 \\ -\ 28 \\ \hline \end{array}$	**g.** $\begin{array}{r} 74 \\ -\ 72 \\ \hline \end{array}$	**m.** $\begin{array}{r} 74 \\ -\ 68 \\ \hline \end{array}$	**s.** $\begin{array}{r} 97 \\ -\ 50 \\ \hline \end{array}$
b. $\begin{array}{r} 97 \\ -\ 35 \\ \hline \end{array}$	**h.** $\begin{array}{r} 50 \\ -\ 22 \\ \hline \end{array}$	**n.** $\begin{array}{r} 38 \\ -\ 15 \\ \hline \end{array}$	**t.** $\begin{array}{r} 55 \\ -\ 39 \\ \hline \end{array}$
c. $\begin{array}{r} 30 \\ -\ 16 \\ \hline \end{array}$	**i.** $\begin{array}{r} 41 \\ -\ 32 \\ \hline \end{array}$	**o.** $\begin{array}{r} 45 \\ -\ 29 \\ \hline \end{array}$	**u.** $\begin{array}{r} 34 \\ -\ 17 \\ \hline \end{array}$
d. $\begin{array}{r} 56 \\ -\ 26 \\ \hline \end{array}$	**j.** $\begin{array}{r} 37 \\ -\ 30 \\ \hline \end{array}$	**p.** $\begin{array}{r} 79 \\ -\ 32 \\ \hline \end{array}$	**v.** $\begin{array}{r} 74 \\ -\ 19 \\ \hline \end{array}$
e. $\begin{array}{r} 40 \\ -\ 33 \\ \hline \end{array}$	**k.** $\begin{array}{r} 72 \\ -\ 53 \\ \hline \end{array}$	**q.** $\begin{array}{r} 60 \\ -\ 14 \\ \hline \end{array}$	**w.** $\begin{array}{r} 28 \\ -\ 28 \\ \hline \end{array}$
f. $\begin{array}{r} 86 \\ -\ 56 \\ \hline \end{array}$	**l.** $\begin{array}{r} 77 \\ -\ 70 \\ \hline \end{array}$	**r.** $\begin{array}{r} 86 \\ -\ 16 \\ \hline \end{array}$	**x.** $\begin{array}{r} 55 \\ -\ 54 \\ \hline \end{array}$

What's the Difference?

Find the differences.

a. $\begin{array}{r} 57 \\ -\ 47 \\ \hline \end{array}$	**g.** $\begin{array}{r} 72 \\ -\ 12 \\ \hline \end{array}$	**m.** $\begin{array}{r} 71 \\ -\ 59 \\ \hline \end{array}$	**s.** $\begin{array}{r} 79 \\ -\ 54 \\ \hline \end{array}$
b. $\begin{array}{r} 75 \\ -\ 23 \\ \hline \end{array}$	**h.** $\begin{array}{r} 88 \\ -\ 24 \\ \hline \end{array}$	**n.** $\begin{array}{r} 30 \\ -\ 18 \\ \hline \end{array}$	**t.** $\begin{array}{r} 95 \\ -\ 48 \\ \hline \end{array}$
c. $\begin{array}{r} 53 \\ -\ 17 \\ \hline \end{array}$	**i.** $\begin{array}{r} 84 \\ -\ 19 \\ \hline \end{array}$	**o.** $\begin{array}{r} 42 \\ -\ 38 \\ \hline \end{array}$	**u.** $\begin{array}{r} 77 \\ -\ 70 \\ \hline \end{array}$
d. $\begin{array}{r} 49 \\ -\ 26 \\ \hline \end{array}$	**j.** $\begin{array}{r} 92 \\ -\ 14 \\ \hline \end{array}$	**p.** $\begin{array}{r} 86 \\ -\ 63 \\ \hline \end{array}$	**v.** $\begin{array}{r} 44 \\ -\ 16 \\ \hline \end{array}$
e. $\begin{array}{r} 62 \\ -\ 56 \\ \hline \end{array}$	**k.** $\begin{array}{r} 65 \\ -\ 36 \\ \hline \end{array}$	**q.** $\begin{array}{r} 96 \\ -\ 45 \\ \hline \end{array}$	**w.** $\begin{array}{r} 36 \\ -\ 24 \\ \hline \end{array}$
f. $\begin{array}{r} 63 \\ -\ 33 \\ \hline \end{array}$	**l.** $\begin{array}{r} 42 \\ -\ 30 \\ \hline \end{array}$	**r.** $\begin{array}{r} 61 \\ -\ 15 \\ \hline \end{array}$	**x.** $\begin{array}{r} 73 \\ -\ 30 \\ \hline \end{array}$

What's the Scoop?

Fill in the missing number on each cone to complete the problem.

1.
10
+
16

2.
17
− 8

3.
+ 4
17

4.
9
+
19

5.
8
−
1

6.
15
+ 4

7.
− 11
7

8.
21
− 16

9.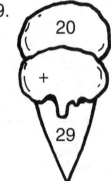
20
+
29

10.
14
− 7

11.
− 13
10

12.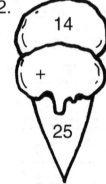
14
+
25

13.
14
− 6

14.
+ 13
19

15.
12
+ 12

16.
18
− 6

Sign In

Place + and – signs between the digits so that both sides of each equation are equal.

1.   6   4   1   2   6   2   =   15

2.   9   1   3   1   4   1   =   5

3.   9   3   4   1   2   3   =   14

4.   5   1   1   3   4   6   =   18

5.   9   8   6   3   5   3   =   8

6.   2   1   8   9   3   5   =   20

7.   5   3   2   4   1   5   =   12

8.   4   9   3   7   3   1   =   11

9.   7   6   2   8   7   1   =   3

10.   9   9   9   2   2   8   =   1

Times Tables

Complete the times tables.

0 x 0 = _____	1 x 6 = _____	2 x 12 = _____	4 x 5 = _____
0 x 1 = _____	1 x 7 = _____	3 x 0 = _____	4 x 6 = _____
0 x 2 = _____	1 x 8 = _____	3 x 1 = _____	4 x 7 = _____
0 x 3 = _____	1 x 9 = _____	3 x 2 = _____	4 x 8 = _____
0 x 4 = _____	1 x 10 = _____	3 x 3 = _____	4 x 9 = _____
0 x 5 = _____	1 x 11 = _____	3 x 4 = _____	4 x 10 = _____
0 x 6 = _____	1 x 12 = _____	3 x 5 = _____	4 x 11 = _____
0 x 7 = _____	2 x 0 = _____	3 x 6 = _____	4 x 12 = _____
0 x 8 = _____	2 x 1 = _____	3 x 7 = _____	5 x 0 = _____
0 x 9 = _____	2 x 2 = _____	3 x 8 = _____	5 x 1 = _____
0 x 10 = _____	2 x 3 = _____	3 x 9 = _____	5 x 2 = _____
0 x 11 = _____	2 x 4 = _____	3 x 10 = _____	5 x 3 = _____
0 x 12 = _____	2 x 5 = _____	3 x 11 = _____	5 x 4 = _____
1 x 0 = _____	2 x 6 = _____	3 x 12 = _____	5 x 5 = _____
1 x 1 = _____	2 x 7 = _____	4 x 0 = _____	5 x 6 = _____
1 x 2 = _____	2 x 8 = _____	4 x 1 = _____	5 x 7 = _____
1 x 3 = _____	2 x 9 = _____	4 x 2 = _____	5 x 8 = _____
1 x 4 = _____	2 x 10 = _____	4 x 3 = _____	5 x 9 = _____
1 x 5 = _____	2 x 11 = _____	4 x 4 = _____	5 x 10 = _____

Times Tables (cont.)

Complete the times tables.

5 x 11 = _____	7 x 4 = _____	8 x 10 = _____	10 x 3 = _____	11 x 9 = _____
5 x 12 = _____	7 x 5 = _____	8 x 11 = _____	10 x 4 = _____	11 x 10 = _____
6 x 0 = _____	7 x 6 = _____	8 x 12 = _____	10 x 5 = _____	11 x 11 = _____
6 x 1 = _____	7 x 7 = _____	9 x 0 = _____	10 x 6 = _____	11 x 12 = _____
6 x 2 = _____	7 x 8 = _____	9 x 1 = _____	10 x 7 = _____	12 x 0 = _____
6 x 3 = _____	7 x 9 = _____	9 x 2 = _____	10 x 8 = _____	12 x 1 = _____
6 x 4 = _____	7 x 10 = _____	9 x 3 = _____	10 x 9 = _____	12 x 2 = _____
6 x 5 = _____	7 x 11 = _____	9 x 4 = _____	10 x 10 = _____	12 x 3 = _____
6 x 6 = _____	7 x 12 = _____	9 x 5 = _____	10 x 11 = _____	12 x 4 = _____
6 x 7 = _____	8 x 0 = _____	9 x 6 = _____	10 x 12 = _____	12 x 5 = _____
6 x 8 = _____	8 x 1 = _____	9 x 7 = _____	11 x 0 = _____	12 x 6 = _____
6 x 9 = _____	8 x 2 = _____	9 x 8 = _____	11 x 1 = _____	12 x 7 = _____
6 x 10 = _____	8 x 3 = _____	9 x 9 = _____	11 x 2 = _____	12 x 8 = _____
6 x 11 = _____	8 x 4 = _____	9 x 10 = _____	11 x 3 = _____	12 x 9 = _____
6 x 12 = _____	8 x 5 = _____	9 x 11 = _____	11 x 4 = _____	12 x 10 = _____
7 x 0 = _____	8 x 6 = _____	9 x 12 = _____	11 x 5 = _____	12 x 11 = _____
7 x 1 = _____	8 x 7 = _____	10 x 0 = _____	11 x 6 = _____	12 x 12 = _____
7 x 2 = _____	8 x 8 = _____	10 x 1 = _____	11 x 7 = _____	
7 x 3 = _____	8 x 9 = _____	10 x 2 = _____	11 x 8 = _____	

Single-Digit Multiplication

Solve the problems.

6 x 6 = _____   9 x 5 = _____   6 x 7 = _____   8 x 0 = _____

3 x 1 = _____   4 x 7 = _____   7 x 3 = _____   8 x 9 = _____

9 x 6 = _____   6 x 8 = _____   8 x 1 = _____   9 x 7 = _____

9 x 9 = _____   8 x 4 = _____   0 x 3 = _____   1 x 9 = _____

3 x 2 = _____   4 x 8 = _____   0 x 4 = _____   3 x 3 = _____

4 x 9 = _____   0 x 5 = _____   7 x 2 = _____   8 x 8 = _____

3 x 4 = _____   0 x 6 = _____   3 x 5 = _____   0 x 7 = _____

2 x 0 = _____   3 x 6 = _____   0 x 8 = _____   0 x 0 = _____

1 x 6 = _____   4 x 5 = _____   0 x 1 = _____   1 x 7 = _____

2 x 9 = _____   4 x 2 = _____   5 x 8 = _____   1 x 4 = _____

4 x 3 = _____   5 x 9 = _____   1 x 5 = _____   4 x 6 = _____

5 x 0 = _____   0 x 9 = _____   8 x 5 = _____   5 x 7 = _____

Single- and Double-Digit Multiplication

Solve the problems.

2 x 2	3 x 8	5 x 1	10 x 0
2 x 3	11 x 5	7 x 4	10 x 8
10 x 3	11 x 9	12 x 5	7 x 5
11 x 8	10 x 4	11 x 10	6 x 0
7 x 6	12 x 8	10 x 5	11 x 11
6 x 1	7 x 7	9 x 0	10 x 6
11 x 12	6 x 2	7 x 8	9 x 1
10 x 7	12 x 0	6 x 3	7 x 9
9 x 2	10 x 8	12 x 1	6 x 4
10 x 7	9 x 3	10 x 9	12 x 2

Column Multiplication

Solve the problems.

96	90	47	25	16
x 6	x 3	x 9	x 1	x 6

40	82	60	71	32
x 8	x 5	x 2	x 7	x 4

68	33	20	24	41
x 8	x 1	x 6	x 9	x 4

46	49	38	24	27
x 2	x 7	x 4	x 3	x 3

56	84	70	58	50
x 7	x 2	x 9	x 7	x 1

21	77	79	86	13
x 2	x 6	x 4	x 3	x 2

22	74	26	14	48
x 6	x 1	x 9	x 7	x 3

42	88	69	43	19
x 4	x 5	x 8	x 3	x 2

By Three

Solve the problems.

173	227	402	420	178
x 6	x 3	x 1	x 8	x 9

324	172	286	509	615
x 8	x 4	x 8	x 4	x 2

533	388	620	662	714
x 8	x 1	x 6	x 3	x 9

835	152	254	851	674
x 3	x 7	x 5	x 1	x 8

138	417	317	458	550
x 2	x 8	x 4	x 7	x 6

594	180	538	728	107
x 5	x 4	x 1	x 6	x 3

833	524	468	947	767
x 5	x 3	x 6	x 2	x 7

632	221	489	141	213
x 3	x 2	x 4	x 9	x 5

Double Time

Solve the problems.

23	90	17	35	14
x 16	x 39	x 79	x 15	x 63

56	73	50	81	51
x 82	x 50	x 28	x 76	x 44

13	31	41	14	80
x 38	x 11	x 96	x 79	x 54

34	46	68	34	23
x 24	x 27	x 40	x 83	x 36

89	24	74	48	70
x 57	x 23	x 19	x 79	x 71

21	67	39	96	18
x 26	x 64	x 42	x 30	x 28

44	22	16	25	28
x 76	x 51	x 39	x 17	x 93

58	99	64	34	36
x 48	x 56	x 48	x 23	x 20

Division Facts

Solve the problems.

1 ÷ 1 = _____	18 ÷ 2 = _____	20 ÷ 4 = _____
2 ÷ 1 = _____	20 ÷ 2 = _____	24 ÷ 4 = _____
3 ÷ 1 = _____	22 ÷ 2 = _____	28 ÷ 4 = _____
4 ÷ 1 = _____	24 ÷ 2 = _____	32 ÷ 4 = _____
5 ÷ 1 = _____	3 ÷ 3 = _____	36 ÷ 4 = _____
6 ÷ 1 = _____	6 ÷ 3 = _____	40 ÷ 4 = _____
7 ÷ 1 = _____	9 ÷ 3 = _____	44 ÷ 4 = _____
8 ÷ 1 = _____	12 ÷ 3 = _____	48 ÷ 4 = _____
9 ÷ 1 = _____	15 ÷ 3 = _____	5 ÷ 5 = _____
10 ÷ 1 = _____	18 ÷ 3 = _____	10 ÷ 5 = _____
11 ÷ 1 = _____	21 ÷ 3 = _____	15 ÷ 5 = _____
12 ÷ 1 = _____	24 ÷ 3 = _____	20 ÷ 5 = _____
2 ÷ 2 = _____	27 ÷ 3 = _____	25 ÷ 5 = _____
4 ÷ 2 = _____	30 ÷ 3 = _____	30 ÷ 5 = _____
6 ÷ 2 = _____	33 ÷ 3 = _____	35 ÷ 5 = _____
8 ÷ 2 = _____	36 ÷ 3 = _____	40 ÷ 5 = _____
10 ÷ 2 = _____	4 ÷ 4 = _____	45 ÷ 5 = _____
12 ÷ 2 = _____	8 ÷ 4 = _____	50 ÷ 5 = _____
14 ÷ 2 = _____	12 ÷ 4 = _____	55 ÷ 5 = _____
16 ÷ 2 = _____	16 ÷ 4 = _____	

Division Facts (cont.)

Solve the problems.

60 ÷ 5 = ___	42 ÷ 7 = ___	96 ÷ 8 = ___	60 ÷ 10 = ___	132 ÷ 11 = ___
6 ÷ 6 = ___	49 ÷ 7 = ___	9 ÷ 9 = ___	70 ÷ 10 = ___	12 ÷ 12 = ___
12 ÷ 6 = ___	56 ÷ 7 = ___	18 ÷ 9 = ___	80 ÷ 10 = ___	24 ÷ 12 = ___
18 ÷ 6 = ___	63 ÷ 7 = ___	27 ÷ 9 = ___	90 ÷ 10 = ___	36 ÷ 12 = ___
24 ÷ 6 = ___	70 ÷ 7 = ___	36 ÷ 9 = ___	100 ÷ 10 = ___	48 ÷ 12 = ___
30 ÷ 6 = ___	77 ÷ 7 = ___	45 ÷ 9 = ___	110 ÷ 10 = ___	60 ÷ 12 = ___
36 ÷ 6 = ___	84 ÷ 7 = ___	54 ÷ 9 = ___	120 ÷ 10 = ___	72 ÷ 12 = ___
42 ÷ 6 = ___	8 ÷ 8 = ___	63 ÷ 9 = ___	11 ÷ 11 = ___	84 ÷ 12 = ___
48 ÷ 6 = ___	16 ÷ 8 = ___	72 ÷ 9 = ___	22 ÷ 11 = ___	96 ÷ 12 = ___
54 ÷ 6 = ___	24 ÷ 8 = ___	81 ÷ 9 = ___	33 ÷ 11 = ___	108 ÷ 12 = ___
60 ÷ 6 = ___	32 ÷ 8 = ___	90 ÷ 9 = ___	44 ÷ 11 = ___	120 ÷ 12 = ___
66 ÷ 6 = ___	40 ÷ 8 = ___	99 ÷ 9 = ___	55 ÷ 11 = ___	132 ÷ 12 = ___
72 ÷ 6 = ___	48 ÷ 8 = ___	108 ÷ 9 = ___	66 ÷ 11 = ___	144 ÷ 12 = ___
7 ÷ 7 = ___	56 ÷ 8 = ___	10 ÷ 10 = ___	77 ÷ 11 = ___	
14 ÷ 7 = ___	64 ÷ 8 = ___	20 ÷ 10 = ___	88 ÷ 11 = ___	
21 ÷ 7 = ___	72 ÷ 8 = ___	30 ÷ 10 = ___	99 ÷ 11 = ___	
28 ÷ 7 = ___	80 ÷ 8 = ___	40 ÷ 10 = ___	110 ÷ 11 = ___	
35 ÷ 7 = ___	88 ÷ 8 = ___	50 ÷ 10 = ___	121 ÷ 11 = ___	

Which Is It?

Read the number sentences. Add the correct math sign to each problem.

+	-	x	÷
add	subtract	multiply	divide

1. 5 ☐ 7 = 12

2. 24 ☐ 4 = 6

3. 9 ☐ 3 = 12

4. 18 ☐ 6 = 12

5. 4 ☐ 9 = 13

6. 4 ☐ 9 = 36

7. 10 ☐ 8 = 80

8. 15 ☐ 5 = 3

9. 11 ☐ 4 = 7

10. 8 ☐ 16 = 24

11. 2 ☐ 8 = 16

12. 3 ☐ 2 = 5

13. 22 ☐ 6 = 16

14. 9 ☐ 1 = 10

15. 3 ☐ 3 = 9

Picture Fractions

A **fraction** is a number that names part of a whole thing. The number at the top is the numerator. It tells how many parts of the whole are present. The number at the bottom is the denominator. It tells how many parts there are in all.

Examples:

 $\frac{1}{2}$ (There are two parts in the circle. One part is gray. Therefore, the fraction is $\frac{1}{2}$.)

 $\frac{3}{4}$ (There are four parts in the square. Three parts are gray. The fraction is $\frac{3}{4}$.)

Write a fraction for each picture.

1.  _____

5. 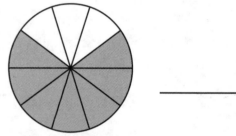 _____

2. _____

6. 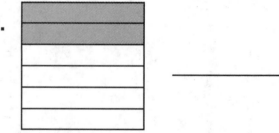 _____

3. 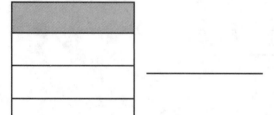 _____

7. _____

4. 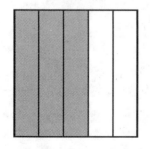 _____

8. 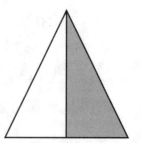 _____

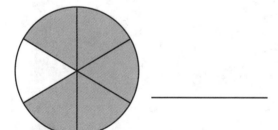

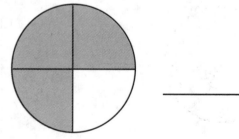

What Time Is It?

Read the time on the clocks. Write the time on the lines.

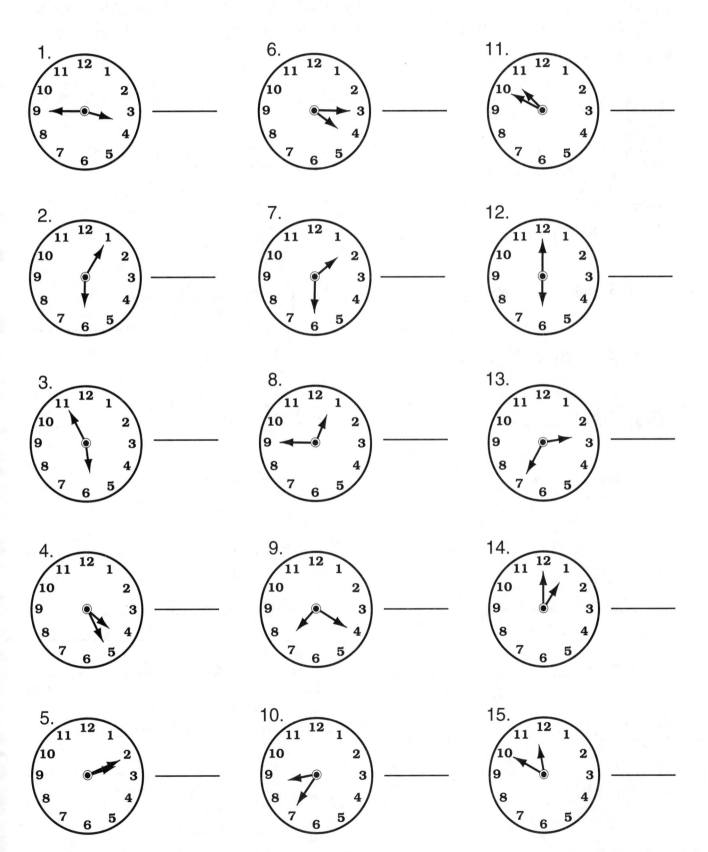

A.M. and P.M.

A.M. is the time after 12 o'clock midnight and before 12 o'clock noon. **P.M.** is the time after 12 o'clock noon and before 12 o'clock midnight. (Midnight itself is **A.M.** and noon itself is **P.M.**) Write **A.M.** or **P.M.** after each of these events to say what time it usually falls in.

1. dinnertime _____

2. getting up _____

3. afternoon nap _____

4. after-school baseball game _____

5. before-school dance class _____

6. breakfast_____

7. evening movie _____

8. evening bath_____

9. after-dinner dessert _____

10. sunrise _____

11. going to school_____

12. sunset_____

13. lunch_____

14. morning cartoons_____

15. going to bed _____

16. after-school piano lessons _____

17. morning exercises _____

18. homework_____

19. afternoon reading_____

20. morning snack _____

21. early recess _____

22. after-school bike ride _____

23. afternoon computer games _____

24. dawn_____

Timely Chore

Each word in the time box refers to a specific time span. List the words in order from the shortest time span to the longest. Then, explain how long each time span is.

Time Span	How Long Is It?

1. _____

2. _____

3. _____

4. _____

5. _____

6. _____

7. _____

8. _____

9. _____

10. _____

11. _____

12. _____

Time Box		
second	hour	millennium
fortnight	day	month
minute	score	century
year	decade	week

Telling Time

Read the time on the analog clock. Write the time on the digital clock.

At What Time Do You. . .

Think about your day. Write at what time of the day you. . .

1. wake up for school? _____

2. eat breakfast? _____

3. start school? _____

4. eat lunch? _____

5. study math? _____

6. have an after school snack? _____

7. play with friends? _____

8. work on homework? _____

9. brush your teeth? _____

10. go to bed? _____

Answer Key

Page 307

person: Adam, Dr. Roberts, farmer, mother, scientist, zoo keeper, artist
place: attic, London, museum, room, Russia, state, playground
thing: comb, door, clock, football, hoe, motor, rainbow

Page 308
1. dancer, air
2. boy, television
3. Mr. Smith, class
4. baby, mother
5. sisters, store
6. school, stories
7. teenagers, skateboards, park
8. dentist, patient
9. dog, fight, cat
10. presents, cake, candles, party

Page 309
Answers will vary.

Page 310
1. I live in the green (house) on Elm Street.
2. My (dog,) Max, and I went for a (walk.)
3. There are three Ryans in my (class.)
4. My (family) is planning a (trip) to the Grand Canyon.
5. "(Mom,) where is my yellow (shirt?)" Jenny asked her (mother.)
6. Where is Primrose Park?
7. The only (vegetable) I like is (broccoli.)
8. Our neighbor's (cat) is named Sylvester.
9. My (teacher) is Mrs. Simms.
10. Ricky, Sam, and Tim are going to play (football) in the (park.)

Page 311
Answers will vary.

Page 312
1. cats
2. dogs
3. houses
4. gates
5. churches
6. monkeys
7. trees
8. classes
9. doors
10. chairs
11. lunches
12. boxes
13. bushes
14. glasses
15. trucks
16. brushes

Page 313
1. pennies
2. ponies
3. berries
4. families
5. factories
6. candies
7. parties
8. cherries
9. babies
10. fillies
11. jellies
12. lilies
13. ladies
14. patties
15. flies
16. stories

Page 314
1. women
2. teeth
3. men
4. children
5. feet
6. mice
7. oxen
8. wives
9. geese
10. loaves

Page 315
1. baby's
2. Mary's
3. boys'
4. tree's
5. Ken's
6. dogs'
7. children's
8. kitten's
9. woman's
10. pan's

Page 316
1. plays
2. flies
3. makes
4. ran
5. popped
6. ran
7. fell
8. eat
9. stood
10. reads

Page 317
woke, jumped, landed, slept, sat, rubbed, grumbled, fell, looked, wondered, slept, ran, grabbed, blew, played, liked, heard, stopped, listened, came, disliked, grabbed, ran, sat, played, floated, played, heard, stopped, listened, came, ran, played, liked, heard, heard, called, went, took, put, put, told, left, went, imagined, heard, stopped, listened, snored, moaned, stuck, heard, covered, slept

Page 318
1. seems
2. is
3. is
4. looks
5. are
6. are
7. were
8. are
9. are
10. is

Page 319
1. A; sings
2. A; kicks
3. A; has
4. L; is
5. L; was
6. A; tipped
7. A; jumped
8. L; is
9. A; walked
10. A; washes

Page 320
1. walked
2. climbed
3. jumped
4. played
5. combed
6. roared
7. smiled
8. folded
9. closed
10. painted
11. color
12. scribble
13. turn
14. cook
15. wash
16. share
17. stack
18. type
19. laugh
20. deliver

Page 321
run—ran; see—saw; eat—ate; come—came; make—made; build—built; sleep—slept; give—gave; take—took; bring—brought; sing—sang

Page 322
1. blew
2. came
3. sang
4. wore
5. took
6. cried
7. made
8. gave
9. fell
10. flew
11. catch
12. read
13. ride
14. drink
15. swing
16. shine
17. pay
18. write
19. sweep
20. tear

Page 323
1. hops, singular
2. shines, singular
3. were, plural
4. roar, plural
5. rides, singular
6. is, singular
7. have, plural
8. are, plural
9. dances, singular
10. are, plural

Page 324
1. read
2. fly
3. swims
4. chases
5. climbs
6. run
7. hike
8. count
9. plays
10. watch

Page 325
1. were
2. was
3. was
4. were
5 was
6. were
7. do
8. do
9. do
10. does
11. does
12. does

Page 326
Answers will vary.

Page 327
1. striped
2. loose
3. Many
4. funny
5. large
6–10: Answers will vary.

Page 328
Answers will vary.

Page 329
1. a
2. an
3. a
4. an
5. a
6. a
7. an
8. an
9. a
10. a
11. An
12. a
13. a
14. An
15. A

Page 330
1. how
2. when
3. where
4. when
5. how
6. how
7. where
8. when
9. how
10. how

Answer Key (cont.)

Page 331
1. <u>after lunch</u>; when
2. <u>softly</u>; how
3. <u>into the basket</u>; where
4. <u>skillfully</u>; how
5. <u>tomorrow</u>; when
6. <u>well</u>; how
7. <u>tonight</u>; when
8. <u>after time ran out</u>; when
9. <u>quickly</u>; how
10. <u>through the afternoon</u>; when

Page 332
1. how; quietly
2. when; tomorrow
3. when; later
4. where; here
5. how; fiercely
6. how; softly
7. how; gracefully
8. when; Yesterday
9. how; well
10. how; quickly

Page 333
1. he
2. she
3. they
4. They
5. her
6. it
7. She
8. He
9. her
10. them
11. them
12. he
13. they
14. it
15. him

Page 334
1. they
2. she
3. he
4. they
5. she
6. she
7. he
8. she

Page 335
1. We
2. us
3. I
4. me
5. us
6. I
7. I
8. we
9. me
10. us

Page 336
1. busy, active
2. nibble, chew
3. flavorful, tasty
4. joyful, happy
5. fall, trip
6. huge, enormous
7. worried, anxious
8. mad, angry
9. talk, chat
10. rush, hurry

Page 337
1. watched
2. shore
3. eat
4. bucket
5. slept
6. asked
7. decorate
8. small
9. big
10. quiet

Page 338
1. neat, spotless
2. sad, unhappy
3. thin, skinny
4. look, see
5. plain, simple
6. strong, powerful
7. cold, chilly
8. big, large
9. cheap, stingy
10. quiet, calm

Page 339
Words will vary.

Page 340
1. happy—sad
2. brave—afraid
3. right—wrong
4. fast—slow
5. big—little
6. rude—polite
7. old—young
8. strong—weak
9. crowded—empty
10. smile—frown
11. close—far
12. loud—quiet
13. ask—answer
14. wild—tame
15. beautiful—ugly
16. hard—easy

Page 341
1. low
2. empty
3. down
4. Few
5. white
6. difficult
7. Everybody
8. No one
9. calm
10. bad

Page 342
Answers will vary but may include:
1. bottom
2. sky
3. false
4. slow
5. enemy/foe
6. plain
7. tight
8. under
9. even
10. whole
11. negative
12. sunset
13. buy
14. thin
15. wet

Page 343
1. pail
2. Two
3. hear
4. wear
5. sew
6. high
7. wood
8. bee
9. blew
10. knew

Page 344
1. aunt
2. tear
3. dew
4. pearl
5. night
6. banned
7. sheer
8. role
9. guest
10. wee
11. doe
12. chilly
13. break
14. fir

Page 345
one, night, road, two, him, knew, where, some, not, too, to, him, their, way, to, in, ate, no

Page 346
red: sad, unhappy; happy, joyful; tender, gentle; huge, big; tiny, small; cold, icy; loud, noisy
yellow: black, white; fast, slow; in, out; up, down; big, little; day, night; good, bad

Page 347
Words will vary.

Page 348
1. A
2. S
3. A
4. S
5. H
6. S
7. A
8. H
9. S
10. H
11. A
12. S
13. S
14. A
15. H
16. S
17. H
18. A

Page 349
1. S
2. A
3. A
4. H
5. H
6. S
7. H
8. A
9. S
10. A
11. H
12. S
13. H
14. S
15. H
16. S
17. A
18. A

Page 350
1. When I went to the store, I saw my teacher, Mrs. Roe, buying strawberries.
2. My family will go to Disneyland in July.
3. I am reading *Old Yeller* this week.
4. My sister, Sarah, says her favorite subject is Spanish.
5. On Wednesday, we will celebrate Groundhog Day.
6. My brother said that Mom was a cheerleader at Roosevelt High School.
7. In August, we're going to visit Aunt Margaret in San Francisco, California.
8. Benjie, my little brother, had a birthday, and we sang, "Happy Birthday to You."
9. My friend, Rosa, speaks Spanish, and I speak English.
10. My neighbor, Julia, is going to be an exchange student in Paris, France, next August.

Page 351
names (people and pets): Alexander, Mr. Peterson, Sandy, Spot, Fluffy
places: Rocky Mountains, Colorado River, Plum Street, Russia, South America
days: Monday, Thursday, Saturday
months: November, August, March, February
holidays: Christmas, Thanksgiving, Mardi Gras

Answer Key (cont.)

Page 352
1. The
2. Freddy Wilson's, Peepers, Mrs. Woolsey's
3. As, I, I
4. In, Robin Hood, Lieutenant Bronksy
5. The, Thursday, November, Thanksgiving
6. I, Halloween, Saturday
7. Aunt Susan, Yellowstone National Park
8. Connie, Maple Street, Bismarck, North Dakota
9. Brazil, Argentina, Peru, South America
10. The, Mediterranean Sea, Atlantic Ocean, Spain
11. The, Love, Esther
12. Davis Medical Center, January
13. One, African, Islam
14. Italians, Germans, Caucasian
15. Last, Tuesday, Ruben, Spotty, Tulip Street, Central Park

Page 353
she'll—she will; it's—it is; won't—will not; you'll—you will; you're—you are; isn't—is not; we're—we are; I'll—I will; they'll—they will; weren't—were not; I'm—I am; he's—he is; can't—can not; aren't—are not; they're—they are

Page 354
1. can't
2. he's
3. won't
4. doesn't
5. they're
6. we're
7. shouldn't
8. it'll
9. she will
10. it is
11. must not
12. you are
13. they will
14. have not
15. I will
16. I am

Page 355
1. won't
2. He'll
3. It's
4. Where's
5. didn't
6. Let's
7. can't
8. I'd

Page 356
1. . or !
2. . or !
3. ?
4. .
5. .
6. ?
7. ?
8. !
9. .
10. . or !
11. . or !
12. .
13. ?
14. .
15. ?

Page 357
1. .
2. ?
3. !
4. ?
5. .
6. . or !
7. !
8. .
9. ?
10. ?
11. ?
12. .
13. ?
14. !
15. .

Page 358
1. No, Mary does not like marshmallows.
2. Well, maybe Bernard will try the s'mores.
3. Bobby, would you like to try a s'more?
4. Alice wants a hot dog, potato chips, and a pickle.
5. We played baseball, basketball, and volleyball.
6. Harry, would you like to dance?

Page 359
1. Jack, my brother, does not like to go to the dentist.
2. I like my dentist, Dr. Lee.
3. Dr. Payce, the dentist in the next office, is also a good dentist.
4. On March 2, 1999, Dr. Lee took David and me camping.
5. My first visit to Dr. Lee was on February 27, 1994.
6. By June 30, 2012, I will have become a dentist myself.
7. I was born in Brooklyn, New York and so was Dr. Lee.
8. He visits Chicago, Illinois, every summer.
9. David wishes they would go to Orlando, Florida, each year instead.

Page 360
1. You wear your blue jeans, and I'll wear my black jeans.
2. Your white T-shirt fits better, but your red T-shirt is more colorful.
3. Do you want yellow patches on your jeans, or do you want pink patches?
4. Jill's T-shirt looks great, and Amy's jeans are terrific.
5. I have three pairs of blue jeans, but I want another pair of green jeans.
6. You need to wash your old jeans, and you should iron your new jeans.
7. This white T-shirt is mine, but that white T-shirt is yours.
8. Let's all wear our blue jeans today, and let's wear our red jeans tomorrow.

Page 361
1. Yes, I would love to go to the movie.
2. We have potato chips, cheese, and chili.
3. Grandma, could we please spend the night?

4. This red car belongs to my mom, and this blue car belongs to my dad.
5. John, may I borrow your football?
6. We saw swans, ducks, and an ostrich.
7. Invite Casey, Jackie, and Toby to go with us.
8. No, we can't go to the zoo today.
9. My sister likes hot dogs, and I like pizza.
10. Aunt Irene, my mom's sister, liked the book, but I liked the movie.

Page 362
1. Tasha's birthday is March 4, 1981.
2. Dennis, my best friend, lives in San Francisco, California, but he is moving to Oakland.
3. Our teacher, Mr. Hill, took us on a field trip to Boston, Massachusetts.
4. July 16, 1973, is my parents' anniversary.
5. The Davis family is moving to Orlando, Florida, on July 13, 2001.
6. My friend, Mrs. Allen, is a nurse.
7. The airplane will land in Paris, France, after taking off from London, England.
8. He visits Chicago, Illinois, every summer, but this year he will go to Montreal, Canada.

Page 363
1. cat's food
2. bird's nest
3. Kenny's bike
4. Mr. Stout's store
5. Janie's radio
6. Don's book
7. coach's baseball
8. teacher's desk
9. class' closet
10. Mrs. Davis' pencil

Page 364
1. "Yes, Ryan," Mom answered, "Matt can come over after lunch."
2. "Thanks, Mom," Ryan answered.
3. no quotation marks
4. Mom said, "While you play basketball, I'll bake cookies."
5. no quotation marks
6. no quotation marks

Answer Key (cont.)

Page 365
1. Bobby yelled, "Mom, where are my blue jeans?"
2. "A plane is flying overhead," said Jim's dad.
3. Mindy said, "Look at the turtles."
4. "Watch out!" yelled Sara. "The dog will get out!"
5. no changes
6. "Grandma," Joey cried, "will you tie my shoe?"
7. The boys yelled, "Come out and play!"
8. Mother said, "Change the channel, boys."
9. no changes
10. "Can you ride a bicycle?" asked Joseph.

Page 366
Have you ever been on a farm? Mrs. Young took her third grade class to Mr. Frank's farm on Tuesday, morning. They saw cows, chickens, and horses. Mr. Frank wanted to know if any students would like to ride a horse. Leslie screamed, "I do!" Also, John and Carl wanted to ride. Mrs. Young's class will never forget the special day on the farm.

Page 367
Dear Pen Pal,

I love to go to the circus! On May 6, 1999, the circus came to my hometown of Jackson, Wyoming. A parade marched through our streets, and soon the big top could be seen. Ken, my best friend, and I went to watch the performers prepare for opening night. We saw clowns, acrobats, and even the ringmaster. What a sight! Have you ever seen anything like it? You should go if you ever get the chance.

I also really enjoy playing baseball. My favorite team is the New York Yankees, but I also like the St. Louis Cardinals. When I grow up, I want to be a baseball pitcher, first baseman, or shortstop. Do you like baseball? What do you want to do when you grow up? I wish you could see my cool baseball card collection, but Ken's collection is even better.

Oh, I almost forgot to tell you about my family! There are four people in my family. They are my mom, my dad, my brother, and me. Scruffy, my cat, is also a family member. In August 2000, my grandpa will probably move in with us. I can't wait for that! Didn't you say your grandma lives with you? I'll bet you really like that.

Well, that's all for now. Please, write back to me soon. See you!
Your pal,
Brent

Page 368
1. (doctor) checked
2. (sister) ate
3. (actor) read
4. (neighbors) mowed
5. (hiker) climbed
6. (child) brushed
7. (family) swam
8. (singer) stepped
9. (poet) wrote
10. (grandmother) visited

Page 369
1. Blake
2. the paintbox
3. the colors
4. Blake
5. green
6. orange
7. Blake
8. color
9. Mom
10. the painting

Page 370
1. is very cold
2. jump into the water
3. splashes us
4. is cold
5. gets out of the water
6. does a handstand underwater
7. claps for him
8. has a leak in it
9. throws the inner tube onto the shore
10. sits on the inner tube
11. deflates with Tonia on it
12. laughs with Tonia
13. jumps into the water
14. swims as fast as he can

Page 371
Subject and predicate choices will vary.

1. S	6. S	11. S
2. S	7. P	12. P
3. P	8. P	13. S
4. S	9. P	14. P
5. P	10. S	15. S

Page 372–375
Answers will vary.

Page 376
complete sentences: 2, 3, 5, 7, 9, 10, 14, 15

Page 378
1. ! exclamatory
2. . declarative
3. ? interrogative
4. ? interrogative
5. . declarative
6. ! exclamatory or . imperative
7. ! exclamatory or . imperative
8. . declarative or ! exclamatory
9. ? interrogative
10. . imperative or ! exclamatory
11. ? interrogative
12. ! exclamatory or . declarative
13. ! exclamatory
14. . imperative
15. ? interrogative

Page 379
1. The cat chased the bird. (or) The bird chased the cat.
2. I wrote a letter to my friend.
3. The family made a puzzle.
4. The baker baked a cake. (or) A baker baked the cake.
5. A penguin jumped into the sea.
6. The puppets sang a song to the audience.

Page 380
1. I'm going swimming after school!
2. Chris opens the door.
3. Will we go to the store tomorrow?
4. My iguana ate my homework.
5. Juanita helps me.
6. Can you come with me?
7. Maria dances every day.
8. I have a cat.
9. That bicycle looks brand new!
10. Do you like candy?

Page 381
Sentences will vary.

Page 382
1. I have many things in my room.
2. There is a box of clothes under the bed.
3. A rug is in front of the closet.
4. Sentence will vary.
5. I can see trees from my window.
6. Sentence will vary.
7. Sentence will vary.

Page 383
1. It is windy today. I should fly my kite.
2. I like to read. *James and the Giant Peach* is my favorite book.
3. Where are you going? When will you be home?
4. The boy ran home after school. Then he did his homework.

Answer Key (cont.)

5. The clown danced in the parade. He gave balloons to all the children.
6. My sister really enjoys camping. I do, too.
7. The puppies cried for their mother. They were hungry.
8. I don't feel like going to bed. I want to stay up to watch my show!
9. Who is there? What do you want?
10. They wanted to climb the tree. The branches were too high to reach.

Page 384
1. The monkeys danced to the peddler's music.
2. My sister cried for my mother. She wouldn't stop.
3. My favorite game to play is Chinese checkers.
4. The students wondered what the teacher had planned for the day.
5. They were late to the party. Everyone was worried about them.
6. The birds were singing in the trees. The flowers looked colorful in the sun.
7. He knew that it would be an exciting day the moment he saw the pony.

Page 385
1. My cousin spent the night at my house.
2. John said that I could look at his snake.
3. Jim entered the bicycle race.
4. What a race it was!
5. Did he wear a helmet?
6. Who won the race?

Page 386
"Today," Mrs. Banks announced, "you are going to make your own butter." She asked C. J. and Juan to pass out the spoons, napkins, knives, and empty margarine tubs. Sonya, Erin, and Scott chose to help pour the cream. "You will only need two tablespoons of cream," warned Mrs. Banks. Next, she told us to attach the lid and shake it hard. In a few minutes, each of us had a lump of butter. We spread it on crackers. It was a tasty treat.

Page 387
Here is one possibility. Some variations are possible.

Our class went on a very special field trip. We saved up money from recycling newspapers and aluminum cans until we had enough for a group rate to Disneyland. Isn't that exciting?

We also had to save up enough for the bus, which wasn't too expensive. When the day finally came, we were so excited! We sang songs like "Bingo" and "The Ants Go Marching In." All the way there the bus driver said he was going to go crazy, but he was just kidding. He was also going to Disneyland, and he was happy about that.

When we got there, Marisa said, "I see Space Mountain!" Then Luke said, "I see the Matterhorn!" Then Hector said, "I see Splash Mountain!" and, of course, then Olivia said, "I see Big Thunder Mountain!"

The bus driver said, "Maybe they should call it Mountainland instead." Nobody said anything because just then we all saw the Monorail go by. "I want to go on the Monorail," Cassie said, but Mrs. Martinez said that we had to go through the entrance first.

After we went through the entrance, everybody forgot about the Monorail. We were divided into groups so we could go wherever our group wanted to go. We could join with other groups, too, whenever we wanted to. We all wore bright, orange shirts so it wouldn't be too hard to find each other. Mrs. Martinez took a group and so did Mr. Rawlings, Miss White, Mrs. Hojito, and Bill, the bus driver. Guess what? I was in Bill's group! I'll never forget this day. Our group had more fun than any other group because Bill went on all the rides with us, and he didn't complain at all. In fact, he said, "I'm having too much fun!" Isn't that great? Bill even rode the Bobsleds with us, and he went on Autopia, too. He didn't get sick on Dumbo or the merry-go-round, and he even went on Splash Mountain, Thunder Mountain, and Space Mountain. On Indiana Jones, he covered his eyes when a snake hissed at him, and on the Jungle Cruise he shrieked when a hippopotamus blew water on him. He made us all laugh all the time. At the very end, Bill got motion sickness on the Teacups. Someone was coming to pick him up and to bring a new bus driver. That meant we got to go back into Disneyland for one more hour. We felt sorry for Bill, but we were glad to have another hour.

Page 388
hat, bug, door, house, fan, ladder
1–10. Answers will vary.

Page 389
There are many possibilities. The following are some ideas:

___*an:* ban, can, fan, man
___*ark:* bark, dark, hark, lark, mark
___*eat:* beat, feat, heat, meat, neat
___*ame:* came, dame, fame, game, lame
___*ear:* bear, dear, fear, gear, near
___*our:* dour, four, hour, pour, sour
___*ine:* dine, fine, line, mine, pine
___*ice:* dice, lice, mice, nice, rice
___*up:* cup, pup, sup

Page 390
plant, train, braid, dress, tree, drain, clown, crayon, snake

Page 391
Possible answers include the following.

bl: block, blind, blue, blow
br: brown, brook, bright, bring
cl: clown, clap, clean, clutter
cr: cry, creep, cringe, crave
dr: drive, drink, drown, drip
fl: fly, flip, flounce, flit
fr: French, fry, free, frost
gl: glee, glean, glad, glow
gr: green, grass, grow, grape
pl: please, play, plot, plan
pr: pray, prim, promise, proper
sl: slow, slide, sled, slant
sp: space, spice, sport, speck
st: stand, stop, stick, stall
str: street, strand, strap, string
tr: train, trap, trim, trout

Page 392
1. chick or thick
2. choose
3. chop or shop
4. shape
5. math or mash
6. thank or shank
7. cheese
8. check
9. thirst
10. whistle or thistle
11. bath or bash
12. wish or with
13. whip, chip, or ship
14. bench
15. washing
16. trash

Page 393
a (red): tape, table, name, whale, ate
e (purple): treat, eat, free, seem, he, she, sleep, meet, bee, team
i (yellow): mine, sigh, nice, find, try
o (green): show, open, so
u (blue): you, fuse, huge, cube, music

Answer Key (cont.)

Page 394

a (purple): cat, and, fan
e (blue): men, when, met
i (red): thin, flip, bit
o (yellow): stop, pot, nod, mob, box, on
u (green): club, nut, cup

Page 395

top hat (long): bay, bike, cake, coat, dime, flown, meat, mule, side, tree, use
cap (short): chick, fish, frog, hat, jump, nest, net, pond, six, sun, track

Page 396

1. pain
2. hay
3. pail
4. train
5. layer
6. pay
7. aim
8. day

Page 397

1. boy
2. toy
3. joint
4. joy
5. soil
6. coin
7. royal
8. boil

Page 398

1. monkey
2. cookie
3. money
4. donkey
5. candy
6. puppies
7. baby
8. happy

Page 399

1. dirt
2. hurt
3. worm
4. arm
5. fur
6. torn
7. hair
8. sharp

Page 400

1. cane
2. site
3. cape
4. tube
5. dote
6. note
7. rate
8. lobe
9. bite
10. cube
11. grime
12. fine
13. bathe
14. vane
15. plane

Page 401

1. write
2. witch
3. whole
4. dumb
5. knot
6. notch
7. knew
8. comb
9. honest
10. lamb
11. ghost
12. whale
13. wrench
14. batch
15. whip
16. hour
17. catch
18. wrong
19. wrinkle
20. match
21. knight
22. knee
23. crumb
24. knife
25. thumb
26. knit

Page 402

alphabet, awful, cough, dolphin, elephant, elf, enough, fantastic, fish, fun, giraffe, laugh, muff, phonics, rough, taffy, telephone, tough

Page 403

f sound: cough, enough, rough, slough*, tough, trough
silent: daughter, dough, knight, light, naughty, night, right, sigh, sight, slough*, taught, though, high
*Note that *slough* can be pronounced both ways, and each way has a different meaning.

Page 404

1. ache
2. back
3. bank
4. beak or beach
5. cane
6. cut
7. crumb
8. dock
9. jack
10. keep
11. key
12. kind
13. look
14. make
15. neck
16. nickel
17. pack
18. pocket
19. scare
20. school
21. skin
22. sock
23. spoke
24. stomach
25. walk
26. rake

Page 405

far; run; doll; pass; will; book; dirt; lion; big; hang; ring; sun

Page 406

1. alone—known
2. bowl—roll
3. coat—wrote
4. home—roam
5. leak—week
6. maid—frayed
7. plate—great
8. seize—bees
9. sigh—fly
10. soap—rope
11. tail—bale
12. thought—taught

Page 408

The picture is a red bell on a blue background.

Page 409

There are many answer possibilities: honeymoon, playground, headlight, moonlight, railroad, sailboat, rattlesnake, rainbow, plywood, takeover, salesperson

Page 410

1. out
2. step
3. head
4. side
5. pot
6. fire
7. ball
8. down
9. store
10. ball
11. light
12. side
13. out
14. back
15. where

Page 411

compound words (red): blackboard, catnip, mailbox, campground, butterfly, popcorn

Page 412

one-syllable words: star, How, I, what, you, are, up, the, world, so, high, Like, a, in, the, sky, star, How, I what, you, are

Page 413

1. ham-mer
2. win-dow
3. but-ter
4. let-ter
5. car-pet
6. mon-key
7. pil-low
8. num-bers
9. doc-tor

Page 414

one syllable (red): house, quilt, move, big, car, boat, blue, tree, blank, wish, game, peach, dream, flash
two syllables (blue): story, over, farmer, pitcher, children, finger, sewing, motor, pizza, wagon, glasses, bottle, shoulder, rabbit, grandma, drawing, trailer
three syllables (green): eleven, alphabet, elephant, directions, video, octopus, computer, camera, vanilla

Page 415

I-rish; mag-a-zine; a-live; gas-o-line; tel-e-phone; o-pen; a-gain; Can-a-da; o-cean

Page 416

1. regular
2. spell
3. pride
4. use
5. possible
6. loyal
7. known
8. arrange
9. maid
10. plane
11. joy
12. form
13. cycle
14. stop
15. royal

Page 417

1. dance
2. bank
3. skate
4. collect
5. dream
6. build
7. teach
8. visit
9. act

Page 418

prefix: un; un-wrap
prefix: re; re-fill
prefix: dis; dis-cover
prefix: non; non-sense
prefix: pre; pre-school
prefix: mis; misspell

Page 419

Answers will vary.

Answer Key (cont.)

Page 420

	Prefix	Root	Definition
1.	re	read	to read again
2.	un	prepare	not prepared
3.	pre	school	schooling before regular school
4.	mis	spell	spelled incorrectly
5.	under	water	watered less than enough
6.	over	joy	exceedingly filled with joy
7.	mis	judge	judged wrongly
8.	over	eat	to eat more than enough

Page 421

1. *suffix:* ness; kind-ness
2. *suffix:* ful; care-ful
3. *suffix:* ful; help-ful
4. *suffix:* less; seed-less
5. *suffix:* ly; clear-ly
6. *suffix:* ful; health-ful

Page 422

1. *suffix:* ous; joyous
2. *suffix:* less; careless
3. *suffix:* less; thankless
4. *suffix:* ous; famous
5. *suffix:* ous; mountainous
6. *suffix:* less; thoughtless

Page 423

yellow: invite, rerun, nonfat, untie, unpaid, discover
blue: careless, joyful, meaningful, kindness, thoughtless, famous

Page 424

bears; enough; already; forty; bird; reading

Page 425

school, face, combed, hair, red, blue, jeans, laid, shoes, because, knots, Finally, kitchen, cereal, very, pack, peanut, sandwich, apple, cookies, ready, brush, teeth, there, was, to

Page 426

1. clue
2. correct
3. correct
4. line
5. freeze
6. boat
7. sail
8. correct
9. correct
10. women or woman
11. fish
12. cookie
13. monkey
14. correct
15. correct
16. each
17. loud
18. girl
19. correct
20. low

Page 427

Answers may vary.

1. school
2. skinny
3. pretty
4. tomorrow
5. eggs
6. asleep
7. fifteen
8. green
9. apple
10. all
11. floor
12. troop
13. quills
14. shells
15. noon

Page 428

1. mar or ram
2. ate or eat
3. came
4. lap
5. nap
6. star or ants
7. keep
8. pace
9. read or dare
10. meat, mate, or team
11. thin
12. smile or limes
13. tip
14. top
15. cars
16. rat or art
17. mate, meat, or tame
18. sit
19. net
20. lips

Page 429

1. goat, goose, or gopher
2. golf
3. gondola
4. gold
5. gone
6. Golden Rule
7. golden retriever
8. goal
9. goober
10. go-between
11. gobble
12. goblin
13. gorgeous
14. gorilla
15. goblet
16. goggles
17. gown
18. tango
19. gourd
20. goldfinch or goose

Page 430

Answers will vary.

Page 431

Page 432

1. goo
2. loose
3. dinner
4. choose
5. meet
6. comma
7. supper
8. dessert
9. loot
10. bee
11. feed
12. good
13. soon
14. inn
15. loop
16. corral

Page 433

1. n
2. b
3. h
4. e
5. l
6. j
7. f
8. a
9. o
10. d
11. m
12. i
13. k
14. g
15. c

Page 434

1. north
2. Street
3. railroad
4. South America
5. master of ceremonies
6. cash on delivery
7. Wednesday
8. ante meridiem (before noon or morning)
9. chapter
10. dozen
11. quart
12. package
13. maximum
14. Avenue
15. September
16. year
17. building
18. number
19. temperature
20. Post Office

Page 435

1. record´
2. de´sert
3. content´
4. con´test
5. refuse´
6. read (red)
7. close (cloz)
8. con´duct
9. sub´ject
10. ad´dress

Page 436

1. mat
2. mate
3. tine
4. tin
5. fed
6. feed
7. us
8. use
9. meet
10. met

Answer Key (cont.)

Page 437
1. ghost
2. male or mail
3. post
4. lazy
5. place
6. row
7. fuel
8. total
9. oak
10. spray
11. veil or vale
12. repair
13. reply
14. observe
15. why

Page 438
cart, friend, ghost, house, jump, light, moon, river, silent, tunnel, umbrella, vest

cane, cell, deer, dog, game, grass, lion, loop, lunch, same, science, sort

Page 439
The first and third lists are in alphabetical order.

Page 444
1. B
2. C
3. A
4. B
5. A
6. A
7. B
8. C
9. C
10. A
Sentences will vary.

Page 445
1. C
2. B
3. B
4. A
5. D
6. B
7. A
8. D
9. C
10. C
Sentences will vary.

Page 446
1. C
2. A
3. C
4. B
5. A
6. C
7. B
8. C
9. A
10. A
Sentences will vary.

Page 447
1. visitor; Sentences will vary.
2. forty-nine
3. ten
4. fifty
5. orange, tan

Page 451
from left to right: 3, 2, 6, 4, 1, 5

Page 452
a. 4
b. 1
c. 6
d. 3
e. 8
f. 2
g. 7
h. 5

Page 453
1. At first, the new pony lay quietly on the ground.
2. Then, she lifted her nose into the air.
3. Next, she put her front hooves firmly on the grass.
4. Finally, her wobbly legs pushed her up.

5. The new pony was standing on her own!

Page 454
1. They cleaned their rooms.
2. They washed the family's car.
3. They got ready to go to the zoo.
4. They visited the sharks.
5. They went to the wolf den.
6. They met their mother at the alligator exhibit.

Page 456
There are many ways to travel. People can travel by plane, boat, or train. Cars and buses are other ways to travel. Bicycles, tricycles, scooters, and skateboards are good for getting around. A fun way to travel is on a horse or a donkey. Some people can even travel in a spaceship!

Page 457
1. chores
2. favorite foods
3. school
4. pet peeves
5. ice cream
6. homework
7. favorite rides
8. travel
9. summer
10. sports

Page 458
The lion roars.
The alligator sleeps.
The bear eats a fish.
Ice cream is a nice treat.

Page 459
1. C
2. D
3. A
4. B
5. E

Page 461
Barn owls are fully grown by about 12 weeks of age.

Page 462
1. Answers will vary.
2. Yes, it did.
3. Answers include: be friendly, smile, say hello, share, be kind, don't wait for others to talk to you, go up to them first

Page 463
1. A very young boy named Mark.
2. He visited the American Zoo and saw baby penguins hatch.
3. He was near the penguin exhibit when they hatched.
4. Sentences will vary.

Page 464
1. George Washington
2. He was known as a great leader.
3. He was a good general and president.
4. Sentences will vary.

Page 465
Their tickets were lost!—They lost their tickets.
The boys rode the bus to the game.—The bus took the boys to the game.
My favorite book is that one.—That book is my favorite one.
My blue shirt has a rip.—My blue shirt is torn.

Page 466
1. He forgot to chill the sandwiches overnight.
2. The sandwiches spoiled.

Page 467
1. She climbed down her bedpost.
2. She was glad her mother did not see the mess under her bed.
3. She arranged the dollhouse furniture.
4. They ate her leftover cookies from her bedtime snack.
5. She actually found cookie crumbs in her dollhouse.

Page 468
1. He said that he could eat a horse.
2. He said that he did not eat much lunch today.
3. He is looking for some food to eat.

Page 469
1. Jack and Wendy do not like the Fun House.
2. They think it is too scary, and they want to leave.
1. Mary really wants the dress, and she is jealous.
2. Mary says that she does not like the dress, but she wants to know if there are any more. Also, by asking so much about it, she leads others to believe that she is really interested.

Page 470
1. rooster
2. movie
3. computer
4. rose
5. guitar

Page 471
Conclusions and drawings will vary.

Page 472
Conclusions and drawings will vary.

Page 473
1. C
2. E
3. I
4. F
5. L
6. K
7. A
8. G
9. B
10. D
11. J
12. H

Page 474
Answers will vary.

Answer Key (cont.)

Page 475
1. fact
2. opinion
3. fact
4. opinion
5. opinion
6. opinion
7. opinion
8. fact

Page 476
opinions (green)
I think panthers are beautiful.
They are scary.
A panther would be a great pet.
No it wouldn't.
This is the best trip we have ever taken.
I think it is fun, too.
I think they're the best animals here!
My favorite is the reindeer.
We learned a lot at the zoo today.
facts (red)
Panthers belong to the cat family.
They weigh more than 100 pounds.
It is against the law to keep a wild animal as a pet.
The zoo has many animals for us to see.
There are six different types of monkeys at this zoo.
They live where the weather is very cold.
Tomorrow we will write stories about the things we have learned.

Page 477
Answers will vary.

Page 478
1. excited
2. sad
3. silly
4. worried
5. happy

Page 479
1. two
2. Tracy and his father
3. Tracy
4. "He" in the first sentence

Page 480
1. check
2. no check
3. check
4. check
5. no check

Page 481
1. 3
2. 1
3. 1
4. 3

Page 482
Answers will vary.

Page 483
1. chicken = cowardly
2. piece of cake = easy
3. teacher's pet = particular favorite
4. hot water = trouble

Page 484
1. everything
2. annoy
3. scared
4. free
5. send a message (write or call)
6. good gardener
7. not listen
8. eat sparingly
9. quit
10. study hard
11. understand
12. study
13. remain expressionless in the face of something funny
14. physically hit the center of a target or say/do something profound or astute
15. be merciful or generous

Page 485
1. chalkboard or sidewalk
2. quack
3. cook
4. south
5. seeing or sight
6. fish
7. stadium or field
8. hand
9. hammer
10. far
11. girl
12. jungle

Page 486
1. quack
2. skin
3. goal
4. swim
5. bird
6. coloring
7. night
8. year
9. winter
10. head

Page 487
1. bird
2. racket
3. Elizabeth
4. poem
5. long or tall
6. Abraham
7. nut
8. soft
9. sand
10. window
11. read
12. teeth
13. snow
14. cut
15. shoe
16. screw
17. ring
18. hands
19. oink
20. minute

Page 488
1. trees
2. boys' names
3. streets
4. cities
5. bugs
6. books
7. feelings
8. countries
9. toys
10. clothes
11. oceans
12. shoes
13. vegetables
14. sandwiches
15. sports

Page 489
wood: oak, pencil, board, forest, walnut, lumber, maple
metals: tin, iron, nail, aluminum, steel, copper, bronze
water: bay, sea, pond, lake, river, ocean, creek
space: countdown, Mars, moon, orbit, astronaut, weightless, rocket
colors: tan, red, blue, green, scarlet, beige, chartreuse
furniture: lamp, couch, mirror, chest, rocker, dresser, cabinet

Page 490
Answers and paragraph will vary.

Page 492
Summaries will vary.

Page 497–505
Answers will vary.

Page 506
1. B
2. C
3. A

Page 507–520
Answers will vary

Page 521
1. S
2. S
3. M
4. S
5. M
6. S
7. S
8. M
9. S
10. S

Page 561
1. 2 hundreds, 6 tens, 3 ones
2. 5 hundreds, 2 tens, 6 ones
3. 3 hundreds, 4 tens, 0 ones
4. 4 hundreds, 5 tens, 8 ones
5. 6 hundreds, 0 tens, 1 ones

Page 562
1. 194
2. 362
3. 98
4. 422
5. 503
6. 501
7. 272
8. 486

Page 563
1. 50
2. 60
3. 90
4. 20
5. 70
6. 10
7. 20
8. 400
9. 600
10. 200
11. 900
12. 800
13. 300
14. 600
15. 200
16. 260

Page 564
1, 3, 5, 7, 9, 11, 13, 15, 17, 19, 21, 23, 25, 27, 29, 31, 33, 35, 37, 39, 41, 43, 45, 47, 49, 51, 53, 55, 57, 59, 61, 63, 65, 67, 69, 71, 73, 75, 77, 79, 81, 83, 85, 87, 89, 91, 93, 95, 97, 99

Page 565
2, 4, 6, 8, 10, 12, 14, 16, 18, 20, 22, 24, 26, 28, 30, 32, 34, 36, 38, 40, 42, 44, 46, 48, 50, 52, 54, 56, 58, 60, 62, 64, 66, 68, 70, 72, 74, 76, 78, 80, 82, 84, 86, 88, 90, 92, 94, 96, 98, 100

Answer Key (cont.)

Page 566
1. 4
2. 13
3. 10
4. 12
5. 7
6. 6
7. 3
8. 8
9. 3
10. 10
11. 14
12. 8
13. 6
14. 11
15. 15
16. 5
17. 2
18. 8
19. 14
20. 7

Page 567
a. 45
b. 90
c. 78
d. 74
e. 69
f. 71
g. 142
h. 136
i. 98
j. 161

Page 568
$32 + 13 = 45$
$27 + 12 = 39$
$26 + 13 = 39$
$16 + 24 = 40$
$34 + 14 = 48$
$15 + 28 = 43$

Page 569
a. $12 + 14 + 22 = 48$
b. $28 + 32 + 46 = 106$
c. $27 + 23 + 52 = 102$
d. $14 + 33 + 21 = 68$

Page 570
a. 77
b. 132
c. 46
d. 82
e. 73
f. 142
g. 89
h. 72
i. 93
j. 57
k. 125
l. 137
m. 142
n. 53
o. 74
p. 66
q. 74
r. 102
s. 147
t. 74
u. 51
v. 93
w. 55
x. 109

Page 571
a. 143
b. 131
c. 91
d. 117
e. 186
f. 157
g. 123
h. 163
i. 145
j. 129
k. 185
l. 106
m. 156
n. 100
o. 93
p. 132
q. 201
r. 174
s. 150
t. 182
u. 174
v. 119
w. 111
x. 170

Page 572
a. 24
b. 64
c. 30
d. 2
e. 25
f. 33
g. 6
h. 10
i. 62
j. 37

Page 573
a. 12
b. 59
c. 9
d. 13
e. 46
f. 29
g. 7
h. 33
i. 12
j. 66

Page 574
$42 - 13 = 29$
$34 - 11 = 23$
$54 - 20 = 34$
$26 - 13 = 13$
$27 - 12 = 15$
$48 - 29 = 19$

Page 575
a. $25 - 15 = 10$
b. $96 - 45 = 51$
c. $41 - 32 = 9$
d. $93 - 48 = 45$

Page 576
a. 21
b. 62
c. 14
d. 30
e. 7
f. 30
g. 2
h. 28
i. 9
j. 7
k. 19
l. 7
m. 6
n. 23
o. 16
p. 47
q. 46
r. 70
s. 47
t. 16
u. 17
v. 55
w. 0
x. 1

Page 577
a. 10
b. 52
c. 36
d. 23
e. 6
f. 30
g. 60
h. 64
i. 65
j. 78
k. 29
l. 12
m. 12
n. 12
o. 4
p. 23
q. 51
r. 46
s. 25
t. 47
u. 7
v. 28
w. 12
x. 43

Page 578
1. 6
2. 9
3. 13
4. 10
5. 7
6. 19
7. 18
8. 5
9. 9
10. 7
11. 23
12. 11
13. 8
14. 6
15. 24
16. 12

Page 579
1. $6 + 4 - 1 - 2 + 6 + 2 = 15$
2. $9 + 1 - 3 + 1 - 4 + 1 = 5$
3. $9 - 3 + 4 - 1 + 2 + 3 = 14$
4. $5 - 1 + 1 + 3 + 4 + 6 = 18$
5. $9 - 8 + 6 + 3 - 5 + 3 = 8$
6. $2 - 1 + 8 + 9 - 3 + 5 = 20$
7. $5 + 3 + 2 - 4 + 1 + 5 = 12$
8. $4 + 9 + 3 - 7 + 3 - 1 = 11$
9. $7 - 6 + 2 + 8 - 7 - 1 = 3$
10. $9 + 9 - 9 + 2 - 2 - 8 = 1$

Page 580
$0 \times 0 = 0$
$0 \times 1 = 0$
$0 \times 2 = 0$
$0 \times 3 = 0$
$0 \times 4 = 0$
$0 \times 5 = 0$
$0 \times 6 = 0$
$0 \times 7 = 0$
$0 \times 8 = 0$
$0 \times 9 = 0$
$0 \times 10 = 0$
$0 \times 11 = 0$
$0 \times 12 = 0$
$1 \times 0 = 0$
$1 \times 1 = 1$
$1 \times 2 = 2$
$1 \times 3 = 3$
$1 \times 4 = 4$
$1 \times 5 = 5$
$1 \times 6 = 6$
$1 \times 7 = 7$
$1 \times 8 = 8$
$1 \times 9 = 9$
$1 \times 10 = 10$
$1 \times 11 = 11$
$1 \times 12 = 12$
$2 \times 0 = 0$
$2 \times 1 = 2$
$2 \times 2 = 4$
$2 \times 3 = 6$
$2 \times 4 = 8$
$2 \times 5 = 10$
$2 \times 6 = 12$
$2 \times 7 = 14$
$2 \times 8 = 16$
$2 \times 9 = 18$
$2 \times 10 = 20$
$2 \times 11 = 22$
$2 \times 12 = 24$
$3 \times 0 = 0$
$3 \times 1 = 3$
$3 \times 2 = 6$
$3 \times 3 = 9$
$3 \times 4 = 12$
$3 \times 5 = 15$
$3 \times 6 = 18$
$3 \times 7 = 21$
$3 \times 8 = 24$
$3 \times 9 = 27$
$3 \times 10 = 30$
$3 \times 11 = 33$
$3 \times 12 = 36$
$4 \times 0 = 0$
$4 \times 1 = 4$
$4 \times 2 = 8$
$4 \times 3 = 12$
$4 \times 4 = 16$
$4 \times 5 = 20$
$4 \times 6 = 24$
$4 \times 7 = 28$
$4 \times 8 = 32$
$4 \times 9 = 36$
$4 \times 10 = 40$
$4 \times 11 = 44$
$4 \times 12 = 48$
$5 \times 0 = 0$
$5 \times 1 = 5$
$5 \times 2 = 10$
$5 \times 3 = 15$
$5 \times 4 = 20$
$5 \times 5 = 25$
$5 \times 6 = 30$
$5 \times 7 = 35$
$5 \times 8 = 40$
$5 \times 9 = 45$
$5 \times 10 = 50$

#6455 Practice and Learn

Answer Key (cont.)

Page 581

5 x 11 = 55	7 x 4 = 28	8 x 10 = 80	10 x 3 = 30	11 x 9 = 99
5 x 12 = 60	7 x 5 = 35	8 x 11 = 88	10 x 4 = 40	11 x 10 = 110
6 x 0 = 0	7 x 6 = 42	8 x 12 = 96	10 x 5 = 50	11 x 11 = 121
6 x 1 = 6	7 x 7 = 49	9 x 0 = 0	10 x 6 = 60	11 x 12 = 132
6 x 2 = 12	7 x 8 = 56	9 x 1 = 9	10 x 7 = 70	12 x 0 = 0
6 x 3 = 18	7 x 9 = 63	9 x 2 = 18	10 x 8 = 80	12 x 1 = 12
6 x 4 = 24	7 x 10 = 70	9 x 3 = 27	10 x 9 = 90	12 x 2 = 24
6 x 5 = 30	7 x 11 = 77	9 x 4 = 36	10 x 10 = 100	12 x 3 = 36
6 x 6 = 36	7 x 12 = 84	9 x 5 = 45	10 x 11 = 110	12 x 4 = 48
6 x 7 = 42	8 x 0 = 0	9 x 6 = 54	10 x 12 = 120	12 x 5 = 60
6 x 8 = 48	8 x 1 = 8	9 x 7 = 63	11 x 0 = 0	12 x 6 = 72
6 x 9 = 54	8 x 2 = 16	9 x 8 = 72	11 x 1 = 11	12 x 7 = 84
6 x 10 = 60	8 x 3 = 24	9 x 9 = 81	11 x 2 = 22	12 x 8 = 96
6 x 11 = 66	8 x 4 = 32	9 x 10 = 90	11 x 3 = 33	12 x 9 = 108
6 x 12 = 72	8 x 5 = 40	9 x 11 = 99	11 x 4 = 44	12 x 10 = 120
7 x 0 = 0	8 x 6 = 48	9 x 12 = 108	11 x 5 = 55	12 x 11 = 132
7 x 1 = 7	8 x 7 = 56	10 x 0 = 0	11 x 6 = 66	12 x 12 = 144
7 x 2 = 14	8 x 8 = 64	10 x 1 = 10	11 x 7 = 77	
7 x 3 = 21	8 x 9 = 72	10 x 2 = 20	11 x 8 = 88	

Page 582

6 x 6 = 36	9 x 5 = 45	6 x 7 = 42	8 x 0 = 0
3 x 1 = 3	4 x 7 = 28	7 x 3 = 21	8 x 9 = 72
9 x 6 = 54	6 x 8 = 48	8 x 1 = 8	9 x 7 = 63
9 x 9 = 81	8 x 4 = 32	0 x 3 = 0	1 x 9 = 9
3 x 2 = 6	4 x 8 = 32	0 x 4 = 0	3 x 3 = 9
4 x 9 = 36	0 x 5 = 0	7 x 2 = 14	8 x 8 = 64
3 x 4 = 12	0 x 6 = 0	3 x 5 = 15	0 x 7 = 0
2 x 0 = 0	3 x 6 = 18	0 x 8 = 0	0 x 0 = 0
1 x 6 = 6	4 x 5 = 20	0 x 1 = 0	1 x 7 = 7
2 x 9 = 18	4 x 2 = 8	5 x 8 = 40	1 x 4 = 4
4 x 3 = 12	5 x 9 = 45	1 x 5 = 5	4 x 6 = 24
5 x 0 = 0	0 x 9 = 0	8 x 5 = 40	5 x 7 = 35

Page 583

2 x 2 = 4	3 x 8 = 24	5 x 1 = 5	10 x 0 = 10
2 x 3 = 6	11 x 5 = 55	7 x 4 = 28	10 x 8 = 80
10 x 3 = 30	11 x 9 = 99	5 x 12 = 60	7 x 5 = 35
11 x 8 = 88	10 x 4 = 40	11 x 10 = 110	6 x 0 = 6
7 x 6 = 42	12 x 8 = 96	10 x 5 = 50	11 x 11 = 121
6 x 1 = 6	7 x 7 = 49	9 x 0 = 0	10 x 6 = 60
11 x 12 = 132	6 x 2 = 12	7 x 8 = 56	9 x 1 = 9
10 x 7 = 70	12 x 0 = 12	6 x 3 = 18	7 x 9 = 63
9 x 2 = 18	10 x 8 = 80	12 x 1 = 12	6 x 4 = 24
10 x 7 = 70	9 x 3 = 27	10 x 9 = 90	12 x 2 = 24

Page 584

96 x 6 = 576	90 x 3 = 270	47 x 9 = 423	25 x 1 = 25	16 x 6 = 96
40 x 8 = 320	82 x 5 = 410	60 x 2 = 120	71 x 7 = 497	32 x 4 = 128
68 x 8 = 544	33 x 1 = 33	20 x 6 = 120	24 x 9 = 216	41 x 4 = 164
46 x 2 = 92	49 x 7 = 343	38 x 4 = 152	24 x 3 = 72	27 x 3 = 81
56 x 7 = 392	84 x 2 = 168	70 x 9 = 630	58 x 7 = 406	50 x 1 = 50
21 x 2 = 42	77 x 6 = 462	79 x 4 = 316	86 x 3 = 258	13 x 2 = 26
22 x 6 = 132	74 x 1 = 74	26 x 9 = 234	14 x 7 = 98	48 x 3 = 144
42 x 4 = 168	88 x 5 = 440	69 x 8 = 552	43 x 3 = 129	19 x 2 = 38

Answer Key (cont.)

Page 585

173 x 6 = 1,038	227 x 3 = 681	402 x 1 = 402	420 x 8 = 3,360	178 x 9 = 1,602
324 x 8 = 2,592	172 x 4 = 688	286 x 8 = 2,288	509 x 4 = 2,036	615 x 2 = 1,230
533 x 8 = 4,264	388 x 1= 388	620 x 6 = 3,720	662 x 3 = 1,986	714 x 9 = 6,426
835 x 3 = 2,505	152 x 7 = 1,064	254 x 5 = 1,270	851 x 1= 851	674 x 8 = 5,392
138 x 2 = 276	417 x 8 = 3,336	317 x 4 = 1,268	458 x 7 = 3,206	550 x 6 = 3,300
594 x 5 = 2,970	180 x 4 = 720	538 x 1= 538	728 x 6 = 4,368	107 x 3 = 321
833 x 5 = 4,165	524 x 3 = 1,572	468 x 6 = 2,808	947 x 2 = 1,894	767 x 7 = 5,369
632 x 3 = 1,896	221 x 2 = 442	489 x 4 = 1,956	141 x 9 = 1,269	213 x 5 = 1,065

Page 586

23 x 16 = 368	90 x 39 = 3,510	17 x 79 = 1,343	35 x 15 = 525	14 x 63 = 882
56 x 82 = 4,592	73 x 50 = 3,650	50 x 28 = 1,400	81 x 76 = 6,156	51 x 44 = 2,244
13 x 38 = 494	31 x 11 = 341	41 x 96 = 3,936	14 x 79 = 1,106	80 x 54 = 4,320
34 x 24 = 816	46 x 27 = 1,242	68 x 40 = 2,720	34 x 83 = 2,822	23 x 36 = 828
89 x 57 = 5,073	24 x 23 = 552	74 x 19 = 1,406	48 x 79 = 3,792	70 x71 = 4,970
21 x 26 = 546	67 x 64 = 4,288	39 x 42 = 1,638	96 x 30 = 2,880	18 x 28 = 504
44 x 76 = 3,344	22 x 51 = 1,122	16 x 39 = 624	25 x 17 = 425	28 x 93 = 2,604
58 x 48 = 2,784	99 x 56 = 5,544	64 x 48 = 3,072	34 x 23 = 782	36 x 20 = 720

Page 587

1 ÷ 1 = 1	14 ÷ 2 = 7	4 ÷ 4 = 1	35 ÷ 5 = 7
2 ÷ 1 = 2	16 ÷ 2 = 8	8 ÷ 4 = 2	40 ÷ 5 = 8
3 ÷ 1 = 3	18 ÷ 2 = 9	12 ÷ 4 = 3	45 ÷ 5 = 9
4 ÷ 1 = 4	20 ÷ 2 = 10	16 ÷ 4 = 4	50 ÷ 5 = 10
5 ÷ 1 = 5	22 ÷ 2 = 11	20 ÷ 4 = 5	55 ÷ 5 = 11
6 ÷ 1 = 6	24 ÷ 2 = 12	24 ÷ 4 = 6	
7 ÷ 1 = 7	3 ÷ 3 = 1	28 ÷ 4 = 7	
8 ÷ 1 = 8	6 ÷ 3 = 2	32 ÷ 4 = 8	
9 ÷ 1 = 9	9 ÷ 3 = 3	36 ÷ 4 = 9	
10 ÷ 1 = 10	12 ÷ 3 = 4	40 ÷ 4 = 10	
11 ÷ 1 = 11	15 ÷ 3 = 5	44 ÷ 4 = 11	
12 ÷ 1 = 12	18 ÷ 3 = 6	48 ÷ 4 = 12	
2 ÷ 2 = 1	21 ÷ 3 = 7	5 ÷ 5 = 1	
4 ÷ 2 = 2	24 ÷ 3 = 8	10 ÷ 5 = 2	
6 ÷ 2 = 3	27 ÷ 3 = 9	15 ÷ 5 = 3	
8 ÷ 2 = 4	30 ÷ 3 = 10	20 ÷ 5 = 4	
10 ÷ 2 = 5	33 ÷ 3 = 11	25 ÷ 5 = 5	
12 ÷ 2 = 6	36 ÷ 3 = 12	30 ÷ 5 = 6	

Page 588

60 ÷ 5 = 12	42 ÷ 7 = 6	96 ÷ 8 = 12	60 ÷ 10 = 6	132 ÷ 11 = 12
6 ÷ 6 = 1	49 ÷ 7 = 7	9 ÷ 9 = 1	70 ÷ 10 = 7	12 ÷ 12 = 1
12 ÷ 6 = 2	56 ÷ 7 = 8	18 ÷ 9 = 2	80 ÷ 10 = 8	24 ÷ 12 = 2
18 ÷ 6 = 3	63 ÷ 7 = 9	27 ÷ 9 = 3	90 ÷ 10 = 9	36 ÷ 12 = 3
24 ÷ 6 = 4	70 ÷ 7 = 10	36 ÷ 9 = 4	100 ÷ 10 = 10	48 ÷ 12 = 4
30 ÷ 6 = 5	77 ÷ 7 = 11	45 ÷ 9 = 5	110 ÷ 10 = 11	60 ÷ 12 = 5
36 ÷ 6 = 6	84 ÷ 7 = 12	54 ÷ 9 = 6	120 ÷ 10 = 12	72 ÷ 12 = 6
42 ÷ 6 = 7	8 ÷ 8 = 1	63 ÷ 9 = 7	11 ÷ 11 = 1	84 ÷ 12 = 7
48 ÷ 6 = 8	16 ÷ 8 = 2	72 ÷ 9 = 8	22 ÷ 11 = 2	96 ÷ 12 = 8
54 ÷ 6 = 9	24 ÷ 8 = 3	81 ÷ 9 = 9	33 ÷ 11 = 3	108 ÷ 12 = 9
60 ÷ 6 = 10	32 ÷ 8 = 4	90 ÷ 9 = 10	44 ÷ 11 = 4	120 ÷ 12 = 10
66 ÷ 6 = 11	40 ÷ 8 = 5	99 ÷ 9 = 11	55 ÷ 11 = 5	132 ÷ 12 = 11
72 ÷ 6 = 12	48 ÷ 8 = 6	108 ÷ 9 = 12	66 ÷ 11 = 6	144 ÷ 12 = 12
7 ÷ 7 = 1	56 ÷ 8 = 7	10 ÷ 10 = 1	77 ÷ 11 = 7	
14 ÷ 7 = 2	64 ÷ 8 = 8	20 ÷ 10 = 2	88 ÷ 11 = 8	
21 ÷ 7 = 3	72 ÷ 8 = 9	30 ÷ 10 = 3	99 ÷ 11 = 9	
28 ÷ 7 = 4	80 ÷ 8 = 10	40 ÷ 10 = 4	110 ÷ 11 = 10	
35 ÷ 7 = 5	88 ÷ 8 = 11	50 ÷ 10 = 5	121 ÷ 11 = 11	

Answer Key (cont.)

Page 589

1. 5 + 7 = 12
2. 24 ÷ 4 = 6
3. 9 + 3 = 12
4. 18 – 6 = 12
5. 4 + 9 = 13
6. 4 x 9 = 36
7. 10 x 8 = 80
8. 15 ÷ 5 = 3
9. 11 – 4 = 7
10. 8 + 16 = 24
11. 2 x 8 = 16
12. 3 + 2 = 5
13. 22 – 6 = 16
14. 9 + 1 = 10
15. 3 x 3 = 9

Page 590

1. 1/3
2. 1/4
3. 5/6
4. 3/5
5. 7/10
6. 2/6
7. 3/4
8. 1/2

Page 591

1. 3:45
2. 6:05
3. 5:55
4. 4:25
5. 2:10
6. 4:15
7. 1:30
8. 12:45
9. 7:20
10. 8:35
11. 10:50
12. 6:00
13. 2:35
14. 1:00
15. 11:50

Page 592

1. P.M.
2. A.M.
3. P.M.
4. P.M.
5. A.M.
6. A.M.
7. P.M.
8. P.M.
9. P.M.
10. A.M.
11. A.M.
12. P.M.
13. P.M.
14. A.M.
15. P.M.
16. P.M.
17. A.M.
18. P.M.
19. P.M.
20. A.M.
21. A.M.
22. P.M.
23. P.M.
24. A.M.

Page 593

1. second: one–sixtieth of a minute
2. minute: 60 seconds
3. hour: 60 minutes
4. day: 24 hours
5. week: seven days
6. fortnight: two weeks
7. month: approximately four weeks (28–31 days)
8. year: 365 days
9. decade: 10 years
10. score: 20 years
11. century: 100 years
12. millennium: 1000 years

Page 594

5:15	2:35
3:30	6:55
1:40	8:10
12:05	9:25
7:30	11:50